INSIGHTS
INTO
EVOLUTIONARY
ASTROLOGY

ABOUT ROSE MARCUS

Rose Marcus hosted one of the first of Jeffrey Wolf Green's schools of evolutionary astrology, in 1994. In 2001, she established her own school, the Canadian School of Evolutionary Astrology. She also holds CAP (Certified Astrology Professional) accreditation from the International Society for Astrological Research (ISAR). Rose has a deep passion for evolutionary astrology, which seeks to understand the birth chart from the perspective of the soul's trinity work: to extract current life purpose from the learning and lessons of the past, to calibrate the intended forward (to set conscious intention), and to optimize on the choice-making and potentials of the present.

Over the years Rose has written forecasts for numerous publications and projects; she also offers in-depth monthly forecasts on her website. In addition to her teaching, lecturing, and private consultation work, Rose's media activities include regular appearances on local television in Vancouver.

For more information please visit her website, www.rosemarcus.com.

Insights
into
Evolutionary
Astrology

A Diverse Collection of Essays
by Prominent Astrologers

Edited by

Rose Marcus

Llewellyn Publications
Woodbury, Minnesota

First Edition
First Printing, 2010
Cover background: Vintage sun ray © 2009 Matt Knannlein/iStockphoto.com; Zodiac map © 2009 Classix/iStockphoto.com
Cover design by Ellen Dahl
Interior map illustrations © iStockphoto.com/John Woodcock

Llewellyn is a registered trademark of Llewellyn Worldwide Ltd.

Chart wheels were created using Solar Fire Gold by Esoteric Technologies Pty Ltd., published by Astrolabe, Inc., www.alabe.com.

Library of Congress Cataloging-in-Publication Data

Insights into evolutionary astrology : a diverse collection of essays by prominent astrologers / edited by Rose Marcus. — 1st ed.
　　p.　cm.
　Includes bibliographical references (p.　　).
　ISBN 978-0-7387-1986-3
　1. Astrology and reincarnation.　I. Marcus, Rose.
　BF1729.R37I58 2010
　133.5—dc22
　　　　　　　　　　　　　2010014353

Llewellyn Worldwide Ltd. does not participate in, endorse, or have any authority or responsibility concerning private business transactions between our authors and the public.

　All mail addressed to the author is forwarded, but the publisher cannot, unless specifically instructed by the author, give out an address or phone number.

　Any Internet references contained in this work are current at publication time, but the publisher cannot guarantee that a specific location will continue to be maintained. Please refer to the publisher's website for links to authors' websites and other sources.

Llewellyn Publications
Llewellyn Worldwide Ltd.
2143 Wooddale Drive
Woodbury, MN 55125-2989
www.llewellyn.com

Printed in the United States of America

ACKNOWLEDGMENTS

A heartfelt thank you to my colleagues who have contributed to this book, for their amazing patience through a very lengthy completion process and for the gift of their writings, which I am proud to share in this published form. Thank you also to hard-working editors Maggie (Magi) Frost, Adina Mather, Jinny Rodrigo, and Mikal Shook, and also to Llewellyn production editor Brett Fechheimer, designer Donna Burch, and the rest of the helpful staff.

On behalf of all the authors in this book, namaste to our cherished circle of friends, teachers, and healers, and to all those in the EA circle who have supported our conferences and individual work through the years. A special thanks to my lovely daughters, Jasmin and Kiri, for allowing me to spend so much time at the computer!

Deepest gratitude goes to the teachings of Paramahansa Yogananda, whose spiritual guidance has kept many of us in the EA circle humbled and inspired.

Thank you, Jeffrey Wolf Green, for being the bright beacon, for your teachings, and for your unswerving love and encouragement that has continued to fuel me these many years.

—Rose Marcus

CONTENTS

Introduction

BY ROSE MARCUS

This book, *Insights into Evolutionary Astrology*, is a collection of essays written by top astrologers from the Jeffrey Wolf Green school of study. It is intended that the offerings in this book will distinguish this school from other branches of astrology, and that the content will also clearly demonstrate how Jeffrey's pioneering body of work differs from that of other teachers who have now joined the evolutionary astrology banner.

The book begins with a discourse on the nature of the Soul by the founder of evolutionary astrology, Jeffrey Wolf Green. His essay succinctly describes the four natural evolutionary momentums that propel the Soul's growth. In Deva Green's chapter, "From Cataclysm to the Awakening of Latent Capacities," she elaborates on these four momentums with detailed examples, such as Barack Obama's compelling political rise to the White House.

Jeffrey also outlines for us the how the Soul evolves through the creation process of necessity and desire—or, in other words, fate, karma, and free will. Along with a dissertation on the various evolutionary conditions, Jeffrey describes the core principles of natural law and details how the exposure to societal norms and man-made laws has progressively shaped and conditioned the evolving ego. These key points provide a foundation for an expanded understanding of how the astrological archetypes may be funneled into expression at any given time. This brilliant chapter will be of interest to students of astrology, students of life, and spiritual questers alike.

This book demonstrates what has been largely overlooked or omitted in most astrological practice. It is essential to recognize that an individual's consciousness is reflective of that individual's stage of evolution. Jeffrey Wolf Green places particular emphasis on this key point as the bottom-line determinant for understanding how an individual will respond to life and to his or her chart. A crucial first step for chart analysis lies in the gathering of basic information. Clues to the evolutionary state will come from an observation of the interests, activities, concerns, ambitions, lifestyle, and personality of the client. Background—such as family relationships, ancestry, and religious, spiritual, economic, and cultural influences—provides essential context. Previous experiences and histories retained within the memory pools of the subconscious condition an individual's expression and response mechanisms.

Chart interpretation can be daunting when one considers the myriad of possible expressions and manifestations for any chart symbol. Jeffrey always reminds students that astrology, like any science, must be based in observation and correlation, and that one size does not fit all. Once an assessment of the evolutionary state has been made, chart analysis can become more precise. Jeffrey Wolf Green devised a step-by-step method for analyzing the influence of the conditionings of the past in relation to future potentials and present integration.

In chapter 3, "Evolutionary States," Kim Marie uses one example to provide a thorough, in-depth analysis of the three main evolutionary states. Her chapter clearly demonstrates how greatly the analyses of charts—and the experiential realities of life—can differ when evolutionary states are factored into the equation.

Sexuality, the root of our instinctual self, is one of the core ways that evolution is advanced. In his chapter, "Relationships and Sexuality in Astrology," Maurice Fernandez provides an overview of the sexual dynamics of each of the twelve zodiacal signs. He first describes the intrinsic qualities of the purely biological dynamic correlated to the Soul's intent for evolution through each one of the archetypes. Next, he describes how the influences of social morality and sexual politics add complexity to the natural selection process and how these factors can easily create distortions in the behavior responses of each of the signs.

Astrologers have often been challenged to determine how the manifestations of self-expression for two people with similar charts can vary so greatly. Kristin Fontana demystifies this topic in her chapter, "Twins: Similar Charts, Worlds Apart!" In what should be a common practice for any chart delineation, the primary key to interpretation of twin charts, or of any two charts that are especially close in similarity, is first to assess the evolutionary state of the individuals or entities in question. Again, evolutionary states, which are one of the essential formulas of Jeffrey Wolf Green's teachings/methodologies, are fundamental to the deeper understanding of the chart and the individual. They are a key tool to the unlocking of information that can easily be overlooked or misdiagnosed.

Additionally, as most students of astrology know, planet rulerships are a basic tool of astrological study. Evolutionary astrology reminds the student how important rulerships are in any chart interpretation and how they are an essential qualifying piece of information, especially in reference to house cusps. The examples in Kristin Fontana's chapter will also provide fuel for thought as to the choice of house systems. While each house system has its merits and choosing one is a matter of personal preference, Jeffrey Wolf Green advocates the use of the Porphyry house system, which uses the primary angles of the chart (the Ascendant/Descendant and Midheaven/Nadir angles) as the primary divisions from which the inner angles (the houses of the quadrants: 2, 3, 5, 6, 8, 9, 11, 12) are equally divided.

Past-life therapist Patricia L. Walsh has combined her work in deep-memory regression therapy with her study of evolutionary astrology. She has spent many years gathering and documenting actual case studies, amassing an impressive collection that readily validates the core principles of evolutionary astrology and Jeffrey's specific methodologies. The examples in her chapter, "When Planets Square the Nodal Axis: Insights from a Past-Life Therapist," include demonstrations of "skipped steps," another key notable of Jeffrey's techniques. Her case studies demonstrate how an individual will continue to work through a central or core dynamic from lifetime to lifetime. Patricia Walsh's marriage of these two fields of study distinguishes her work as truly pioneering.

While the Moon's nodes are commonly included in chart delineation, the nodes of the planets have been largely overlooked. The analysis of planetary nodes, which move very slowly over great lengths of time, can provide rich information pertaining to the background of our bigger-picture collective evolution. For example, the planetary nodes for Jupiter through Pluto occupy approximately the same degrees for all of us born in the twentieth century. A look at the planetary nodes through natal-chart contacts, by house positions and aspects, will demonstrate how this bigger-picture information animates within our individual psyche fabric. In chapter 7, "Time's Arrow," Mark Jones simplifies what can often be viewed as a daunting topic and provides a valid case for why planetary nodes should be added to your astrological research.

The final offering in this book is my own chapter on the archetype of Capricorn, the predominant sign archetype that will dictate the evolution of the collective journey through 2024. Capricorn correlates to the conditionings of consciousness; to social, economic, and political landscapes; and to the marking of time, of history, and of reality itself. This chapter includes a full discussion of the Capricorn archetype, Pluto's transit through Capricorn, and the upcoming cardinal transit triggers that will intensify the Capricorn themes and experiences. Also included is a brief look at the geodetic regions that will be animated by Pluto's tour through Capricorn.

I hope this book will serve to expand astrological understandings and skills, and that it will encourage the reader to conduct further independent examination into the field of evolutionary astrology.

Blessings,
Rose Marcus
May 2010

1

Evolutionary Principles of the Soul's Evolution

BY JEFFREY WOLF GREEN,
FOUNDER OF EVOLUTIONARY ASTROLOGY

The following is a review of the key astrological principles involved in evolutionary astrology. The key principles that are reviewed here are (1) the natural law of evolution and the two primary ways it manifests, (2) exactly what a Soul is, (3) how the natural law of evolution manifests from within the Soul, (4) the "ego" that the Soul manifests in each life (5), the four natural evolutionary conditions or stages of a Soul's evolution, (6) sociological or cultural conditioning, (7) the four natural ways that the Soul affects its evolutionary necessities (the issue of fate, karma, and free choice), and (9) the nature of aspects.

EVOLUTION

The simplest way to validate the natural law of evolution is based on the universal human experience, in which all of us know that we are in a continuous state of becoming. This is not a function of belief or a need to believe. It is simply a fact. Of course anyone can observe the natural law of evolution in countless ways as applied to the totality of Creation. We can observe it relative to the evolution of the human life form, we can observe it in the lives of plants and animals, and we can observe it through fundamental changes over great lengths of time to the Earth itself as an evolving planet. We can observe it through our telescopes pointed out into the universe, and we can even observe it at a molecular level of life. Evolution simply comes down to and means the changing of form, the changing of structure, the changing of energy, and the change of anything. The very word *change* implies evolution.

Evolution is always preceded by another natural law called *involution*. What this means is that for a change, or evolution, to occur relative to some structure, form, energy pattern, dynamics, etc., it is always preceded by an involution, which simply means the ending or destruction of something that pre-exists. That which pre-exists, when evolution or change becomes necessary, implies and means that some pre-existing something—a dynamic, structure, and so on—is promoting a state of stagnation or non-growth. In all life forms, in anything that exists as phenomena within the totality of Creation, there exists another natural law called *survival*. When this natural law is ignited or stimulated, for whatever reasons, it will always cause the natural law of involution, leading to evolution, to occur, so that the ongoing survival of a life form, structure, and so on can occur.

The natural laws of evolution and involution have two ways of manifesting. One way is a slow, progressive, non-cataclysmic process of change. The *law of uniformity* is one way; the other way, of course, is cataclysmic change, in which the very nature of the process of involution leading to evolution is intense and abrupt. This differs from the evolution reflected in the natural law of uniformity, which allows for gradual change over time. Cataclysmic evolution creates a sudden change that is immediate and stark. Again, these two natural ways of evolution are observable by anyone as facts that do not require any belief at all. The natural law of evolution and involution correlate astrologically to Pluto.

THE SOUL

The word *Soul* has had an equivalent in almost every human language that has ever been on Earth. So, what is it? Can we open up the brain and find it? No, obviously we cannot. But we cannot open up the physical body and find emotion either. Yet we know we all have emotions. Can we open up the brain and find thought? No. Yet we all know we have at least a thought or two in our heads. Can we open up the body and find sadness, or depression, or happiness, or love? No. Yet we all know that these things exist within us. Obviously, then, we are dealing with the nature of energy. The Soul is energy, which is no different from the energy of consciousness itself.

We cannot open up the brain and find consciousness. Consciousness is one of the greatest "mysteries" of all to scientists, for they cannot explain its origins or even how it came to be. Consciousness correlates astrologically to Neptune. This is exactly the starting point for what we call religion and philosophy: the human need to contemplate and consider, within the desire to know, where we come from and why. In turn, this becomes the causative factor for "beliefs," where beliefs are the result of human pondering upon the origin of life itself. But is there a difference between beliefs and actual knowing? Is there a way to know the answer to the big cosmic questions versus the need to believe in an answer? The happy news is that there is. For example, by the sheer fact that there is a manifested Creation that exists as fact, there must also be truths that inherently exist due to the fact of the manifested Creation in the first place. By the fact of its existence, most of us can easily reason that there has to be something that is the origin of Creation. In generic language we could call that something the origin of all things, or the Source, and in religious terminology it is called God or the Goddess.

Consciousness is certainly part of the manifested Creation. It exists. That which is the origin of consciousness, of itself, must also be conscious. Thus the totality of consciousness emanates from this Source. As an observable fact we all know that consciousness is in all living things, all life forms. And all of these life forms have the appearance of being separate from all other life forms yet are simultaneously connected to them. Two plants next to each other appear separate, yet they are simultaneously connected to one another by the sheer fact of being plants. So, on the one hand there is in fact the individualizing aspect of consciousness. Yet, on the other, there is the universal aspect of consciousness, which binds all the individual aspects of consciousness together.

Another way of illustrating this is the famous story of the wave and the ocean. Most of us would agree that it is the ocean that is the origin of the wave. Yet from the point of view of the wave, if the individualizing aspect of consciousness was centered there, within itself, the wave appears and seems separate. In other words, if the center of gravity for consciousness were within the wave, then from that center of gravity the wave appears, and is experienced, as something separate from its own source, the ocean. On the other hand, if the center of gravity within consciousness were the ocean itself, then the ocean simultaneously experiences its totality while experiencing the individualizing aspects of itself as manifested in the waves that emanate from it.

In the very same way, then, the Universal Consciousness, which is the origin of all consciousness, has created and manifested the totality of manifested Creation, which of course includes the human being and the consciousness within it. And within human consciousness, there exists a natural individualizing aspect. This individualizing aspect occurs as a natural result of the fact that the human life form has a distinct and individual form relative to its root. The human life form as a seed, so to speak, produces many other branches; the distinction is no different from the ocean and the wave. Thus, each human life form has its own individualizing consciousness that is called the Soul. The Soul, then, is an immutable consciousness, or energy, that is naturally part of the Universal Consciousness that has created it in the first place. *Immutable* here means that which cannot be destroyed. Why? Because energy can never be destroyed, it can only change form—evolve.

So how does the Soul evolve? What dynamics are inherent within it that are the cause of its own evolution? Within all human Souls there exist two antithetical desires, where desire is the determinant of evolution. One desire is to return to the origin of all of Creation. And the other desire is to separate from that which is the origin of all things. This simple inner dynamic within the Soul is also the natural cause, or law, of free choice, or free will. The evolution of the Soul is simply based on a progressive elimination of all separating desires to the exclusion of only one desire that can remain: to return to the origin of all things. This does not require any belief system at all, nor any religion that one must belong to. This simple truth, because it is a function of natural law, can be validated by anyone through his or her own life experience.

Isn't it true, for example, that any of us can have whatever separating desire that we can imagine? We can have a desire for a new lover, a new career post, a new possession, and so on. And we may have the ability to manifest that which we desire. And when we do there is in fact a sense of satisfaction that comes from the actualizing of that which we have desired. But what soon replaces it? Is it not the sense of dissatisfaction, the sense of wanting something more? It is precisely this sense of dissatisfaction, the sense of wanting something more, that echoes the ultimate desire to return to the origin of all things, the only desire that will bring to us that ultimate satisfaction. All of us have this universal experience.

So how can we know, independent of belief systems, that there in fact exists an ultimate Source? The human being knew long, long ago—before the manifestation of religions and complicated cosmologies, through inner contemplation, inner "looking"—that when the breath in the body, inhale and exhale, became very, very shallow, even stopped, there would then appear within the interior of its consciousness a light. This occurred as a natural function of the breath shallowing or stopping. Naturally. Much later in human history this was to be called the famous "third eye." And it is this very light that symbolized and connected the individual consciousness reflected in the Soul to the Universal Consciousness that is the origin of all things. The human being also learned long ago that by merging its own individual consciousness, or Soul, with that light, its consciousness would then expand in such a way that the individual consciousness itself became universal and was then able to consciously experience that ultimate Source of All Things; the wave has returned to the ocean.

The point here, again, is that human beings can know and validate these natural laws through their own actual experience; doing so does not require belief systems of any kind. The key to doing this is to gradually shallow and stop the breath altogether. Anyone can do this.

If you doubt this, or wonder how, try the following natural method: On your inhaling breath simply mentally affirm the number one. On your exhaling breath simply mentally affirm the number two. The "secret" here is to concentrate as hard as you can on the numbers one and two. It is with this act of concentration, intensified by desire manifesting as will, that progressively your breath will in fact begin to shallow and even stop. Remember that consciousness is energy and cannot be destroyed. It can only change form. Thus, unlike what some may think, when the breath is stopped it does not mean that you have to die. Consciousness is not dependent on the human form. When the breath is stopped, the inner light, which is intrinsic to consciousness, will soon begin to appear. And as it does so, simply move into it with the conscious act of surrender. Surrendering to it will then allow for a merging of your own consciousness with that Universal Consciousness as symbolized in the light. Anyone can do this, and then know for himself or herself this natural truth.

It is this natural law of breath, when stopped or deeply shallowed, that allows for what all the great teachers of relatively recent centuries—when compared to how long the human being has actually been on the planet—have said. As Jesus said, "When thine eye is single, thy whole body is also full of light."

Symbolically speaking, our two physical eyes correlate to the two motions of breath: inhale and exhale. It is the inhaling and exhaling of the breath that keep one's consciousness utterly involved and enmeshed in the duality, or polarity, of life itself. Likes and dislikes, happy and sad, love and hate, etc., correlate to and demonstrate this natural law. The numbers one and two correlate to the natural law of finitude and duality, cause and effect. Yet between one and two there exists an interval, or zero. The interval, or zero, correlates to the Universal Consciousness, or infinity. Thus when the breath stops or becomes very, very shallow, the interval is then perceived. What is perceived in the single eye (or what has been called the third eye)— that which naturally exists within the interior of consciousness—can be accessed and merged with our Soul. When this occurs, the law of duality ceases to exist. The ultimate satisfaction is then realized. The Soul correlates astrologically to Pluto.

From the point of view of natural laws, it is interesting to note, historically speaking, that advanced mathematics like algebra, trigonometry, quantum physics, and so on, could not have been realized unless there was an "idea" or conception called zero. In the third century AD in India, mathematicians conceived of the number zero. And, of course, from the point of view of Indian cosmologies, this occurred as a direct extension of their natural understanding of the origin of Creation. Out of nothing, or zero, the manifested Creation (the unmanifested/manifested, the causeless cause) occurred.

THE EGO

Coming into human form, the Soul will then manifest what is known as the ego. The ego correlates astrologically to the Moon. The ego is also pure energy. We cannot open the brain and find it. Unlike the energy of the Soul, which is sustained from life to life until the final merging with the Source occurs, the energy of the ego in any life is dissolved after each life is lived.

The analogy of the wave and the ocean again serves to illustrate this point. The ocean can be equated with the Soul, and the wave can be equated with the ego. Of course the ocean, Soul, is manifesting the waves, ego, life after life. And just as the waves can rise and fall, in any given life that the Soul creates, the ocean is sustained. In other words, the egos that the Soul manifests in each life rise from birth but finally dissolve back into the ocean, Soul, upon the completion of each life. Its energy is not destroyed but simply absorbed back into the energy that created it in the first place.

The ego created by the Soul thus allows for the individualizing aspect of the Soul in each life. In each life the ego is created by the Soul in such a way as to serve as the vehicle through which the evolutionary intentions of the Soul in any life occurs. Each ego that the Soul creates is oriented to reality in such a way that the very nature of the orientation serves as the vehicle through which the life lessons occur and are understood by the Soul. In each life, the ego allows for a self-image of the Soul to occur relative to the individualizing aspect of the Soul.

An analogy to a movie projector will suffice to illustrate this point. If I have a movie projector loaded with a reel of film and a screen in front of the movie projector, and I turn on the machine, generating light from it, I will have no distinct imagery on the screen unless I also have a lens within the projector. Without the lens, what manifests from the machine is simply diffuse light. Thus the lens serves as a vehicle through which the inherent images on the film can be focused and given distinct shape, form, and images. In the very same way, the ego that the Soul generates in each life allows for a vehicle, or lens, through which the inherent images that exist within our Soul take form. This natural law of consciousness is thus the cause that allows for individual self-perception and the word *I* itself.

The Soul, Pluto, also correlates to the genetic code, RNA and DNA, chromosomes, and enzymes. In each life the Soul is the determinant for the entire genetic code of the life, the human form, that it is being born into. Each life that the Soul chooses is a continuation of that which has come before, where each new life correlates to the ongoing evolutionary lessons or intentions of any given Soul. Thus, the body type that includes which race to be born into, the appearance of it, the culture to be born into, the parents of origin, and the specific and individual nature of the emotions, feelings, psychology, desires, and so on, correlate to the Soul's intentions reflected in the genetic code in total in each life. This is all then given individual form in each life via the egocentric structure, the Moon, that the Soul creates in each life. Thus any person can then say things such as, "This is who I am," "This is what I need," "This is what I'm feeling," "This is what I'm trying to learn." And so on. The individualizing aspect of the ego is what the Soul creates in each life.

When death occurs in any given life, as stated earlier, the ego that the Soul has created for a life then dissolves back into its origin, the Soul. Since both are energy, and energy cannot be destroyed, where does the Soul go upon the physical death of the body? In other words, where is it on an energetic level? We have heard the term *astral plane*, and the words *heaven* and *hell*. Obviously, what these types of words refer to are other realities or planes of existence. There are, in fact, other energetic realities or planes of existence. Simply speaking, the astral plane is an energetic plane of existence that all Souls go to after the completion of physical lives on places like Earth. Energetically, this plane of existence is much less materially dense than places like Earth.

After physical death, the Soul "goes to" the astral plane in order to review the life that has just been lived and to prepare for yet another birth on a place like Earth. Upon the completion of a life on Earth, the ego dissolves back into the Soul in such a way that the center of gravity within the consciousness, within the astral plane, is the Soul itself. For most folks, living lives in the material plane we call Earth, the center of gravity of consciousness is the ego itself. This is why the vast majority of people who are alive feel within themselves that they are separate from everything else; the center of gravity being the ego-centric "I." In the astral plane the center of gravity shifts to the Soul itself, so that when death occurs in any given life the memory of the ego of that life is sustained.

This memory of the ego is necessary for the Soul, for it is the memory of the ego that allows the Soul not only to review the life that has just been lived but also serves as the basis for the next life to be lived, relative to the continuing evolution of the Soul itself; in each life we all pick up where we have left off before. Thus, this memory of the ego in each life serves as the causative factor of what type of ego-centric structure the Soul needs to create in the next life. In essence, it is the memory of the ego that the Soul draws upon, and the images contained therein serve as the basis of the next ego that the Soul needs to generate in each successive life to promote its ongoing evolution.

Astrologically speaking, this is symbolized by Pluto, the Soul, and the south and north nodes of the Moon. The South Node of the Moon correlates to the prior egocentric memories of the Soul that determine the natal placement of the Moon in each life and the current ego, and the North Node of the Moon correlates to the evolving ego of the Soul—the nature and types of inner and outer experiences that the Soul needs and desires in order to facilitate its ongoing evolution. In turn, this will then constitute the new egocentric memories and images that the Soul will draw upon when a life has been lived and is terminated at physical death.

Most of us are aware that the Moon also correlates to one's family of origin in any given life. It should be clear, then, that upon the death of the physical body, the Soul goes to the astral plane and again meets important family members and others close to the Soul. This is also why, for many Souls, we continue to meet those family members upon rebirth into yet another physical life on places like Earth. It is the memory of the ego, now combined with the memory of family, that is the determinant in this phenomenon. And this phenomenon is sustained until there is no longer any evolutionary or karmic need to sustain such relationships.

THE EVOLUTIONARY CONDITIONS OR STATES

A crucial principle to review concerns the four natural evolutionary conditions, or stages, of a Soul's evolution. One of the great problems of modern astrology is a total ignorance of this natural law. As a result, much if not most of astrological understanding correlates with the one-size-fits-all approach. In and of itself this approach does a total disservice not only to astrology in general, but also to the very people it attempts to help. This approach flies in the face of common sense, not to mention life itself. It is like saying if I have Venus square Pluto, then the meaning of that astrological pairing would be the same for all. This approach never takes into account the individual context of anything.

Let us remember a core truth about astrology: it only works relative to observed context. If the one-size-fits-all approach were in fact true, then, for example, when Uranus transited Pisces in the 1920s, the same social themes would have existed all over the planet. In reality, they did not, because of individual context. In Germany, for example, and its context following World War I, there manifested an almost total breakdown in the social order, where one literally had to haul wheelbarrows of money just to buy a loaf of bread. Yet at the same time, in the United States, the Roaring Twenties manifested because of the specific context of America at that time. This was, in essence, fueled by the invention of non-secured personal credit.

The evolution of the Soul is based on the progressive elimination of all separating desires to the exclusion of the only desire that can remain: to return home to that which is the origin of all Souls in the first place. Based on this natural law, there are four natural evolutionary conditions—with three subdivisions in each—that correlate to the Soul's evolutionary journey. If you doubt this, simply stand back in a Uranian way from any society, country, culture, or tribe, and observe it. Any detached observer will then be able to notice four natural evolutionary conditions.

These four conditions are:

1. Roughly 4 to 5 percent of all Souls are in what I have previously called the dimly evolved state. This means one of two things: either Souls that are evolving into human consciousness from other forms of life such as animals and plants, or Souls that are de-evolving backward into this condition due to karmic causes.

2. Souls that have evolved into what can be called the "consensus" state of evolution, which accounts for roughly 70 percent of all Souls on the planet at this time.

3. The individualized state of evolution, where *individualized* is used in a Jungian sense of the word. This accounts for roughly 20 percent of all Souls.

4. The spiritual state of evolution that accounts for roughly 4 to 6 percent of all Souls on the planet.

It is extremely important to understand that no astrologer can determine which evolutionary condition exists for any Soul by simply looking at the birth chart alone. The astrologer must observe and interact with the client in order for this determination to be made. A good way to do this in a counseling situation, when a client has come to the astrologer, is simply to ask the client why they are there, and what questions they have. Generally, the very nature of the questions that the client has will cue the astrologer as to what evolutionary condition exists for that client. For example, if one client asks, "When can I expect enlightenment?" and another asks, "When will I have my new BMW?" there clearly is an observed difference reflecting the level of evolutionary progression of the Soul.

The Dimly Evolved State

Those Souls that are evolving into human consciousness from other forms of life—typically animal and plant, since animals and plants essentially have the same emotional and nervous systems as humans—are characterized by a very limited sense of self-awareness. This self-awareness is usually limited to the time and space that they personally occupy. When one looks into such Souls' eyes, they typically express a density within the pupils, like a film effect. These Souls are generally very joyous and very, very innocent, and can bring great love to those who are close to them. Terminology used to describe these types of Souls includes terms like *cretinism*, *very low IQ*, *mongoloid*, *mental retardation*, and the like. The root desire within this evolutionary stage or state is the desire to be normal—where "normal" means to be like most other people, the consensus state.

Conversely, due to karmic causes, it can occur that Souls can be de-evolved, which means that such Souls are forced back into this state. This then becomes very problematic for such Souls, because they had previously evolved beyond this stage. Thus, such Souls now experience great and humiliating limitations because of the de-evolution. As a result, these Souls are extremely angry and some can go about creating great disturbances for other people. These Souls can also be classified by the terminology listed in the previous paragraph. But the great difference is that when one looks into the pupils of these Souls' eyes, one will notice a great, quite piercing white light manifesting from the pupils. And, within that light, one will inwardly experience the intense anger within such a Soul.

The Consensus State

Astrologically speaking, this state correlates to Saturn because of the underlying desire to conform to the consensus of any society, culture, tribe, or country. Thus, such Souls' entire orientation to reality—including their values; their sense of meaning in life; their morality, customs, norms, and taboos; and their sense of what is right and wrong—is simply an extension of the prevailing consensus of whatever society they are born into. In essence, the reality for such Souls is merely an extension of the external conditioning that any consensus group of people provides. They cannot step out of the box, so to speak. For example, if a scientist claims that astrology is bogus, then all those who are within the consensus state will have the same opinion.

Within the consensus state—like all the other states—there are three subdivisions that we must account for. Each subdivision reflects the ongoing evolution of a Soul through the entire evolutionary state, which then leads to the next evolutionary state with its three subdivisions—until the final liberation of a Soul occurs relative to the exhaustion of all separating desires ultimately reflected in the third subdivision of the spiritual state of evolution. The way that evolution occurs through each state is by exhausting all the desires that are intrinsic to the nature of each evolutionary state or condition. Within the consensus state, the root desire that propels the evolution of the Soul forward, from the first subdivision through the third, is characterized by the desire to get ahead—to get ahead of the system, which of course means the consensus society that they belong to.

Souls within the first subdivision of the consensus state are characterized by a limited sense of self-awareness that is essentially limited to the time and space that they occupy, a limited awareness of the dynamics of the community that they inhabit, and an even more limited awareness of the dynamics of the country they live in—and yet they are incredibly self-righteous relative to the values, morality, and consensus religion of the existing society of their birth, how life is interpreted according to those beliefs, the judgments issued because of those beliefs, and so on. There simply is no ability to separate themselves from any of this; it is as if they are social automatons. An apt analogy for these Souls is to the worker bees in a beehive. Typically, they are in the lowest social stratum of their society of birth.

As evolution proceeds for these Souls relative to the desire to get ahead, it will lead them into the second subdivision, because that root desire means they will want more from society than simply remaining within its lower strata. These Souls, of course, perceive from the point of view of the lower strata that there are others who have more than they have. This perception is more or less limited to others having more possessions of a grander nature than they have, social positions within society they themselves do not have and thus more social freedom, and so on. Yet, that limited perception fuels the root desire to get ahead and to have more. In order for this desire to be realized, they must learn even more about how society and its dynamics work. This then requires an expansion of their personal awareness in order for this learning to take place. It is the very fact of the evolutionary necessity to expand their awareness that propels the evolution of the Soul into the second subdivision within the consensus state.

In the second subdivision it then becomes necessary for the Soul to learn even more about the nature of society in order to use the social system to its own evolutionary advantage—to get ahead. The reality for such Souls is still totally defined by the consensus of society: its values, morality, religions, judgments, what is right and wrong, and the like. Yet by desiring to get ahead, the Soul must expand its personal awareness of the nature of the dynamics of how the society that it is part of is put together: its rules, regulations, what is required for this ambition or that one to be actualized, and so on. The Soul thus becomes ever more aware of others, of the community that it is part of, and the country that it lives within.

This expanding awareness also includes the beginning of becoming aware of other countries and the differences in values, morality, religions, and so on as reflected in these other societies. Thus personal awareness, self-awareness, expands because of the heightened awareness of others relative to the Soul's desire to get ahead. This evolutionary stage correlates to the middle strata within the social order of any given society. As the Soul evolves through this state, it increasingly becomes aware of the upper strata of society, of those who are in positions of power and leadership, of those who have great material abundance, and, as result, the desire to get ahead fuels the ongoing evolution of the Soul into the third subdivision within the consensus state.

In order for the Soul to evolve into the third subdivision within the consensus state, it demands an increasing awareness of how society works in total. Because of this, personal awareness expands through evolutionary necessity in order for the Soul's desires, defined by ambitions, to get ahead and be realized. The Soul's personal awareness has now expanded to the point that it is very aware of the totality of the community and society that it belongs to, of the country that it lives in, and this also includes a progressive awareness of other countries, other cultures, and of the relativity of morality, values, religions, and so on, as reflected in other countries and cultures. Even though this awareness progressively includes the relativity of morality and values, it does not mean that the Soul in this subdivision considers other countries, values, beliefs, and religions equal to its own society and country of birth. In fact, within this subdivision the self-righteousness born out of conformity, the underlying hallmark of the consensus state in total, is sustained: we are right, and they are wrong. In total, the consensus state correlates to what is called *nationalism*.

In this final subdivision within the consensus state, the Soul desires to be on top of society, to have positions of social importance and relative power, prestige, and material abundance. This subdivision includes the politicians, the CEOs of corporations, important positions in the business world, mainstream religious leaders, and so on. These Souls include the upper strata of society. As the Soul evolves through this last subdivision, it will finally exhaust all the desires that are inherent within it. As a result, the meaning of life itself will progressively be lost, as those desires no longer hold any meaning.

At the very end of the journey through this state, the Soul will finally question whether or not there must be more to life than this. This very question implies an awakening alienation from the consensus, from normal life as defined by the consensus. It is this awakening alienation from normalcy defined by the consensus of any society that now triggers the beginning of a new desire that will propel the Soul into the individuated evolutionary state—the desire to liberate from all external conditioning that has previously defined the Soul's sense of reality in general and its sense of personal identity, or individuality, specifically.

The Individuated State

Astrologically speaking, the individuated state correlates to Uranus, because the Soul desires to liberate or rebel against the consensus state it is now evolving away from. Instead of the Soul being defined by the consensus to shape its sense of reality in general, and its personal identity specifically, the Soul now desires to discover who and what it is independent of such conditioning. Earlier I stated that if a Soul were in the consensus state, and a scientist said astrology is bogus, this would then be the automatic belief of those Souls who are within the consensus state. If that same scientist said this to a Soul within the individuated state, the response would be something like "No, thank you, I will think for myself."

Souls in this evolutionary state inwardly feel different—different from the majority of the society and country of their birth. Because of the desire to liberate from the consensus, the awareness of Souls in this state progressively expands to include ever-larger wholes or frames of reference.

This expansion of awareness begins because the Soul no longer can identify with the consensus of the society of birth. As a result, the Soul now feels a progressive detachment from society, like standing on the outside and looking in. This then allows the Soul to objectify itself relative to personal awareness and self-perception. Rebelling against consensus beliefs, values, morality, and so on, the Soul now begins to question the assumptions that most people hold dear to their hearts that correlate to what reality is and is not. Such Souls now begin to experiment by investigating other ways of looking at and understanding the nature of life itself. This is a reflection of the independent thinking that characterizes this evolutionary state. And it is through this independent thinking and investigating of all kinds of different ways of understanding life—including investigating ideas, beliefs, and philosophies from other lands and cultures—that allows for an ever-increasing expansion of their consciousness and, thus, their sense of personal awareness. As a result of this, such Souls no longer feel at home in their own land, their country of birth.

In the first subdivision, the Soul will typically try to compensate for this inner feeling of being different—of not belonging to the consensus—and the inner sense of alienation by trying to appear normal. This compensation will then cause the Soul to structure its outer reality much as Souls do in the consensus state: normal kinds of work, normal kinds of friends, the normal appearance, and so on. Yet inwardly these Souls feel and know that they can no longer personally identify with that compensatory reality that they attempt to sustain. This compensation manifests in this subdivision because, after all, the consensus is just where the Soul has been. It therefore constitutes a sense of security relative to the inner feeling of being detached and different. We must remember that for most people the sense of security for life is a function of self-consistency. And self-consistency is a function of the past. As a result, the compensation manifests as a reaction to this increasingly new feeling of being different, of not belonging anymore to the consensus. This feeling creates a sense of insecurity in this subdivision because is it brand-new; the Soul has not been here before. Yet this very act of compensation creates a very real state of being in a living lie.

Even as this compensatory behavior occurs, the Soul nonetheless will be questioning everything deep within itself, the privacy of its own inner life. Typically, such Souls will read all kinds of books that contain ideas that go way beyond the norm as defined by the consensus. Many, depending on cultural possibilities, will take classes or workshops that have the same theme or intention. Some will seek out these kinds of alternative environments in order to find and bond with others of like mind, others who feel just as they do. This compensatory behavior will progressively give way, and collapse in on itself, as the Soul evolves further through this subdivision. The Soul will progressively distance itself from the consensus and begin to form relationships with other alienated Souls just like itself. Because of the necessity of work, or a job, most of these Souls will either do any kind of work just to get by, without identifying with such work in any way, or they will actualize a work that is individualistic and symbolic of their own individuality.

In the second subdivision, the underlying archetype of Uranus as it correlates to rebellion is at its highest. This rebellion is so extreme that the Soul has now thrown off almost any idea or philosophy that has come before at any level of reality. Such Souls end up in a kind of existential void and typically hang out with other such alienated Souls, which has the effect of reinforcing the total state of rebellion from all of reality other than the reality that they have now defined through the existential void. These Souls will exhibit a deep fear of integrating into society in any kind of way, for the fear suggests to them that if they do so that somehow that very same society or reality will absorb their hard-won, at least to them, individuality, which is defined through the act or rebellion in this stage. As a result, these Souls typically hang out on the fringes of society, hurling atom bombs of criticism at it in order to reinforce their sense of personal righteousness defined by their alienation from the consensus. Because of the natural law of evolution, which is always preceded by an involution, these people at some point will realize that their fear of integrating into reality, into society, is just that: a fear only. Once this is realized, they will begin to make the effort to integrate back into society but with their individuality intact. At that point, the Soul will then evolve into the third subdivision within the individuated state.

In the third subdivision, the Soul will begin to manifest within society or reality as truly unique and gifted people from the point of view of the consensus. This means that such Souls will have in some way a unique gift, or capacity, to help the consensus itself evolve, by integrating that capacity or gift within the consensus. Yet these people will not inwardly feel identified with the consensus; they are standing inwardly very distant from it. The consciousness of these Souls has progressively expanded through the individuated state in such a way that they are aware of the entire world and the relativity of beliefs, values, morality, and so on. As a result, they feel within themselves that they are world citizens, much more than a singular citizen of their country of birth. The inner pondering as to the very nature of existence and Creation, of who they really are, essentially define the nature of their consciousness. Progressively, these people begin to really open up their consciousness to the universal, the cosmos, to God/Goddess. Not the God/Goddess defined through consensus religions but the real or natural God/Goddess. A perfect example in relatively recent history that reflects such a Soul is Albert Einstein. Another example is Carl Jung.

The Spiritual State

Astrologically speaking, this evolutionary state correlates to Neptune, because now the root desire becomes to consciously know, not just believe in, and unite with the Source of All Things—the universal, God/Goddess. Because of this root desire, the consciousness now progressively expands into the universal, the cosmos, in such a way that the very nature of the interior consciousness within the Soul becomes conscious of the living universe within—the wave within the ocean, and the ocean within the wave. Progressively in this spiritual state of evolution, the very center of gravity within the Soul's consciousness shifts from the subjective ego to the Soul itself. Once the center of gravity shifts to the Soul, then in the context of any given life the Soul is able to experience its specific individuality as reflected in the ego while simultaneously experiencing, being centered in, the Soul—the ocean that is aware of the waves that it manifests.

The Soul contains within itself all the prior-life memories that it has ever lived. And the Soul has its own identity or ego. This identity or ego is not the same as the ego that the Soul creates in any given life on places like Earth. The ego of the Soul is one's eternal identity. An easy way for any of us to understand this occurs when we dream. Obviously, when we dream we are not identified with our subjective ego. After all, we are asleep. The subjective ego has temporarily dissolved back into the Soul when we sleep. So the question becomes, who and what is doing the dreaming? Obviously, it can only be the Soul with its own ego that thus allows the Soul to know itself as a Soul that is eternal. Another way to validate the same thing occurs when we sometimes wake up from sleeping and cannot immediately remember who we are—the current subjective ego, the "I," of this life. It takes some effort to actually remember the subjective "I" when this occurs. So, again, the question becomes, who and what must make the effort to remember the subjective "I" in the current life? It can only be our Soul.

As evolution proceeds in this spiritual state, there is a progressive shift in the center of gravity within the Soul's consciousness. When this shift firmly takes hold, then the Soul, in any given life, is experiencing its eternal self or ego while simultaneously experiencing the subjective ego, and the individuality attendant to it, which it has created for its own ongoing evolutionary reasons and intentions. This is very similar to standing at the beach when the sun goes down, at that moment when the sun is equally half above and half below the horizon. In this state of consciousness, the Soul is aware from within itself of all the prior lives that it has lived, and at the same time aware of the specific life, ego, that it is currently living.

Progressively, as evolution proceeds in the spiritual state of evolution, the Soul also becomes consciously aware of the Source of All Things. This occurs as the consciousness of the Soul becomes truly universal, the inner experience of the entire universe within one's own consciousness. This state of cosmic consciousness allows one to actually experience the very point of the manifested Creation itself: the interface between the unmanifested and the manifested. As this occurs, the Soul then also becomes aware of all the natural laws that govern and correlate to the very nature of Creation itself. In the most advanced states of evolution, the Soul, now being utterly identified with these natural laws of Creation, is then able to harmonize with those laws in such a way as to use those laws at will, in conjunction with the will of all things—that which is the very origin of those natural laws.

In the first subdivision within this spiritual state, the Soul progressively becomes aware of just how small it is, because of the increasing universal dimensions that are occurring within its consciousness. This is vastly different from being the center of one's own universe as reflected in the consensus state, for example. In and of itself, this has a naturally humbling effect on the Soul and thus the current subjective ego, Moon, which it has created. It is exactly this naturally humbling archetype that thus allows progressively for the center of gravity to shift within the Soul's consciousness from the subjective ego to the Soul itself, and ultimately to a conscious union with the Source of All Things.

As a result, the Soul desires to progressively commit itself to the desire to reunite with the Source. As this occurs, the Soul will progressively commit itself to devotional types of spiritual practice in this subdivision. Within this, the Soul desires to commit itself to various forms of work that all correlate to being of service to the larger whole, of service to others in some way. Many will naturally want to orient to various forms of the healing arts or to start centers in which the healing arts are in some way the focus. The core issue here is that the Soul desires to do work on behalf of the Source of All Things and to use the work as a vehicle through which the Source can be inwardly experienced because of the nature of the work. In the East this is called *karma yoga*.

In this first subdivision, the Soul becomes progressively aware of all that it needs to improve upon within itself. A heightened state of awareness occurs that makes the Soul aware of all of its imperfections and, as a result, the Soul can now become highly self-critical. Even though this is natural, it also creates a potential danger or trap to the Soul, in that this heightened state of critical self-awareness can cause the Soul to not feel good enough or ready to do the task, or work, that it is being inwardly directed to do. This then sets in motion all kinds of excuse-making, always manifesting as perfectly rational arguments, for why the Soul will not do what it should do when it should do it. The way out of this trap is to realize that the path to perfection occurs by taking one step at a time.

As evolution progresses through this first subdivision, the Soul will increasingly have direct perception of the single eye, or the third eye, which is inherent to consciousness. As a result, this perception allows the Soul to merge with that single eye in such a way that various types and states of cosmic consciousness will occur, which will lead into the second subdivision within the spiritual state or state of evolution.

As the Soul evolves into the second subdivision, it has already had various kinds of inner cosmic or universal kinds of experiences within its consciousness. However, in this state the final shift in the center of gravity within consciousness from the subjective ego to the Soul itself has yet to occur. In this state the shift manifests more like a rubber band, where the point of gravity keeps going back and forth from the subjective ego to the Soul. The problem that this generates is that the progressive inner experiences within the consciousness of the universal, of the cosmic, of the Source, fuel the subjective ego in such a way that the Soul feels more evolved than it actually is. This can then set in motion, in varying degrees of intensity, "spiritual delusions of grandeur" from an egocentric and Soul point of view. When this occurs, such Souls will then feel that they have a spiritual mission to fulfill on behalf of others, of the world itself.

It is important to remember in trying to understand this subdivision that as the Soul gets ever closer to the Source, the light, whatever egocentric impurities remain within the Soul must be purged. As a result, the closer the Soul becomes to reuniting with its own origin, the more these impurities will manifest through the current-life subjective ego that the Soul's own ego contains.

These impurities can be many things depending on the specific nature of each Soul, but all Souls in this subdivision will share one common impurity: the ego of the Soul that is still identifying itself as somehow separate from that which has created it. This ongoing delusion is thus reflected in the subjective ego that the Soul creates. This common impurity will then be exhibited in specific psychological behaviors that essentially boil down to such Souls pointing the way to themselves as the vehicle of salvation, or to knowing God/Goddess, while at the same time pretending that they are not. In other words, they are extremely good salespeople that peddle God/Goddess as the hook in order to have themselves revered as the way to actually know God/Goddess. There is always a hidden or secret egocentric agenda within these Souls that is masked by the overlay of whatever spiritual or religious teaching they are representing. Examples of this point, in modern history, would be Bhagwan Shree Rajneesh, Elizabeth Clare Prophet, JZ Knight (Ramtha), Da Free John, Rasputin, and the like.

As the Soul evolves through this subdivision, it finally realizes the nature of this root impurity. As a result, it experiences a natural guilt, and this guilt is then used by the Soul to create its own downfall in order to atone for that guilt. The downfall can occur in many different ways, depending on the specific nature of the circumstantial life that the Soul has generated. This downfall caused by guilt and the need to atone for that guilt thus serves as the final evolutionary development that allows the Soul to evolve into the third subdivision within the spiritual state.

In the last and final subdivision within the spiritual state, the Soul is now finally and firmly identified with that which has created it: the Source of All Things. The center of gravity within consciousness has finally centered within the Soul, not the subjective ego created by the Soul. At this point in the evolution of the Soul, all subsequent evolution through this final subdivision will be focused on the elimination of any separating desires that the Soul still has. Because of this final shift within consciousness to the Soul itself, the Soul is inwardly attuned to the Source of All Things in such a way that it perceives itself as but a singular manifestation of the Source. Simultaneously, the Soul perceives all others, all of Creation, as manifestations of that Source. Thus the Soul's inner and outer responses to life itself, how life is understood and interpreted, how it comes to understand the nature of the life it is currently living, how it understands the purpose for the current life, and how it comes to make decisions relative to the life being lived are all based on this inner attunement and alignment with that which has created it.

As evolution begins in this final subdivision, the Soul inwardly feels and knows that it is here to serve the Source in some way. It knows that it cannot just live for itself. It knows that it has some kind of work to do on behalf of the Source. The consciousness of the Soul at this point is entirely structured to give to others, and to give purely without any ulterior agenda or motive involved. The nature of the work will always involve the theme of teaching or healing in some way. Because the Soul is now consciously identified with the Source, the very nature of the Soul's own vibration radiates in such a way that many others are drawn to it like a magnet. Many other Souls are drawn magnetically to these Souls because they also reflect and radiate a fundamental wisdom of life, a deep compassion for the human condition. This occurs because, after all, these Souls have traveled a very long evolutionary journey, which has taken them through almost every kind of life experience imaginable. Such Souls are naturally very unassuming and humble, and have no desire whatsoever for any kind of acclaim to their ego. Quite the opposite: they shy away from such things and always remind anyone who tries to give them acclaim of any kind that all things come from God, or the Source. Such Souls only point the way home, and never to themselves.

Conversely, these Souls can also attract to themselves others who project onto them all manner of judgments, projection of motives, intentions of who they really are, and wholesale persecution. The reason this occurs is because the very nature of these Souls is fundamentally pure and full of the inner light of the Source. As a result, their own inner light has the effect of exposing the impurities in others, of others' actual reality versus the persona that is created, of others' actual intentions and motives for anything. Accordingly, those who do this kind of projection and so on feel threatened by these types of Souls, for they know that they themselves are fundamentally dishonest and that they are invested in having others believe in whatever persona that they are creating to hide their actual reality. Feeling threatened thus causes these types of people to manifest this type of behavior at these Souls.

In the beginning of this subdivision, the nature of the work that the Soul does, the amount of people who are destined to help in some way through the vehicle of teaching or healing, is relatively small and limited to the immediate area in which they live. Progressively, this will evolve from this limited application to involve increasingly larger circles in which the nature of the work on behalf of the Source increases. In the end, this increasing circle will include the entire world. And at the very end of evolution in this subdivision, these Souls will be remembered by countless others long after the physical life of the Soul is over; the nature of their life and the teachings that they represented will be remembered. Examples of these types of Souls are individuals such as Jesus, Yogananda, Lao-Tzu, Buddha, Mohammed, Saint Teresa of Avila, and so on.

It is important to remember, again, that these are the natural evolutionary conditions that reflect the current reality of all people on Earth. For those who wish to employ evolutionary astrology, it is essential that you make the necessary observations of any given person to determine their evolutionary state, and then to orient yourself to their natal chart accordingly. One size does not fit all.

ABOUT JEFFREY WOLF GREEN

Through his deep spiritual insights and his counseling, teaching, and recorded and published works, Jeffrey Wolf Green's prolific work in astrology has inspired a multitude and led to the creation of what is known today as the EA (evolutionary astrology) movement. In 1994 he established the Jeffrey Wolf Green School of Evolutionary Astrology, a certification program that is now also available as a correspondence course. Upon his retirement in 2001, he passed the teaching of his school program to a select few graduates, whose works are also included in this book.

Jeffrey Wolf Green's life experience is as extraordinary as his visionary works. He served in Vietnam, studied in a matriarchal monastery in Nepal and a Vedantic temple in the United States, and was initiated into the sacred practices of the Navajo by a master shaman. He has lectured in many countries the world over, and his books have been translated into many languages. He is the father of four and now lives in secluded retirement.

Jeffrey Wolf Green is the author of:

Pluto, Volume I: The Evolutionary Journey of the Soul (Llewellyn, 1985)

Pluto, Volume II: The Soul's Evolution Through Relationships (Llewellyn, 2000)

Uranus: Freedom from the Known (Llewellyn, 1988)

Measuring the Night, Evolutionary Astrology and the Keys to the Soul, Volumes One & Two; co-authored with Steven Forrest (Seven Paws Press, 2001)

2

From Cataclysm to the Awakening of Latent Capacities:
Four Main Ways That Pluto Affects/Instigates Our Evolutionary Growth

BY DEVA GREEN

There are two distinctly different types of evolution. One type is *uniform*, which correlates with slow but progressive change, and the other type is *cataclysmic*, which obviously correlates to traumatic events, after which we experience an evolutionary leap in our growth. These two types of evolution can be validated simply by examining our own life experiences. They are vastly different from one another in terms of how we experience them.

In addition, there are four ways that Pluto instigates change. The following list is also described in *Pluto, Volume 1: The Evolutionary Journey of the Soul*, by Jeffrey Wolf Green.

OVERIDENTIFICATION

1. When we become overly identified with some area in our lives, either on an emotional level or from an egocentric point of view,

an emotional shock of some nature must occur to enforce the necessary change. Often, this is linked with a traumatic or cataclysmic event. Cataclysmic events occur when the Soul has resisted the necessary evolutionary growth to such an extent that the event must manifest in order for growth to continue. There are two reasons for experiencing any kind of cataclysmic or traumatic change: one is evolutionary necessity, and the other is karmic retribution. These two reasons for experiencing a traumatic event are vastly different from one another.

FORMING A RELATIONSHIP

2. Evolution occurs through forming a relationship with something that we perceive we need but feel that we don't currently have. Evolution takes place as we encounter our personal limitations (our personal strength and weaknesses). This merging process can occur through forming a relationship with anything outside ourselves that we feel we need. It is through this merging that a Plutonian osmosis occurs; we extract the essence of that with which we have formed a relationship and we take it inside ourselves. In this way we can, potentially, create a positive and healthy evolutionary experience and grow past our evolutionary blocks and limitations. This inner metamorphosis is linked with non-cataclysmic, or uniform, change: slow yet progressive change.

GROWING AN AWARENESS OF STAGNATION

3. We encounter times in our life in which we experience an intense personal stagnation, and become aware that we are in fact not growing anymore. Frustration builds when we are only aware of the symptoms but not the causes. We tend to tune out everything else in our life as we try to uncover the cause of

this block. As we uncover the source of the block, unconscious content suddenly pours into conscious awareness, and we finally become aware of the source of the block. This process is very analogous to the volcano that suddenly turns active. It is through this process of overcoming these psychological blocks and allowing the necessary changes to take hold that the Soul evolves.

LATENT OR DORMANT CAPACITIES IGNITED

4. Evolution can occur during times in our lives when we become aware of a latent or dormant capacity within the Soul that was previously not conscious. We suddenly become aware, or conscious, of this hidden capability, and it now requires strength and perseverance to actualize the capacity, which in turn creates evolution.

Another important point to remember is that these evolutionary processes do not occur as isolated events, but can, in fact, occur simultaneously. This evolutionary phenomenon will be demonstrated later in this chapter.

Two extremely important factors that we must remember when counseling a person through these difficult experiences are the individual's natural evolutionary condition and their cultural/religious conditioning. These two factors cannot be overstated when working with a client and his or her birth chart, because it will dramatically change the person's ability to understand and work through the emotional dynamics that these experiences will bring up within the Soul. A person in the early individuated state, for example, will have a harder time working through cataclysmic events that occur than will a person in the later stages of the individuated state or early spiritual state. This is due to strong conditioning patterns that may still be in place. Also, the individual may have less experience in trying to overcome and understand these traumatic events. As we evolve, the desire to understand and to change negative or destructive emotional patterns in ourselves that are creating difficult and traumatic life experiences becomes stronger. In other words, as we evolve, our desire to understand and change negative aspects of ourselves becomes increasingly stronger. Sooner or later, we no longer need to experience these traumatic events. Eventually, our gained wisdom can be shared and passed down to others who are suffering.

As we evolve, so does our attitude and orientation toward change evolve. Our resolve to understand what our lessons are for this life grows also. This occurs as the desire to know the Creator, or the Source, grows stronger and deeper within the Soul. Thus, if and when a cataclysmic event does take place, the person will be better able to handle and adjust to the changes that are taking place, and, one hopes, will be better able to take responsibility for his or her own actions. In different cultures, victimization is not promoted or taught, and so people will naturally take responsibility for themselves.

Different cultures teach different attitudes toward change and personal growth. For example, here in the United States, are people not taught to resist and fear any change, and don't they attempt to live a life that is relatively devoid of any change? Are not material wealth and the accumulation of many possessions what provide ultimate meaning and value for many in this society? In other cultures this is not the case; in fact, the exact opposite is taught. In India, for example, spiritual growth and a personal commitment to a spiritual path and to the Source are taught from birth. This is why it is so important to understand clients' cultural/religious backgrounds as well as their evolutionary states when looking at their birth charts and when counseling an individual through traumatic changes. We can encourage and motivate each other to overcome negative emotional dynamics that keep cycles of repetitive trauma going in our lives and that create some truly horrific events. The keywords here are *courage* and *faith*, and above all remember to have self-compassion and compassion for others. We are only responsible for our own actions, not anyone else's.

It is vital to consider the three main reactions to our evolutionary growth as described by Jeffrey Wolf Green in his book *Pluto, Volume 1: The Evolutionary Journey of the Soul*. These reactions directly impact the types of Plutonian experiences that we will have.

THE THREE REACTIONS

1. Totally resisting growth that is uncommon
2. Changing in some ways and not in others. This is by far the most common choice.
3. Totally embracing the necessary changes and evolutionary growth in an open and nonthreatening way. This, of course, is an uncommon choice.

It is our response to our evolutionary-growth needs that create the types of experiences we will have. If my Soul desires to change/purge certain negative dynamics, yet I am resisting the necessary change, then the possibility of a cataclysmic event will be very likely. In this case, the desire to change overrides the resistance, and the change will happen after the cataclysmic event. Such a case will teach us to stop resisting necessary growth, and to try our best to maintain a positive and open attitude toward change. The keyword here is *desire*. If the desire to change, to return to and merge with the Source, is strong enough, then it will happen, and if the resistance or desire to stay separate from the Source is strong enough, then that will happen, too.

On the following pages are real-life case studies and a discussion of the four main ways that Pluto instigates evolutionary growth. The natal chart of each individual will be briefly interpreted in order to provide a clear understanding of the Soul's evolutionary intentions for the life. The current evolutionary intentions for the Soul's life are symbolized in the natal birth chart by Pluto's polarity point, the

North Node, and its planetary ruler. Pluto's polarity by house and sign position symbolizes the evolutionary intention for the life itself. The North Node by house and sign position, and aspects to other planets, symbolizes the evolving egocentric structure that the Soul will create in order to actualize the evolutionary intentions reflected by Pluto's polarity point. The planetary ruler of the North Node by house and sign position, and aspects to other planets, symbolizes how the Soul will consciously actualize the North Node. The Pluto transits that occurred for each individual at the time of the evolutionary event are illustrated as well. It cannot be stressed enough: significant evolutionary events and Pluto transits can only be put into proper context when we can grasp the core evolutionary intentions for the individual's life.

FORMING A RELATIONSHIP

The most common way that Pluto affects/instigates evolution is when we form a relationship with something outside ourselves that we think we need. This implies that we have identified that there is something that we do not currently have that generates growing desire. By forming this type of relationship, a deep inner metamorphosis occurs. It allows us to experience ourselves in a positive and in a negative way in the context of encountering our personal strengths and weaknesses. This process leads to greater heights of personal awareness and development. By forming these types of relationships we will also experience moments of power and powerlessness. The feelings of power and powerlessness are associated with aspects of ourselves that are known and familiar, and are also associated with aspects of ourselves that are not—and represent the unknown, along with the areas that we may need to work on.

This type of growth is associated with non-cataclysmic, uniform change. The most common form of this type of evolution is forming a relationship with another person, but again, it can be anything that represents something we currently think we need but do not already have. The bottom line to remember when encountering this type of evolution is whether we are choosing to merge with something in a codependent way, and are in fact creating yet another negative and traumatic experience. This, of course, is in sharp contrast to merging with something or someone in a self-reliant manner.

When we merge with something or someone in a self-reliant manner, we are in fact re-empowering ourselves and creating a very positive and Soul-strengthening experience. This is the critical point to address regarding this type of evolution, and it is an important point to remember, both in our own lives and when counseling others. Due to the common conditioning patterns of our typical Western culture, forming relationships in this manner usually leads to the dynamic of use. Typically, people will use each other to get what they want, and as soon as the need that created the relationship is fulfilled they terminate the relationship. This method of using another to fulfill one's own needs without reciprocity isn't always conscious, but unfortunately it is a common reality in this society.

A positive example of this type of evolution is when Swami Kriyananda, a well-known and respected disciple of Paramahansa Yogananda, first met his guru. In his own autobiography, *The Path*, Kriyananda describes the powerful inspiration and evolution within his Soul that occurred through reading Yogananda's autobiography and being accepted as a disciple. In fact, he describes that reading Yogananda's autobiography impacted him so deeply that he boarded a cross-country bus the next day to go to Los Angeles to meet the great guru and to become his disciple. Clearly, this was a very crucial time in his own personal spiritual journey, and his encounter with Yogananda was a very significant evolutionary event.

Kriyananda is in the third-stage spiritual evolutionary condition. In his natal chart, Pluto is conjunct the North Node in Cancer in the first house. Pluto conjunct the North Node symbolizes that the areas

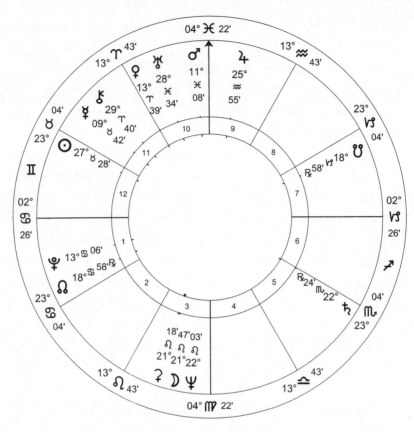

Chart 1: Kriyananda
May 19, 1926, 7 a.m. / Teleajen, Romania

associated with the sign and house position of Pluto conjunct the North Node are areas within the Soul that he has worked to transform prior to the current life, and he is meant to continue in that direction in the current life. Every other contributing factor in the birth chart is to be interpreted in the context of achieving the actualization of Pluto conjunct the North Node. Pluto's polarity point does not apply. The planetary ruler of the North Node is the Moon in Leo in the third house conjunct Neptune in Leo in the third house. The South Node is in Capricorn in the seventh house, ruled by Saturn in Scorpio in the fifth house retrograde. Venus is in Aries in the eleventh house square the nodal axis, and Pluto. From this natal signature we can see that Kriyananda is a pioneer in his time in the context of inspiring countless people to begin the spiritual quest, and also to overcome the hardships and traumatic events in their own lives through the books he has written and the lectures he has given around the world (Pluto in Cancer in the first house conjunct the North Node, ruled by the Moon in Leo in the third house conjunct Neptune).

Kriyananda has founded many ashrams and spiritual centers in which those who sought spiritual guidance and who desired to devote their lives to service to the Creator could live together (Venus in Aries in the eleventh house, square the nodal axis). It can be seen in this natal signature that in the evolutionary past, Kriyananda has inherited positions of social power and authority from the father, and was a part of the noble or ruling class. In the noble class, marriages are arranged in order to keep social power, and these relationships clearly did not meet his deepest emotional needs. He reacted to these life circumstances through rebellion against the responsibilities and duties of his social position and marriage (Venus in the eleventh house square the nodal axis). Kriyananda needed to independently embrace truths of a timeless and transcendent nature (North Node in Cancer in the first house conjunct Pluto, ruled by the Moon in Leo in the third house conjunct Neptune).

At the time when Kriyananda first meet Yogananda, became his disciple, and lived at Self-Realization Fellowship (SRF) headquarters, transiting Pluto was in Leo and moving through the natal third house. It was also approaching a conjunction aspect to the natal Moon/Neptune conjunction. The Moon is the planetary ruler of the North Node conjunct Pluto. Pluto was also forming a trine to Venus in Aries in the eleventh house, which squares the nodal axis, and Pluto. Any planet that is square the nodal axis symbolizes a skipped step from an evolutionary point of view. The node that last formed a conjunction with the planet symbolizes the areas through which the Soul will resolve the skipped step relative to house and sign position of the "resolution node." The planetary ruler of the resolution node will facilitate this process.

The specific Pluto transits described here correlate to critical junctions in Kriyananda's evolutionary journey because they are transiting key planets in the natal chart (the planetary ruler of the North Node that is conjunct Pluto, and a planet—Venus—that is square the nodal axis). Clearly, this was a very significant period of time in Kriyananda's life from an evolutionary point of view. He describes the impact that Yogananda's book *Autobiography of a Yogi* had on him in this way: "*Autobiography of a Yogi* is the greatest book I have ever read. One perusal of it was enough to change my entire life. From that time on my break with the past was complete. I resolved in the smallest detail of my life to follow Paramahansa Yogananda's teachings."

The transiting Pluto was trine the natal Venus is Aries in the eleventh house, which squares the nodal axis, and Pluto. This signature reflects unresolved karma within intimate relationships. Venus square the nodal axis reflects that the Soul's inner and outer relationship patterns in general represent areas of a skipped step in the context of the house and sign positions of the North and South Nodes.

The skipped step resolves around the need for freedom and independence in order for self-discovery and recovery to occur (Venus in Aries in the eleventh house, North Node in Cancer in the first house conjunct Pluto) and the need to be in a relationship based on mutual independence, giving, sharing and inclusion, and equality (South Node in Capricorn in the seventh house). The South Node in Capricorn in the seventh house is the resolution node, ruled by Saturn in Scorpio in the fifth house retrograde. The skipped steps relative to his inner and outer relationship patterns, and within intimate relationships specifically, will occur through integrating into society as an equal and through approaching relationships from the standpoint of equality, and giving, sharing, and inclusion. Previously, Kriyananda had approached relationships from an authoritarian standpoint in the context of the need to be in control of the relationship, and to control his emotions as well. He was in denial that he needed to be in an intimate relationship at all, and spent a majority of his time either on his own or in the spiritual organization SRF. This orientation to life constituted unconscious emotional security and was blocking further evolution. A core life lesson symbolized in the chart is to create a new self-image and identity that is independent from any external organization or spiritual group.

Another crucial evolutionary intention for this life is to learn fundamental self-reliance through his relationship to the Creator in the context of purging any dependency upon an external organization. This intention is symbolized by the planetary ruler of the South Node in Capricorn in the seventh house and Saturn in Scorpio in the fifth house retrograde, forming an opposition to the Sun in Taurus in the twelfth house. An opposition symbolizes the intention to "throw off" the dynamics that are associated with the planets that are in opposition by house and sign position. In addition, Kriyananda was always held in a special light by others whom he taught and befriended (South Node in Capricorn in the seventh house). It is because of this dynamic that his deepest emotional needs were not truly met (Venus in the eleventh house square Pluto and the nodal axis, and the North Node in Cancer in the first house). He did rebel against being put in this confining role, and threatened to disown his spiritual name (Venus is Aries in the eleventh house square the nodal axis).

Venus in the eleventh house symbolizes that unresolved trauma has occurred within intimate relationships in the evolutionary past. With Venus in square to the nodal axis and Pluto, there is a vital need to resolve that trauma through a commitment to another in an intimate relationship, and the need to allow himself to fully access his emotional body. This again is a core skipped step that must now be resolved. The total break from the past that occurred during this time is symbolized by the transiting Pluto forming a trine to Venus in Aries in the eleventh house, and its approach to a conjunction with the Moon in Leo in the third house conjunct Neptune. The Moon is the planetary ruler of the North Node conjunct Pluto. In the context of finding the inner courage and strength to break free from the past and to create brand-new life circumstances, the actions that were undertaken reflects his cooperation with the evolutionary intentions for the life.

Venus in the eleventh house symbolizes the need to be in a community where he could form bonds with others of like mind who were also devoting their life to serving the Creator. As mentioned before, a core evolutionary intention for the current life is to create a new self-image and identity that is free and independent from any external organization or spiritual group. In this way, his self-image and identity will reflect his cosmic identity as a reflection of the Creator. He will find himself able to relate with others on a much more personal level as the emotional body is accessed in all its totality (North Node/Pluto conjunction in Cancer in the first house, and the planetary ruler of the North Node the Moon conjunct Neptune in Leo in the third house). Through his relationship with his guru, he realized that he no longer needed to rebel in a negative manner against oppressive life circumstances that had been created. He was able to come out of his authoritarian role in relationships in general, and open up to his emotional body in a way that he had not been able to do previously in his life.

Pluto transiting Venus symbolizes that a metamorphosis of the Soul's inner and outer relationships will manifest through eliminating all dependencies upon a partner to fulfill projected needs. The evolutionary intention of Pluto/Venus transits is to learn to fulfill our needs from within instead of projecting needs onto a partner. In so doing, all imbalances, extremities, and codependencies within relationships will be eliminated. The inner relationship will be transformed as the

Soul learns self-reliance through meeting its own need from within. The inner relationship is now positive, and the Soul will approach relationships in a self-secure manner. In addition, Pluto/Venus transits symbolize that an intense examination of the Soul's values will manifest. Generally speaking, any values that promote a dependency upon monetary wealth to create emotional security, a relationship to fulfill projected needs, and values that no longer reflect the Soul's true meaning in life in general will occur during this transit. In this way, an evolution of the Soul will occur as values based on conditioning patterns of the past are purged. An awareness of new needs relative to relationships most commonly manifests as well.

In Kriyananda's case, the skipped step was recovered through his decision to move to Los Angeles and live at SRF headquarters. His relationship with the other members at SRF and his guru promoted the awareness of his own limitations, and how to evolve past those limitations. Transiting Pluto's forming trine to Venus symbolizes the ease of integration of this evolutionary process, and also the total awareness of the past that led to the current life circumstances. Thus, he knew what steps to take in order to continue his evolutionary journey. In other words, he became aware of his limitations and weaknesses relative to his inner and outer relationship patterns, and became aware of how to evolve past these limitations in order for a state of consistent growth to manifest.

At the time, Pluto was transiting the third house in Leo. Pluto's transit of the third house symbolizes the evolutionary intention to reformulate the mental or intellectual structure through eliminating old and rigid mental patterns in general. The need to absorb information that allows this metamorphosis to manifest is intensified. Kriyananda recounts that by reading Yogananda's book, previous preconceived notions, biases, and opinions that he held were exposed and he was able to grow to greater heights through an expansion of the mental mind. He also realized that his guru had already "struck at the heart of my deepest weakness, that of intellectual doubt."

It was during this time that Kriyananda first began the process of lecturing and writing, as well as editing Yogananda's own writings in order to have these writings published. In fact, Yogananda authorized him to teach Kriya Yoga to others. Kriyananda fulfilled much of his unresolved karma in the context of relationships in this way. Transiting Pluto in Leo symbolizes the evolutionary need to creatively actualize the special purpose through linking it with a socially relevant need. In this way, the creative actualization process will be transformed, and in alignment with the Soul's evolutionary/karmic intentions. The need to take control of the special purpose in life itself and creatively actualize it is now intensely felt. The creative purpose itself deepens when Pluto transits the Sun, the fifth house, or is in the sign of Leo. It was during this time that Kriyananda realized that his special purpose was based on service to Yogananda through spreading his teachings. Clearly, an expansion of his Soul was occurring through absorbing information of this nature and allowing old and rigid mental patterns to be eliminated. The creative actualization process was deepened through the new mental patterns and transformative information that was absorbed through Yogananda's teachings.

Pluto transiting the Moon symbolizes that a metamorphosis of the self-image must occur through purging all sources of external emotional dependencies and security patterns. The evolutionary intention is to internalize emotional security, and to create a positive and healthy self-image. The Soul must become aware of what constitutes emotional security and for what reasons. As mentioned before, the self-image that is intended to be actualized must be free and independent from any external organization or spiritual group. The previous overidentification with an external organization will be transmuted through establishing internal emotional security. In addition, the awareness of emotional needs that have previously been stifled and repressed commonly manifest during this Pluto transit. It was during this transit that Kriyananda became aware of deep emotional needs that could only be fulfilled through a relationship with the Creator, and by living closely with his guru in order to serve him. He describes the feelings of "coming home" when he read *Autobiography of a Yogi*, and arrived at SRF. He had realized his true "spiritual home" was within himself through his relationship with Yogananda (transiting Pluto conjunct the natal Moon/Neptune conjunction). In this way, he was eliminating emotional dependencies upon any external circumstance in order to create emotional security.

His self-image was transformed as new dimensions of himself were revealed to him through his guru, and his deepening connection to the Source. His primary experience of internal security and nurturing was his connection to the Source and his guru. The Moon correlates to the family environment in general, and it was during this transit that Kriyananda realized that his relationship with his guru, and all the other Masters, created a true "spiritual family" in which his unique essence was fully embraced and nurtured (Pluto/North Node conjunction in Cancer/first house, planetary ruler the Moon/Neptune conjunction in Leo in the third house). In addition, the SRF community was founded upon the principle of living in the spirit of "universal brotherhood."

As mentioned before, the Moon is the planetary ruler of the North Node conjunct Pluto, which reflects that this specific Pluto transit was a highly critical point in this individual's life from an evolutionary point of view. The evolutionary intentions symbolized by the Pluto/North Node in Cancer in the first house will be actualized through the Moon conjunct Neptune in Leo in the third house. In other words, this specific Pluto transit was intended to evoke the awareness within the Soul of the current limitations relative to the self-image and emotional-security factors in general that were blocking the actualization of the evolutionary intentions for the life. With the Moon/

Neptune conjunction, ultimate meaning could not be projected externally in any way, and had to be established totally from within the Soul through his relationship with the Source. Clearly, his close and personal relationship with Yogananda promoted this awareness, and the cooperation with these evolutionary intentions is evident.

This is a positive example of how forming a relationship with something we perceive we need and merging with it, or extracting its essence through osmosis within ourselves, can effect evolution. This individual was able to accomplish a tremendous amount of evolutionary growth through his relationship with Yogananda. This type of evolution can be difficult at times, but it is associated with uniform or non-cataclysmic change. Again, the intention of this illustration is to demonstrate that these metamorphic events are meant to propel the Soul toward the current evolutionary intentions for the life. The Soul's evolutionary intentions are, again, symbolized in the birth chart by Pluto's polarity point. The evolutionary intentions will be consciously actualized by the North Node by house and sign position and aspects it is making to other planets. The North Node will be actualized by its planetary ruler by house and sign position, and aspects it is making to other planets. The point here is to remember to put these events in that context when looking at a birth chart when counseling a client through difficult changes, and to guide the person in that direction.

CATACLYSMIC EVOLUTION

By far the most difficult and troubling way Pluto affects the Soul's evolution is by cataclysmic events. Sometimes we experience traumatic events of such magnitude that, for most of us, there is no choice but to change after the event. The point to remember here is that these events only occur for two reasons:

1. If we have resisted the necessary growth to such an extent that it takes the cataclysmic event to enforce the change. As men-

tioned before, if the Soul desires to do a lot of growth in this life, yet one resists this growth, then a traumatic event will occur in order to enforce the necessary change.

2. Cataclysmic events prompted by karmic causes (karmic retribution). Every action has a reaction. This is the natural law of cause and effect. The deepest dimension or bottom line of this type of evolution serves to enforce the severing and removal of all our dependencies and attachments. In essence, anything that we have become overly identified with on an emotional level from an egocentric point of view in such a way that it is preventing further growth is forcibly removed from our lives through the cataclysmic event. Ultimately, this is why these events are so difficult and painful.

Next, let's look again at the chart of Kriyananda, and examine the evolutionary intentions to experience a cataclysmic event that are based on evolutionary necessity. The cataclysmic event occurred when he was "excommunicated" from SRF under very wounding and false allegations. As mentioned before, his evolutionary intentions are to transmute any external source of emotional security and establish internal emotional security from within the Soul (Pluto conjunct the North Node in Cancer in the first house). The self-image must be free and independent from any external organization or spiritual group (Venus in Aries in the eleventh house square Pluto and the nodal axis).

The previous unresolved karma within intimate relationships will be resolved through initiating relationships of mutual independence and total equality, in which both partners can nurture and love each other for who they intrinsically are as individuals (Venus in Aries in the eleventh house, square the nodal axis of South Node in Capricorn in the seventh house, and the North Node in Cancer in the first house conjunct Pluto). An intimate relationship of this nature would promote full access to the emotional body, and allow the previous unresolved trauma within relationships to heal (Venus in the eleventh house square the nodal axis).

Kriyananda writes in *The Path* about the very painful experience of being ostracized from the organization that he had previously devoted his life to serving. He describes that time as the darkest period of his life, yet he also understood that, ultimately, this event was occurring for a good purpose. He clung to a positive attitude throughout the traumatic experience. He writes, "As I learned to depend on God wholly once more, the greatest storm in my life passed. It left my heart feeling cleansed, strengthened, and lovingly grateful . . . I realized that grace was indeed what my loss—the greatest imaginable for me at the time—had brought me."

This demonstrates this individual's very evolved evolutionary state, and how our own attitude and approach to cataclysmic events will dramatically impact our experience of such events.

At the time of his removal from SRF, the transiting Pluto was in Virgo in his natal fourth house, forming an opposition to the natal Mars in Pisces in the tenth house. It was forming a semi-sextile to his Pluto in Cancer in the first house conjunct the North Node. The transiting Pluto was also forming a trine to the South Node in Capricorn in the seventh house. The opposition that the transiting Pluto formed to Mars symbolizes the evolutionary intention to begin a brand-new cycle of becoming. This new cycle will occur through a metamorphosis of the subjective desire nature, and how the desire nature is acted upon or acted out.

The key during Mars/Pluto transits is to act upon the instinctual desires that feel right on a gut level, and not to act upon those instinctual desires that do not feel right on a gut level. The knowledge of why specific actions were or were not taken will occur after action is initiated. Any desires and instinctual impulses that are based upon a re-creation of the past in general, and are linked with emotional security on that basis, must be purged in order for a new cycle of evolution to manifest. Often, the individual is subjected to projected anger by others, or the individual projects anger at others who are incorrectly perceived as the source of limitation and stagnation.

Again, the evolutionary intention of Mars/Pluto transits is to begin a brand-new cycle of evolutionary becoming through initiating a new direction in life in general. Instinctual urges or desires within the Soul will emerge to break free from the current limitations and restrictions in life. If this desire is resisted, an identity crisis will manifest because of a loss of perspective. With his Mars in Pisces in the tenth house, it is interesting to note that this cataclysmic event did occur within a spiritual organization, and with the transiting Pluto in Virgo in his fourth house opposing his Mars, he was thrown out (opposition) of a community that was previously his home (transiting Pluto in the fourth house). The transiting Pluto in Virgo, and its aspect to Mars in Pisces in the tenth house also symbolizes persecution, which certainly did occur. Kriyananda described that a loss of perspective and identity crisis occurred during this time. With Mars in Pisces in the tenth house, the evolutionary intention is to transmute the dependency and overidentification with the external spiritual organization, and the identity patterns and associations of the past that it created (North Node in Cancer in the first house conjunct Pluto).

This individual experienced projected anger by the members of SRF who excommunicated him. On a positive note, he wrote that this traumatic event did provide an opportunity to throw off (transiting Pluto opposing Mars) the current limitations he was experiencing at that time. He was able to act upon new instinctual urges and desires that manifested in such a way that a new direction in his life, and a brand-new cycle of evolutionary becoming, could begin. He even wrote that he still loved and was dedicated to those who were truly serving Yogananda and the Creator in SRF. Examples of the new direction he was initiating were demonstrated as he began singing inspirational songs by request of friends, and as he continued to write and lecture as a minister in an ashram where he was invited to live.

Kriyananda writes that on an instinctual level he understood that the Master (Yogananda) was guiding him, and that he still had work to do that could not have been accomplished had he not become independent from the organization (transiting Pluto opposing Mars in Pisces/tenth house). Mars in Pisces in the tenth house symbolizes that the Soul intends to bring to culmination the subjective desires of the past that were binding him to old behavioral patterns. This culmination was advanced during the Mars/Pluto transit, and as he learned to establish his own voice of authority from within himself through his evolving relationship with the Creator, he was continually asked to lecture and write by those who perceived his unique wisdom.

The transiting Pluto was forming a semi-sextile to the natal Pluto in Cancer in the first house conjunct the North Node in the same house and sign. As mentioned before, the evolutionary intentions for this life are to create a new self-image that is free and independent from any external organization, and to fully open up the emotional body. In this way, he will be able to approach relationships in a transformed manner (Venus in Aries in the eleventh house square the nodal axis and Pluto). This transit symbolizes a very important juncture in his life from an evolutionary point of view.

The evolutionary intentions symbolized by Pluto's conjunction to the North Node were being directly emphasized at this time, and the individual's cooperation with these evolutionary intentions was critical. Again, he did resolve to understand the dynamics within himself that were creating this traumatic event and to evolve past those dynamics. The semi-sextile in a non-stressful aspect indicates an ease of integration of the evolutionary intentions. There was an ease of integration of these lessons at this time, and the ability to understand what dynamics within himself needed to be changed. His emotional body was actively healed as he initiated the new life path that was independent from the SRF organization, yet still dedicated to spreading the teachings of Yogananda. For example, he was able to write about this experience despite the obvious pain he went through. He was able to communicate with others on a deeply personal level free from the confining spiritual role and self-image of the past. He saw that others were touched through his writing and through his inspirational music. In fact, he eventually wrote a book about spiritualizing the dynamics of marriage (planetary ruler of the North Node conjunct Pluto is the Moon in Leo in the third house conjunct Neptune). The cataclysmic event of being removed from SRF in a forceful manner was intended to induce the awareness of these lessons.

The transiting Pluto was making a trine to the South Node in Capricorn in the seventh house, which is ruled by Saturn in Scorpio in the fifth house retrograde. This transit symbolizes that unresolved dynamics of the past that were blocking evolution at that time were being directly confronted in order to be resolved (transiting Pluto trine the South Node in Capricorn in the seventh house). His old and habitual manner of approaching relationships, which was authoritarian in nature and based on controlling his emotions and the relationship, were being exposed within the Soul in order to transmute the limitations that are created by such dynamics. He was forced to examine himself in very deep ways in order to understand why the current cataclysmic event was occurring (Pluto forming a trine to the South Node, and the planetary ruler of the South Node is Saturn in Scorpio in the fifth house retrograde). The trine is a non-stressful aspect which symbolizes an ease of integration of the evolutionary intentions.

In addition, this individual was able to understand the totality of the past that had led to the current moment, and what steps to take to continue the actualization of the current evolutionary intentions. He continued to lecture and write, but he was no longer dependent upon, or overly identified with, any external organization. He wrote that after the immediacy of this traumatic event, he experienced an evolutionary leap that he honestly admitted he would not otherwise have made. A type of inner rebirth was experienced, one that had confronted and transmuted the limitations of the past, and grew to greater heights of evolution. As described previously, he was able to relate to others on a much more personal level, and was no longer confined by the special "spiritual role" of the past.

This is a positive example of how cataclysmic events induce the Soul's growth through the severing of any dynamic that the Soul has overly identified with from an egocentric point of view, and is thus blocking further evolution. Again, there are two causes of experiencing cataclysmic events: karmic retribution and evolutionary necessity. This specific example is related to evolutionary necessity. However, it is important to note that karmic retribution does not mean that an individual has intentionally hurt another person. Please do not interpret your own cataclysmic changes or that of others around you in this manner unless it is clear that this is the case. Tremendous harm can come when we think in this manner, and it can actually lead others to believe that they have done certain things that they actually have not done. This is incredibly damaging and must be avoided at all costs. It is critical to make this distinction when dealing with clients and other people in general. This example is simply meant to illustrate how cataclysmic events are meant to instigate the evolution of the Soul, and how dramatically our own response toward evolutionary change and growth will impact our experience of the event itself. This example is also intended to make the clear distinction between the two types of causes of cataclysmic events from an evolutionary point of view.

AWARENESS OF STAGNATION

A very difficult way that Pluto affects evolution is when we become increasingly aware that we are stagnating, and our evolutionary growth is stopping. Progressively our lives lose meaning, and we start to withdraw emotionally and can also physically withdraw from active participation in the circumstances of our life. This is a very painful experience not only for ourselves but also for others around us as well. We can no longer find meaning in our life, and can no longer deny facing our current reality. We are typically aware only of the symptoms that we are experiencing, not of the causes. In the worst-case scenarios, this can create catatonia in some people. Most of us do not allow it to progress to this state and seek out some kind of therapy/help when these conditions reach a critical-mass situation. This is an incredibly unsettling and painful experience, because what we are essentially saying is that the way we have structured our lives is not what we really want.

As counselors, we can guide people (and ourselves if we happen to encounter such an experience) toward the awareness of which inner dynamics within themselves are creating the current situation and how to proceed. This process is very similar to a dormant volcano that suddenly becomes active. We are aware of a block (either internally or externally) but not the source of it. We focus all of our energy into uncovering the source of the block and then, suddenly, unconscious content pours into our conscious awareness. The volcano suddenly erupts, and we finally become aware of why we are experiencing the current difficulties. We can then evolve from the knowledge we have gained, and move forward in our lives in a new way.

We are now going to look at the birth chart (chart 2) of a different individual, and see the possibility of this kind of experience occurring. Please note that this individual is in the first stages of the spiritual evolutionary condition, and in her natal chart she has Neptune conjunct Venus and Mercury in Sagittarius/seventh house. From these two facts we can clearly see that she is looking for a deeper meaning/higher purpose to life. However, we can also see that she was looking for it outside herself (especially regarding others) and experienced a tremendous amount of disillusionment relative to this dynamic (Neptune, Venus, Mercury in the seventh house).

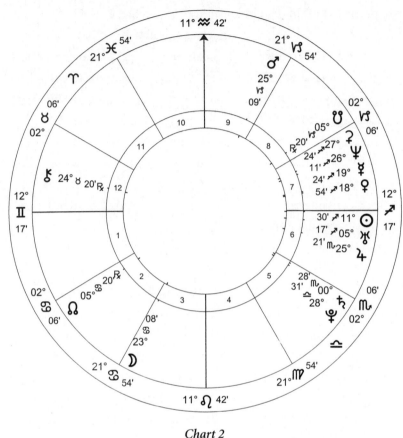

Chart 2
December 3, 1982 / 4:16 p.m. / Seattle, Washington

Also, she has South Node in Capricorn in the eighth and her natal Pluto in the fifth house. From this we can see that there is a strong possibility that the distorted dynamic of looking for recognition and validation from the outer world by conforming to the conditioning patterns of the consensus is still in place (South Node in Capricorn/eighth). She has Sun conjunct Uranus in Sagittarius and in the sixth house, so we can also see that she does sincerely want to serve/help humanity. This desire to live a life dedicated to the path of service will ultimately help her to integrate her Soul's deepest intentions. She must learn necessary lessons in self-objectivity, and to discriminate what her true life's work is (Sun conjunct Uranus in the sixth). Based on this natal signature we can see the likelihood that this individual will come to experience a loss of meaning in her life based on her conditioning patterns in contrast to her true Soul nature (who she actually is). In other words, there was a need in her to go through this difficult experience because of the strong conditioning patterns that were still in place. The previously mentioned astrological signature demonstrates this very clearly.

She chose to attend a well-known university, hoping to graduate with a bachelor's degree in psychology (South Node in Capricorn in the eighth house). She had been hoping to meet a few new close friends, and have at least some meaningful experiences at the university. About six months into the school year, she began to feel a progressive loss of meaning in her life and increasing personal stagnation. She began to emotionally withdraw and felt incredibly lonely and isolated. No matter how hard she tried, she could no longer deceive or delude herself into believing that the university had any meaning for her whatsoever. This was occurring at the same time that her pre-existing close friendships were blowing up. Her growing depression was beginning to lead to an inner state of paralysis. She could no longer function and found herself just going through the motions of life.

At the time, transiting Pluto in Sagittarius was moving through her seventh house and was approaching a conjunction to her natal Venus, making the same aspects in her natal chart as were mentioned previously. She was prompted to an intense self-examination of her values and inner orientation, and began to see how this was connected to her inner relationship with herself. It forced her to a deep examination regarding what had true meaning, and what no longer held any value for her. She needed to admit to herself that she was in fact looking for social recognition and validation from the outside. (Pluto in the fifth house and South Node in Capricorn in the eighth house. The planetary ruler of her South Node is Saturn, which is in Scorpio conjunct her Pluto.)

She had to face the reality that the desire for money as a means to create her bottom-line security was in fact something she needed to purge from her Soul at time. (South Node in Capricorn in the eighth house and North Node in Cancer in the second house correlates to the need to break free from this conditioning and finding ultimate security within herself.) She also needed to see how she was dependent on this system for validation and inner security (transiting Pluto conjunct Venus in the seventh house), and how this was creating a tremendous sense of inner frustration, stagnation, and depression. This orientation to life was essentially narcissistic in nature, and it was only keeping her locked into her own insecurities, dependencies, and narcissistic neediness.

Transiting Pluto forming a conjunction to her natal Venus demanded that she find her sense of self-worth from within rather than look to the outer world to validate her, and also that she not be dependent on social status and monetary wealth for a sense of inner security and meaning. Transiting Pluto also formed a quincunx to her natal Moon in Cancer in the third house. This translated into the fact that a core evolutionary lesson is to create a metamorphosis of her self-image, by facing what constituted emotional security at that time. She needed to examine *why*, and by seeing and objectively viewing the different influences that contributed to her self-image, she came to realize that she was keeping herself tied into her fears and insecurities by living this kind of lifestyle at the university. In other words, this lifestyle was keeping her locked into her negative self-image. The transit to her Moon re-emphasized the need to learn to provide her own emotional security from within, and to provide her own positive reinforcement in terms of arriving at a positive self-image. (Transiting Pluto on her Venus in the seventh house forming a quincunx to her Moon in Cancer in the third house.)

Relative to the transiting Pluto triggering the Venus conjunction to her natal Mercury and Neptune, this was a time of absolutely restructuring her thought process (Mercury) and dissolving (Neptune) all the old mental conditioning patterns that were creating the current troubles for her. Pluto's transit to Neptune correlated to a time in which a necessary disillusionment process was experienced. She needed to face all her delusions about herself and life in general, and to realign her Soul with actual reality. She was being taught a critical and humbling lesson. She was meant to learn that she is a co-creator with God/Goddess, this through the painful experience of disillusionment and through seeing firsthand the consequences of following her separating desires. She came to realize she had been making a lot of excuses for herself. She also came to realize how she rationalized not only her own behavior (Mercury), but also that of others around her, because she did not want to face the actual truth of what was going on within herself and within others. She uncovered a very deep narcissism within herself and also a pattern of victimization, at first blaming the university and others in the outer world for her problems. The uncovering of this kind of thinking and mental structure within herself (Pluto transit to Mercury) was like a very intense Plutonian atom-bomb discovery for her.

With transiting Pluto also approaching a conjunction to her Neptune in the seventh house, she needed to face the fact that the ultimate meaning she projected onto the university and onto others simply didn't exist. She was shocked when she realized that she had been looking for an ultimate "something," that she was looking for somebody or something on the outside to provide ultimate meaning for her. She wasn't seeing herself or others around her clearly, and as Pluto came closer to Neptune this fact was uncovered at point-blank range. She discovered that essentially she had been creating one disillusionment after the other relative to this distorted inner orientation. The Pluto transits brought these pre-existing issues to a head and forced her to deal with them in a stark manner. Progressively, she came to see how all of these issues described above connected to her current life's difficulties. She did eventually make a break from the university and started to follow a life path that is more connected to her Soul, and thus what she felt to be her true life's purpose—one that she feels is directed by God/Goddess. She became sincerely joyful, and this is her reward (Venus) for undertaking the required inner work.

As described earlier, her evolutionary point is in Aries in the eleventh house, and her North Node is in Cancer/second house with the planetary ruler (the Moon) in Cancer in the third house, involving the aspects mentioned before. The experiences of feeling absolutely alone and disillusioned at the university, and of her difficult friendship blow-ups, were both very important. Relative to the eleventh-house polarity point, they enforced the important lessons of objectivity and of detaching from her own narcissistic orientation to life. These experiences guided her to the critical point of actualizing the kind of life that she really wanted to live and was meant to live, versus living a conditioned life (Pluto in the fifth house, South Node in Capricorn in the eighth house).

With the North Node in Cancer in the second house, the primary and essential lessons of self-reliance, self-worth, and learning to provide her own emotional security from within were evoked by this Pluto transit. She learned to validate herself in this manner, and she was no longer dependent on others or society's approval. Relative to the planetary ruler located in Cancer in the third house and making the aspects mentioned before, through this experience she learned to feel secure to communicate what was actually going on inside of her in a straightforward and honest way, and to feel secure within herself in doing so. (Moon in Cancer in the third house, North Node in Cancer in the second house.) Before this she had a hard time honestly sharing/processing the truth and the emotional depth of what she was experiencing and would typically come to a superficial place with others, approaching her emotions through intellectual filters (Moon Cancer/third house).

This individual was not a superficial person; in fact, she carried within her an uncommon depth she craved to share with others. Her conditioning impacted her ability to see people for who they truly were, and for this reason she held back. She also had insecurities about being rejected by others (natally she has Sun/sixth house), as well as fears of her own emotional body and her own judgments about her emotions (South Node in Capricorn/ eighth house and Mars in Capricorn). The build-up of emotional energy that was being repressed eventually blew up on others, which of course is a very unhealthy dynamic. She needed to learn to throw this conditioning off (Moon opposing her Mars in Capricorn in the ninth house, T-square Pluto), and through the difficulty of this experience she eventually did.

This is an example of how Pluto affects our evolution through experiencing a progressive loss of meaning in life and having intense feelings of inner stagnation. Eventually we face the fact that the way we have structured our life is not the way we really want it. Note that these Plutonian experiences do not necessarily occur as isolated events. One can trigger another, or they can occur simultaneously. When others around us, or we ourselves, go through this type of negative and difficult experience, we can still turn it into a positive one by motivating ourselves to do the required inner work so we will never go through it again. The example of this young woman going through these difficult growth experiences at school is a relatively gentle illustration of this type of evolution. However, in general, this is a very difficult and painful type of evolution, and it is associated with cataclysmic growth.

LATENT CAPACITIES AWAKENED

The last and most basic way that Pluto affects our evolution is when we suddenly become consciously aware of a latent or dormant capacity within ourselves. This can be a very exciting but also a very stressful experience, because it requires a tremendous amount of courage and perseverance to develop and actualize our new talent. The new capacity that we become aware of may, in some cases, totally threaten or undermine our current inner and outer structure. In other words, our current sense of inner security is risked at the core level, and we must find the courage to actualize our new capacity no matter what outer changes we need to make.

Let's say, for example, that you are currently working at a local retail store as a manager, yet suddenly you become aware that you have the capacity to be a wonderful counselor for children. This would require a total shift in terms of how you structure your life, inwardly and outwardly. It would require the perseverance to actualize your new goal. In some cases, this can manifest as a deepening of current capacity, or it can manifest as a different dimension of this capacity brought into conscious awareness that needs to be developed. In both cases, it requires courage and a strong will to develop/actualize the new capacity. It is through this hard work and commitment to doing so that our evolution is effected.

The next example (chart 3) is that of Barack Obama. Pesident Barack Obama is in the first-stage spiritual evolutionary condition. He was born in Hawaii and raised mainly by his mother, who was a single parent. Obama's biological father left the family early in young Barack's life, and consequently Obama never developed a relationship with him. He is orientated toward Christianity, and attended an African-American church. He graduated from Harvard Law School but turned down high-paying jobs in order to work in inner-city communities and then to pursue a political career. He also taught law at a university in Chicago.

President Obama's stated mission in political office is to re-empower the middle and working classes by creating a system of equality

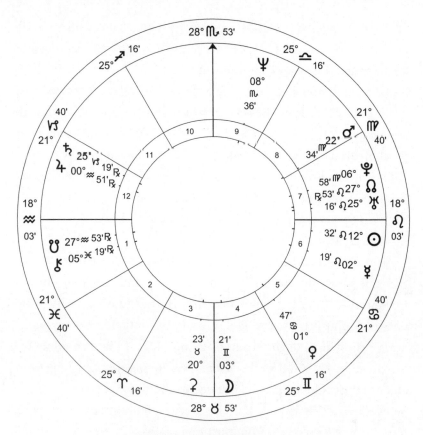

Chart 3: Barack Obama
August 4, 1961 / 7:24 p.m. / Honolulu, Hawaii

and justice, and to create a government that truly serves the best interests of all people. He has dedicated his life to helping those who are
struggling in poverty, people who were essentially abandoned by the
previous government. In his natal chart, Pluto is in Virgo in the seventh house conjunct the North Node in Leo also in the seventh house,
with Uranus in the same house and sign. The planetary ruler of the
North Node is the Sun in Leo in the sixth house. The South Node is in
Aquarius in the first house, and the planetary ruler (Uranus) is in Leo
in the seventh house conjunct Pluto and the North Node. The Moon
is in Gemini in the fourth house square the nodal axis.

From this natal signature we can see that Obama's devotion to God, or the Source, and his desire to purify and perfect himself, manifests through his service to others in a social context (Pluto in Virgo in the seventh house conjunct the North Node in Leo). Obama's core evolutionary intentions are also to have an inner relationship with self and relate to others from a standpoint of true equality. Emotional and psychological extremes, projected needs, and expectations within relationships that create inequalities and imbalances need to be purged from the Soul. Pluto in Virgo symbolizes the need to learn humility from an egocentric point of view and to purge all egocentric delusions of grandeur.

Pluto conjunct the North Node reflects that he has worked on actualizing these core evolutionary intentions in the past, and is meant to continue in the same direction in this life. Pluto's polarity point does not apply because the Soul is meant to continue working on the areas indicated by the house and sign position of Pluto conjunct the North Node. This Soul has been a pioneer in this area for a long time, and has thus attained natural leadership abilities that serve to inspire people toward the same goals. The overwhelming support and positive feedback he received from the public speaks for itself.

Obama's passion for justice and fair play, and his desire to create a social system that is based upon equality, is reflected in the Pluto/North Node conjunction in the seventh house. Obama's bottom line is rooted in the natural law of giving, sharing, and inclusion. It also symbolizes that he needs to eliminate any psychological dynamic of self-doubt that undermines his inherent and natural capacities in the context of leadership (North Node in Leo conjunct Pluto, ruled by the Sun in Leo in the sixth house). This Soul has a natural understanding of group leadership, and of how to operate within a group as an equal with others (South Node in Aquarius in the first house, ruled by Uranus in Leo in the seventh house conjunct Pluto and the North Node).

The South Node in Aquarius in the first house ruled by Uranus in Leo in the seventh house conjunct Pluto and the North Node symbolizes that, in this life, the Soul intends to fully and creatively self-actualize the special purpose and destiny that was not fully actualized prior to the current life. That this process was prematurely "cut off" is demonstrated by Uranus conjunct Pluto and the North Node, the South Node in Aquarius in the first house, and the Moon in Gemini in the fourth house square the nodal axis. In fact, this astrological signature is indicative of assassination in a previous lifetime. Uranus correlates to sudden or quick experiences of trauma, and the seventh house indicates that this was at the hands of another in an extreme way.

The Moon square the nodal axis symbolizes that a skipped step has been created prior to the current life and must now be recovered in order for evolution to continue. These skipped steps will act as a conflicting force in the context of full actualization of the current evolutionary intentions symbolized by Pluto's conjunction to the North Node. The Moon in the fourth house symbolizes that his self-image, his emotional dynamics in general (the emotional body), and specifically his ability to nurture himself from within are skipped steps from the past that must be resolved. It also indicates that his early-childhood environment was critical in the context of forming his self-image.

As mentioned earlier, Obama's father essentially abandoned the family shortly after Obama's birth, and his mother was his sole source of support as he grew up. Not knowing his father had a damaging impact on Obama's self-image, and he has written about his struggle to integrate his own sense of "manhood" or "masculinity" as he matured into adulthood. The Moon in the fourth house specifically correlates with the anima/animus dynamic, or how we integrate both genders equally within ourselves over time. These early childhood conditions had the effect of throwing him back on himself in the context of learning to validate himself from within, and thus learning how to meet his own emotional needs from within instead of projecting these needs externally (Pluto in the seventh house conjunct the North Node in the context of Moon square the nodal axis).

In addition to the above, the South Node in Aquarius in the first house and the planetary ruler Uranus conjunct Pluto and the North Node reflect that trauma was suffered in the family environment that must be resolved. The resolution of that trauma will occur through the dynamics specifically related to the house and sign of Uranus and Pluto conjunct the North Node. The Moon in the fourth house square the nodal axis reflects that the recovery of these skipped steps will occur through the family environment, and through becoming a "full-time" parent. This will allow for the wounds of his past to be healed, and for a positive self-image to manifest. Again, because the planetary ruler of the South Node is conjunct Pluto and the North Node, the resolution of the skipped steps will be integrated through the Pluto/ North Node conjunction. Specifically, he must form long-lasting and committed relationships (Pluto/North Node in the seventh house) through which emotional healing, nurturing, and equal emotional giving and receiving can occur.

At the time of the 2008 election, the transiting Pluto was in Sagittarius in Obama's natal eleventh house, forming a trine to the Pluto/ North Node conjunction in the seventh house. This symbolizes that this is a critical juncture, or time frame, from an evolutionary point of view. A trine is a non-stressful aspect that reflects an ease of integration of the current evolutionary intentions. (However, it is important to note that non-stressful aspects can also manifest negatively as an ease of resistance because of the lack of stress, or tension, to change past patterns of behaviors that are blocking further growth.)

This Pluto transit demonstrates Obama's ability to find the necessary courage and faith to confront the Bush administration and create the necessary support to become the next president of the United States. In so doing, he certainly had to confront his own self-doubt (Pluto in Virgo) and compulsive undermining psychological patterns that had previously created a situation wherein he had not fully actualized his true capacities or potential. In addition, the trine reflects the true re-empowerment of his Soul as he actualized himself through exposing the lies, deception, dishonesty, and corruption of the Bush administration (transiting Pluto in Sagittarius in the eleventh house) by repeating one simple message, which could be summarized as: "Together we can change this country, and we can create a better future in which we are not a nation defined by red states or blue states, but defined as citizens as the United States" (North Node conjunct Pluto in the seventh house conjunct Uranus).

The transiting Pluto in the eleventh house symbolizes the evolutionary intentions to liberate, de-condition, and transform past patterns of behavior that are inhibiting further growth. The process of campaigning, and of being in the forefront of the fight to bring back a condition of equality, justice, and fair play to this nation, was an act of liberation as he continued to give a voice to those who had been abandoned by the Bush administration. Obama, clearly, did not back down or hold back in the context of speaking out during the campaign. In this way, he began to energize toward the creative self-actualization of his special purpose and destiny. The transiting South Node conjunct the planetary ruler of the North Node (the Sun in Leo in the sixth house) reiterates the actualization of these core evolutionary intentions. In essence, this was a time frame in which Obama was actively recovering the skipped steps of the past, and working toward the resolving of all old dynamics that had prevented him from fully fulfilling his special destiny or purpose in this life.

Transiting Neptune forming a conjunction to the South Node in Aquarius in the first house symbolizes that a resolution or culmination of past trauma, and of the unresolved issues of the past in general, was occurring at this point in time. As mentioned before, the current evolutionary intentions to fully self-actualize and fully develop his inherent leadership capacities had been prematurely cut off, and Neptune's conjunction to the South Node in Aquarius reflects that the resolution of the accumulated emotional trauma and unresolved dynamics brought forward from the past was occurring at this point in time.

The transiting Pluto was forming an opposition to Venus in Cancer in the fifth house. This reflects the evolutionary intention to throw off and liberate from past inner and outer relationship patterns that create stagnation, limitations, and blocks toward the achieving of further growth. Venus in Cancer in the fifth house symbolizes the need to establish internal security, a positive self-image, and the need to nurture himself from within. The need to actualize himself through initiating relationships is reflected as well. Again, he would need to learn to validate himself from within in order for creative self-actualization to occur positively. In order to actualize fully the core evolutionary intentions for this life, he must liberate himself (transiting Pluto in the eleventh house) from any insecurities resulting from a negative self-image. His internal and external relationship patterns will be transformed to higher levels of expression as he integrates these fundamental lessons. The positive feedback he has received from his supporters (Venus in the fifth house) provides the necessary motivation to keep moving in this direction. In addition, his family provided a very loving and nurturing support system that allowed these current evolutionary intentions to be actualized (Venus in Cancer/fifth house).

This example demonstrates how the awakening or awareness of latent or dormant capacities within the Soul effects evolution. This is a non-stressful form of evolution, but it does require strength and perseverance to actualize the necessary capacities, because often it threatens the current emotional security patterns at the deepest possible level—in other words, at the Soul level (Pluto). As the Soul actualizes dormant capacities, the current emotional security patterns transform into new ones that are free from the limitations of the past, and thus the individual grows to greater heights. The individual, in turn, can act as a motivating force for others to do the same.

ABOUT DEVA GREEN

Deva Green is the daughter of Jeffrey Wolf Green, the founder and creator of evolutionary astrology. Having been blessed with the ultimate in one-on-one instruction, Deva holds the distinction of being the youngest graduate to date of the Jeffrey Wolf Green School of Evolutionary Astrology, and is now the director of the main school (located in the United States). She began her lecture career at the Third Annual Jeffrey Wolf Green Conference in Sedona, Arizona, in April 2005, and has since been a popular lecturer at NORWAC. She has also taught Introduction to Evolutionary Astrology. Deva Green's first book, *Evolutionary Astrology: Pluto and Your Karmic Mission*, was published by Llewellyn Publications in 2009.

Please visit Deva's website, www.schoolofevolutionaryastrology.com.

3

Evolutionary States

BY KIM MARIE

One of the basic principles of evolutionary astrology is an understanding that Souls incarnate in various states of spiritual evolvement. There are three main evolutionary conditions, or states, of a Soul: the *consensus, individuated,* and *spiritual* states. There also is a fourth, lesser-known evolutionary state called the *dimly evolved,* or *de-evolved,* state.

Evolutionary astrology purports that each Soul has two principal desires: a desire to separate from that which created it and a desire to return to that which created it. These two conflicting desires—to separate and to return—are the source of each incarnation of every Soul. Each individual Soul spends countless lifetimes achieving and exhausting its separating desires—whether it be in the form of a new lover, a new job, a child, a house, etc. Upon achieving a separating desire, a Soul may experience a momentary sense of satisfaction. However, that satisfaction is soon replaced with a sense of dissatisfaction and some type of questioning, or a gut feeling that there must be something more.

A Soul then will manifest another separating desire, and another, and another. This process of achieving and exhausting separating desires, and then the subsequent dissatisfaction, may take place at an unconscious level over the course of many lifetimes. At some point in the process of exhausting separating desires, the desire to return to that which created the Soul starts becoming stronger and stronger. Eventually it is the only desire left.

As Souls embark upon this evolving journey to separate from—and eventually to return to—the Source, God, Goddess, Great Spirit, or whatever term they use for the Divine, they reach these different evolutionary states of Soul consciousness. By taking into consideration the evolutionary state of their clients or students, an astrologer can relate to them at the level their Soul has reached, as opposed to applying the same astrological interpretations to everyone, regardless of their Soul's level of evolution and religious or spiritual beliefs.

For example, an astrological chart with a preponderance of planets in the second house may indicate very different meanings to Souls in different evolutionary states. The second house largely relates to the archetype of self-reliance; however, the progressive evolution of a Soul eventually will transfer those self-reliance issues from lessons about outer security to those of inner security.

In the consensus state, second-house planets may help a Soul learn the basic survival and work skills necessary to hold a job that provides enough food on the table and a roof overhead. Once it has reached the individuated state, a Soul may have still lessons to learn about materialism; however, the emphasis now moves toward pondering upon exactly what it needs to take care of itself, versus what society dictates. A Soul in the spiritual evolutionary state may be releasing material securities and realizing that total inner security and a connection to God/Goddess is most important.

Just as an astrological chart does not show the gender of the Soul it represents, neither does a chart, by itself, reveal the evolutionary state of a Soul, so an interaction between an astrologer and client is a necessity. Through observation and correlation, an astrologer can discern the state of the Soul. This creates a foundation for interpreting an astrological chart, and a basis for communication with clients and students at their own level.

It is not necessary to be an astrologer to understand and discern the different evolutionary states of a Soul. These states are observable by anyone who is willing to take time to understand the nature of a Soul's spiritual journey. Evolution is natural law and a journey all Souls must make, whether it occurs during a single lifetime from birth and growth to decay and death, or over the course of multiple lifetimes in a search for answers to the perennial "why" questions.

As Souls observe and correlate the nature of life and evolution in all species over eons of time, it is only natural to conclude that the Source itself is an evolving force. Just ask the question: why would something perfect create imperfection? Evolution is taking place everywhere, in all kingdoms, in all species, in all Souls, and in God/Goddess itself.

EVOLUTIONARY STATES

The three main evolutionary states of a Soul each can be divided into sub-states to further understand the nature of any Soul. These different evolutionary states are not limited to gender, race, nationality, or culture. An understanding of the evolutionary state will give an astrologer or student clues to the religious or spiritual beliefs of a Soul. It will also help an astrologer to understand how a client is manifesting the separating and/or returning desires.

It also is possible for some Souls to be in transition between one evolutionary state and another, or from one sub-state to another sub-state within an evolutionary state. In a case like this, a Soul would exhibit some traits from one state (or sub-state) to the next evolutionary state (or sub-state). With the awareness that evolution is natural law, most Souls are continually evolving, even when much of the change is occurring at unconscious levels of awareness.

Consensus State

The consensus state includes approximately 70 percent of all Souls on the planet. This is the vast majority of Souls, regardless of gender, race, nationality, or culture. It is known as the consensus state because the Souls in this state are quick to consent, or follow the lead of others. For the most part, they believe what they are told. They have yet to learn how to really think for themselves. They cannot step outside the context of the environment they find themselves living in.

This is the level where formalized, human-made religions exist. If their religious leaders tell them astrology is the work of the devil, the consensus state Souls accept that as the truth. If they are told that a certain race is inferior or a particular country is evil, they also accept that without question.

Separating desires are strongest in the consensus state, although they exist in all evolutionary states. Here, the center of gravity is the ego—in direct opposition to the Soul itself. Identification with self comes from the outside. God is interpreted as an outside perfect male entity, judging Souls via their particular religious conditioning of right and wrong.

Sexual customs are defined and enforced by religious and societal authorities in the consensus state. Over the last few thousand years, consensus-state Souls have been indoctrinated with heavy guilt over any sexual behaviors that are not in compliance with their religious conditionings, which mainly legislate sexuality for procreation only.

The vast majority of religions preach a separation of body and spirit. As natural laws such as sexuality are suppressed, they become distorted through anger and rage. Sexuality in the consensus state is then expressed in many inhumane standards and/or taboos. Natural laws can be suppressed and distorted; however, they cannot be destroyed.

The beginning stages of the consensus state are comprised of Souls that are essentially learning how to function in their society. These are the "worker bees." Their ability to think for themselves is quite limited. Their knowledge of life is based upon what they learn in their family and religious/social environment. There is an overall dependence upon others, including the Souls' religious and social community, to maintain their survival. Psychologically, they can repeat what they have heard, but with no real understanding of what it means or if it is really true.

In the middle stages of the consensus state, Souls are learning how to "keep up with the Joneses." They are learning to understand how their societal system works, and they are trying to play a noticeable role in their communities. They are manifesting a wide variety of separating desires, and they believe that the desire is the goal itself.

The middle stages of the consensus state are responsible for maintaining society on almost all levels, including participation in religious, educational, legal, and societal customs. Psychologically, they support the "system"—whatever their particular cultural, religious, or social conditioning. There is a tendency to defend the past, as security is quite unconsciously dependent upon maintaining the order of things.

By the advanced stages of the consensus state, Souls have figured out how their society works and are learning to lead consensus-state society. These are the Souls who make our laws, customs, and taboos. Many times these are the religious and political leaders. The separating desires of career, home, family, money, etc., constitute their world. Human-made religions are still quite strong here, as these Souls still are heavily invested in outer security. They will become the outer authority figures, although they still are quite insecure on unconscious levels.

Advanced stages of the consensus state are inhabited by Souls who can psychologically manipulate society because they understand how everything works. On a collective level, advanced-stage consensus Souls keep leading society to repeat the past even when they appear to be changing things. This is one of the reasons why evolution takes so long.

All Souls are invested in being secure—that is, in "knowing" their world. The past, no matter how dysfunctional it may be, represents security because it is a known quantity. The future, no matter how much a Soul may desire it, represents insecurity because it is unknown. At any evolutionary state of the Soul, it takes willpower to leave the past behind and move forward into the unknown.

Consensus-state Souls unconsciously defend the past from a need to feel safe and secure. Eventually, often through cataclysmic experiences over several lifetimes, Souls come face to face with the beginning need to look inside themselves.

Individuated State

The individuated state comprises approximately 20 percent of the Souls on the planet, regardless of gender, race, nationality, or culture. This is the level at which Souls begin to individuate and think for themselves. They begin to see that they are somehow different from their peers, family, and society. If someone tells a Soul in the individuated state that astrology is hocus pocus, this Soul can come to the realization that it prefers to decide for itself whether that is true, rather than simply accepting what it is told.

Souls in the individuated state are beginning to question their religious and societal conditioning and upbringing. Here is where returning desires start to become stronger desires—on very subtle levels at first, and then with more and more energy and consciousness. All kinds of belief systems exist in the individuated state, including the belief that there is no God.

Through the individuated state, a Soul will manifest lifetimes of differing religious and spiritual belief systems—adopting, experiencing, and discarding one belief and then the next, on a journey to discover what truth is. This is where Souls learn to distinguish between human-made religions that have been instilled in them and philosophical and spiritual belief systems that they are capable of choosing for themselves.

Here is where Souls start to experience a center of being from within. There is movement from outer ego-based security to inner Soul-based security. Individuated-state Souls may experience confusion and crises when lessons in how to function in society are based upon the security of the outside material world.

Individuated-state Souls pursue all kinds of careers in all walks of life. There can be rebellion against what is expected of them. There can be lifetimes of searching for work that is meaningful. There still can be desires to attain leadership positions as in the consensus state, although those positions may lose their meaning with time. The desire is exhausted. Yet these Souls still may have a desire to be noticed in the outside world.

Sexual rebellion comes through the individuated state as well. As these Souls break free from religious conditioning, they question what is natural for the body and express sexuality in many forms. There is initiation into loving the Soul beyond its current gender expression. Individuated-state Souls begin to realize there is more to sexuality than procreation.

The beginning stages of the individuated state are some of the most insecure times for a Soul. They cannot relate to the consensus state anymore, and yet these Souls still do not have the courage to be different. There is a lot of compromising here as Souls cling to the past, even though it just doesn't work anymore. These are Souls that try to fit in with consensus-state society, and yet feel totally alienated from it. These Souls can create extreme cataclysmic experiences, resisting their movement forward and trying to repeat the past.

Psychologically, Souls in the early individuated state can be quite wounded and confused, as they wonder what is wrong with them.

They sense when something is wrong, yet they do not know what is right. There is intense pressure inward, in order to learn how to relate to themselves from within. There is also pressure to conform, from society, family, religious leaders, and other role models.

Eventually, in the middle stages of the individuated state, Souls start to rebel. The unconscious fear that they will get pulled back into the consensus state allows them to break free from whatever is perceived as conditioning on physical, emotional, mental, and spiritual levels. They may rebel against family, society, religion, or anything else they perceive as a threat to their freedom. They may even rebel against themselves, periodically leaving everything behind.

Souls in the middle stages of the individuated state have trouble maintaining any and all relationships for any length of time. Psychologically, they rebel against any perception of a custom, law, taboo, or socially approved behavior. They have learned how to see the fallacy in human-made religions and social conformity. They have not yet learned how to be inwardly secure from societal pressures.

When Souls evolve into the advanced stages of the individuated state, they learn how to be uniquely themselves. They have a secure knowledge of who they are and who they are not. These Souls are learning to discern their own truth. They may still experience lifetimes of pursuing individual growth, separating desires, and their attendant cataclysms. However, now there is progress and a progressive elimination of the most conscious separating desires.

There is a peacefulness that is often experienced as they begin to accept themselves as who they are—different and unique. They have the psychological awareness to understand much about life, the world, and how societal pressure encourages conformity. Souls in the advanced stages of the individuated state understand how the inner world creates the outer world, and they strive to become more and more conscious of the "why" of everything, as well as its cause and effect.

After lifetimes of pursuing the meaning of life, experiencing many different belief systems, and exhausting countless separating desires, the individuated-state Soul begins to pull it all together into one universal belief system based upon natural, spiritual laws and principles.

Spiritual State

This represents approximately 5 percent of the Souls on the planet, of any gender, race, nationality, or culture. As Souls evolve into the spiritual state, they effortlessly understand the natural, spiritual laws and principles, as opposed to the human-made religions and societal conditioning. They realize that everything is connected to everything else. Souls in the spiritual state tend to gravitate to more and more planetary work.

Spiritual-state Souls comprehend unifying, timeless cosmological principles, and can discern and intuit how different belief systems and religions may have pieces of truth and yet lack the whole truth, or timeless truth. In this state, Souls can understand that astrology is natural law and instinctively recognize the type of correspondence described in the phrase *as above, so below*.

Here the returning desires become stronger than the separating desires. Souls still experience separating desires in the spiritual state; however, they realize the tools that separate one from the Source can also be used to return to the Source. In other words, there is a natural withdrawal from the material world as the desire to return to God/Goddess becomes increasingly stronger and stronger.

In the beginning stages of the spiritual state, we have some of the most humble Souls upon the planet. They begin to truly realize how holy everything and everyone is. The returning desires are becoming increasingly stronger, so there is a need to eliminate whatever is blocking the Soul from returning. This is sometimes manifested as extreme experiences in the physical world to "wake" the Soul up.

Over the course of thousands of years of patriarchal religious conditioning, many Souls have overly developed their spiritual and mental capacities at the expense of their emotional natures. In order for their Soul to progress, their emotions must catch up. Evolutionary astrology has observed that evolution takes place through the emotional body.

Souls in the beginning stages of the spiritual state (and all evolutionary states) can create experiences, consciously and unconsciously, either from karmic payback or from evolutionary necessity, which evolve the process of eliminating separating desires and current patriarchal conditioning. This is very necessary to evolve their Souls in every way—emotionally, mentally, and spiritually. All old emotional wounds must be healed in order for the Soul to become whole on every level.

Spiritual-state Souls will understand that there is still karma to be worked out in relationships. Here is where they learn to evolve karma mates into Soul mates. It is through relationships that Souls can work toward reunion with the Source. The purpose of any relationship for Soul mates is to heal whatever is preventing a Soul from merging with God/Goddess.

Harmony with natural sexual desires must also be healed. Sexuality is natural law, and only the most advanced Souls (roughly 2 percent) have exhausted the separating desire of sexuality. In the beginning stages of the spiritual state, Souls must face their sexual wounds from human-made patriarchal conditioning. This then creates a foundation to understand that sexuality itself is a sacred act of loving God/Goddess through another Soul.

The middle stages of the spiritual state can further the lessons that help the Soul eliminate any final separating desires, usually of an ego nature. In the spiritual state, Souls know the center of gravity is based within their Soul, not their ego, and the ego must merge back to the Source. So any desires that prevent a Soul from merging with God/Goddess must be experienced and exhausted. The most common example is when a Soul believes it is the ultimate source itself. By necessity, a "fall from grace" will be experienced to totally re-merge with the Source on the deepest levels of the Soul.

The hardest lesson any Soul faces is reunion with the God/Goddess. Souls can realize the desire, express the desire, and actually manifest the desire to merge with the Source. However, to totally "let go and let God" is the toughest lesson there is. It is in the middle stages of the spiritual state that a Soul really faces the final barriers (separating desires).

When Souls evolve into the advanced stages of the spiritual state, they are finally eliminating all separating desires and experience only the desire to return. They are finally exhausting the separating desire of sexuality and becoming androgynous. They completely surrender to and merge with the will of God/Goddess. They become known as avatars and masters such as Jesus and Buddha. Their incarnations onto the planet are coming to a close.

Dimly Evolved and De-Evolved States

There is a fourth evolutionary state that most astrologers will rarely encounter in a counseling session. This state is further divided into two sub-states known as the *dimly evolved* and *de-evolved* states, representing approximately 5 percent of the Souls on the planet; again, this is beyond gender, race, nationality, or culture. Many times both the dimly evolved and de-evolved states are found with physical, emotional, and mental handicaps.

The dimly evolved Souls are those who are just evolving into the human species. These Souls will have a dull look to their eyes, and yet their auras will be unconditionally loving. One such possible example could be a Soul with Down's syndrome.

The de-evolved Souls find themselves in a handicapped body for past-life karmic reasons, forced to occupy space and time in harsh, uncomfortable ways. These Souls have glassy, hard eyes, and their auras are very angry and hateful. For whatever personal karmic reasons, they are being forced to experience the world in an environment they cannot control.

Both the dimly evolved and de-evolved sub-states are Souls who almost always find themselves in societal or family care. Their abilities to function freely in the world either are not sufficiently developed or are prevented for karmic reasons.

Understanding these different evolutionary states of the Soul permits one of the most important assessments an astrologer can make. It allows a client or student seeking out astrological help to receive information that is relevant to where their Soul actually exists. Discerning these evolutionary states happens like most talents or activities: it takes time and gets easier with practice. This is most easily accomplished by learning how to really listen to the clients or students express their concerns and desires.

It is not necessary to blurt out what evolutionary state the Soul is in. Rather, it is more meaningful to use direct language, many times in the form of asking questions, which allows the client or student to understand what their next evolutionary step is.

It is helpful to realize that these evolutionary states are not looked at from a "better than" or "less than" judgment. They represent expanding levels of consciousness within Souls. The more any Soul evolves, the more it can take in and understand about its personal environment, society, country, and the world. This brings a responsibility to help those who have not yet reached the same level of awareness. Eventually it brings humility, as a Soul realizes no matter how far it has evolved, there is always another level.

CHART INTERPRETATIONS

An astrological interpretation through evolutionary astrology begins with observation and correlation. A discernment of the evolutionary state of the Soul, as well as basic social, religious, cultural, and parental conditioning, will provide a foundation and starting point for utilizing the "Pluto formula" to understand any Soul's karmic dynamic (past) and evolutionary intent (future).

The first part of the Pluto formula consists of looking at natal Pluto, the South Node of the Moon, and the planetary ruler of the South Node by house, sign, and aspects to grasp where the Soul is coming from by way of past-life patterning. This is known as the *main karmic dynamic*. This shows where the Soul is coming from, and what it will tend to gravitate toward for security reasons.

In all evolutionary states except for the most advanced spiritual states, Souls are unconsciously oriented to the past in order to feel secure. The past is what is known, and somewhere between 75 to 80 percent of a Soul's behavior is directly conditioned by the past, especially past lives.

The second part of the Pluto formula consists of looking at the Pluto polarity point, the North Node of the Moon, and the planetary ruler of the North Node by house, sign, and aspects to understand the *evolutionary intent* of the Soul in this lifetime. This is where the Soul is striving to grow both consciously and unconsciously. It is the next step.

This main karmic dynamic and evolutionary intent of the Pluto formula creates a bottom-line foundation for referencing and understanding any other planetary archetypes and aspects. For more information on the Pluto formula, please refer to *Pluto, Volume 1: The Evolutionary Journey of the Soul* and *Pluto, Volume 2: The Soul's Evolution Through Relationships*, both by Jeffrey Wolf Green.

Evolutionary astrology works closely with the cycle of phases and aspects among planets, in order to understand how long a Soul has been working on the archetype represented in any aspect signature between two planets. The faster-moving planet is always compared to the slower-moving planet in a counterclockwise direction, with the exception that all planets are compared to the Sun, which is the center of life within the Soul.

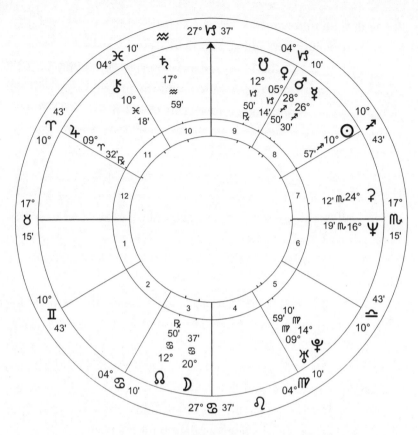

Sara's birth data
December 3, 1963 / 3:31pm EST / Pittsburgh, Pennsylvania

The Moon's nodes are always compared to the planets in a clockwise direction, as their mean motion is in a retrograde direction overall. Please refer to the Pluto books mentioned above for more information on understanding the cycle of phases and aspects.

In order to illustrate the different evolutionary states of the Soul and their foundation in astrological chart interpretation, we will consider the sample chart of a client named Sara, through consensus, individuated, and spiritual states. The social, religious, cultural, and parental imprinting will remain the same in each example. Sara is

Caucasian and was raised in a middle-class environment in the Pittsburgh suburbs with both parents. She was brought up in the Catholic Church.

Consensus-State Interpretation

Here we have a Soul who has spent her most recent lifetimes oriented toward discovering who she is and finding out what is special and unique about herself (fifth house Pluto). Sara also has experienced intense cataclysms of a humiliating nature to help purify her ego's desire for center stage and domination of others (Uranus in Virgo balsamic conjunction to Pluto in Virgo).

Postulating a consensus-state evolution to her Soul would mean that Sara would be preconditioned to believe that her power lies outside of herself. This would be a Soul who has become critical of others in order to feel good about herself and her place in life. Sara would be inclined to compare herself to others, and could feel quite frustrated whenever she perceived someone else as being better than her. In consensus state, Sara could have an outer image of self-importance (fifth house Pluto), which might hide deep feelings of inadequacy (Pluto in Virgo) that she would be unaware of.

The South Node and its planetary ruler show how these Soul lessons from the past played out. Sara would have a need to be in control of every area of her life (South Node in Capricorn, ninth house), and in a consensus state would lean toward traditional beliefs and values, and reliance on outside authorities (Saturn, ruler of South Node, in Aquarius, tenth house). One or both parents might be quite authoritarian, and Sara would receive parental imprinting to become dominant herself. As societal changes progressed, she would hear the message that these changes were making things worse, and she would feel strong pressures to conform, maintain the standards of the past, and resist any growth.

Her Taurus rising would produce an instinct to maintain security at all costs. With South Node in Capricorn, Sara's security would get connected with the material world and especially with her own possessions. She could easily create financial crises for herself from a need to have bigger and better "stuff" than anyone else (fifth house Pluto Soul, Jupiter in Aries waxing trine Sun in Sagittarius, South Node in Capricorn, ninth house). Sara would gravitate toward work that would allow her to be the boss or to receive the most attention.

Sara could be quite fearful of the future and any changes. She would desire to always to be right and in charge, in order to feel secure. Her Mercury in Sagittarius, eighth house, would intuitively find the best arguments to support her position on anything. She could be verbally forceful and ruthless when feeling vulnerable.

With a traditional religious upbringing, fifth-house Pluto Soul, and Neptune in the sixth house, there could be a need to judge others as more sinful, in order to feel good about herself. This could be based upon her own unconsciousness fear of not living up to parental, societal, and religious expectations (South Node in Capricorn, ninth house).

Traditional religious conditioning in the consensus state would tend to suppress Sara's desires to explore sexually in relationships (Sun, Mercury, and Mars in Sagittarius, eighth house). The parental influence could lead to judging the sexuality of others. Because human-made religions generally try to suppress natural sexuality, there could be distorted sexual messages and/or abuse from her father. Sara could exhibit the same sort of sexual behavior she judges as sinful in others, increasing her guilt feelings (eighth house planets in Sagittarius, Pluto in Virgo, fifth house).

Jupiter in Aries, eleventh house, is square the Moon's nodal axis. In evolutionary astrology, this symbolizes skipped steps in Sara's personal beliefs and intuition, especially regarding family and relationships. Sara could receive mixed messages in her parental environment, with one parent dominating and the other being submissive. She would attract partners who either needed her help, in which case she could feel in control, or else she would associate with controlling partners, repeating the submissive-parent pattern (North Node in Cancer, third house, South Node in Capricorn, ninth house).

Her ingrained belief structure would support this, for example in the way traditional religions support the domination of women by men. Sara would face crises with partners, as this patriarchal conditioning about women manifested through inequality in relationships. In consensus state, Sara would have no awareness of manifesting both masochistic and sadistic qualities in her relationships, in order to manipulate her partners into meeting her needs.

With Venus in Capricorn conjunct the South Node, Sara would have a history of suppressing her needs and sensitivity. She could have received parental messages that her needs did not count. Sara might have no idea of her tendency to bounce back and forth between aloof and cold, and emotionally out of control (Moon in Cancer) in relationships.

Inherent in these skipped steps is a need to find her own belief system, which has been suppressed and conditioned by traditional, patriarchal influences. The knowledge of evolutionary states would help to understand that her Soul's ability to break free and liberate herself is relatively limited in the consensus state, even with Jupiter in Aries as the only retrograde planet.

Every crisis in Sara's life would bring up the perennial "why" questions, and her answers would be a rehashing of the current traditional male-God judgments and punishments. In the heat of a current crisis, Sara could make a deal with God to behave a certain way if she could just have her security back in whichever area of her life is in chaos. After the crisis, Sara's behavior would revert back to her old patterns and her guilt would intensify—unconsciously creating yet another crisis.

The Pluto-in-Virgo generation lives from crisis to crisis, until their Souls have evolved enough to break free from the patriarchal conditioning that insists there is a perfect God who will stand in judgment of them. Patriarchal conditioning, via their particular religious imprinting, sets up impossible standards of right and wrong conduct, in order to control Souls through guilt.

When the Pluto-in-Virgo generation evolves to embrace natural laws via the Pisces polarity point, their Souls realize that life is made up of choices and experiences, and then more choices and experiences. The Pisces polarity point leads the Pluto-in-Virgo generation to unconditionally accept and love themselves, so they may evolve and co-create with the Divine, an evolving force itself.

The evolutionary intent for Sara in this incarnation is to detach from and observe her immediate environment in order to see who she really is and how she fits into her world (eleventh house Pluto polarity point). There is a need to become more aware of her actions. There is a need to rebirth her belief system (Pluto polarity point in Pisces). In the consensus state, Sara would only resist this type of inner reflection and project blame for her situations onto others.

These detachment lessons would operate through emotional and mental chaos, causing Sara to feel she is losing her grip on reality (North Node and its planetary ruler, the Moon, both in Cancer, third house). Her evolutionary intent is to totally shake up her world so that she could evolve past her old patterns. To the extent that she is entrenched in the consensus state, Sara would try even harder to cling to the past. She would keep attempting to reinterpret the past, intensifying the emotional heartaches and mental confusion. In consensus-state reality, Sara would be very codependent emotionally (Sun in the eighth house, Moon in Cancer).

If Sara succeeded in breaking free from her Catholic upbringing, her belief system probably would be replaced by another consensus-state religion, such as an evangelical belief structure. Sara's evolutionary intent is to break free from all conditioning of the past, and yet it is that very past that gives her security, so she would continually try to re-create it.

Sara might experience increasing chaos in her everyday world, further straining her nervous system and emotional security (North Node in Cancer, third house). She then would lash out, criticizing and blaming everyone else for her problems. She could experience increasing isolation as a result, forcing her to detach and look at her life (Jupiter in the eleventh house).

In the advanced stages of the consensus state, Sara could be quite ruthless to get what she wants and stay on top. She also would be able to turn on the tears whenever necessary to play the victim role and manipulate her way out of any situation.

At the end of the advanced stages of the consensus state, this chart patterning would start to bring intense downfalls in creativity and relationships due to karmic build-up. The evolutionary intent would be to help Sara's Soul detach—to break free from the past and humiliate herself out of her ego-based needs to be on top and in control (Uranus balsamic Pluto in the fifth house with both in a last quarter square aspect to the Sun in the eighth house). The intent would be to precipitate a transition into the beginning stages of the individuated state.

Individual-State Interpretation

Sara's Soul still would invoke a past-life orientation to work on discovering who she uniquely is. There also would still be strong parental and religious influences toward which her Soul would gravitate, early in life, for security reasons. She still would want to be in control of her environment.

Sara would begin to respond very differently to the evolutionary intent of her Soul. In the beginning stages of the individuated state, she could become very introverted. She might naturally gravitate toward more isolation (South Node in the ninth house) in order to process why she is experiencing traumatic and humiliating events (Uranus balsamic conjunction to Pluto in Virgo, fifth house). There could be a lot of purging within her Soul. If she tried to repeat the past again, it wouldn't work.

Her fifth-house Pluto Soul desires—to be noticed as special and unique—would become much more internalized. Instead of calling attention to herself in order to be noticed by others, as a consensus-state Soul would, Sara could become quite insecure in her behaviors. The need to be noticed would still be vital to her Soul. However, she could become quite critical of herself (Pluto in Virgo) instead of projecting her needs outward so much.

It is hard for a Soul in the beginning stages of the individuated state to act differently from those in the consensus state it is attempting to leave behind. Sara would still participate outwardly in similar social, religious, and relationship roles, and yet inwardly she would feel miserable. She might constantly question why no one ever really loves her, leading her Soul to begin the search for ways to love herself (North Node and its ruler, the Moon, in Cancer, third house).

Because of her Taurus rising, she still would have deeply instinctual needs to be secure, and she would resist making any changes until some crisis forced them upon her. Sara would relate to partners with tremendous insecurity, and relationship inequality still would be the norm. Relationship traumas would increase as her Soul desired (mostly unconsciously) to figure things out. She could alternate between extended periods of being alone, and those of making compromises and suppressing her needs in order to be loved.

Sara has Venus in Capricorn, ninth house in a new phase conjunction to Mars in Sagittarius, eighth house. Her Soul desires to initiate and explore new relationship behavior. Yet, her need to be secure would battle with her desire to move forward.

Sara would continue to face crises involving her belief systems (Jupiter in Aries, eleventh house, square the nodal axis). She could initiate new beliefs in a moment of crisis, and yet not really make the needed changes in her deep-seated beliefs, so she would be inclined to fall back onto old traditions/religions after each crisis passed. She would feel a deep void that "something meaningful" was missing in her life, yet not know what that is.

In the middle stages of the individuated state, Sara could become quite rebellious with this Jupiter signature, discounting all traditional religions and belief systems. She could profess not to believe in a higher power at all, and instead rely on her own practical experience (South Node in Capricorn, ninth house). She would, in effect, become her own higher power (Saturn, ruler of South Node, in Aquarius, tenth house).

The middle stages of the individuated state could begin to create a disbelief in all the traditional philosophies and religions; however, Sara would not yet know what to substitute. Her Soul could be rebelling from past-life memories of persecution via patriarchal religions (Neptune in Scorpio, sixth house). She could initiate many different belief systems, yet not follow through in really understanding or practicing a specific philosophy (Jupiter in Aries square nodal axis in Cancer-Capricorn, third house-ninth house).

Relative to a fifth-house Pluto Soul in the middle stages of the individuated state, Sara would be invested in being however she wanted to be. She could "do her own thing" and be the center of her world. Yet, Uranus balsamic conjunction to Pluto in Virgo would still create traumas and shocks in order to detach and learn how to see the uniqueness of others. At some point Sara would have to face and practice her karmic lessons in learning equality with others (eleventh-house Pluto polarity point).

Patriarchal conditioning through human-made religions has suppressed natural sexuality in all evolutionary states. In the individuated state, Sara's planetary signatures (fifth-house Pluto conjunct Uranus in Virgo; Sun and Mars in Sagittarius, eighth house, Neptune in Scorpio, sixth house) could range from sexual victimization to voyeurism to initiating sacred sexual practices. Here is where observation and correlation are so important to listening and really being able to discern the level at which the Soul is operating, and where the individual client has had actual experience.

The lessons would involve de-conditioning from the patriarchal suppression of sexuality and learning natural, meaningful expressions of sexual urges and feelings. Depending on the evolutionary state of Sara's Soul and the degree to which her Soul is actually breaking free from past conditioning in any evolutionary state, she could express her sexuality in many different ways. Again, observation and correlation are the most important functions an astrologer can perform for a client.

It also might be possible that Sara would be exposed to sexual incest with a parent. In the beginning stages of the individuated state, Sara would think there was something wrong with her to provoke such behavior. By the middle stages of the individuated state, Sara could rebel against incest with appropriate levels of anger—or she could repeat the pattern with her own children.

Her relationship crises would continue periodically throughout her life. The vehicle through which Sara could evolve would be her emotions and her ability to figure out how her inner nature creates her experiences (North Node and its ruler, the Moon, in Cancer, third house). The individuated state would mean Sara was working to let go of her old insecurity patterns, to learn how to really love herself and just be who she naturally is (fifth-house Pluto Soul).

In the advanced stages of the individuated state, Sara would start to figure things out. Every time she faced a "humiliating" experience (Pluto in Virgo) she could detach (eleventh-house Pluto polarity point) and further understand who she is and who she is not (fifth-house Pluto). Sara could face the day-to-day changes she needs to make in order to become more emotionally self-reliant (North Node in Cancer, third house). She could be just fine doing her own thing, and she could learn how to be alone without being lonely. Sara would realize that she must take responsibility for loving herself (Venus in Capricorn). She would instinctually search out new relating patterns (Venus new phase conjunction to Mars).

Sara would still experience crises in her beliefs (Jupiter square the nodal axis, Neptune in the sixth house). Through the various stages of the individuated state, she could have experienced several past lives in exploring different belief systems, facing some type of crisis each time a particular religion or belief system became limiting. Jupiter retrograde in Aries square the nodal axis (eleventh, third, ninth houses) would now mean that Sara needs to detach and initiate a more natural, inclusive belief system—and stick with it.

In the consensus state, this Jupiter retrograde signature signified a need to initiate new belief systems. Now in the advanced stages of the individuated state, Sara would need to cast off her excess religious and spiritual philosophies and really practice the system toward which she most naturally gravitates (South Node in Capricorn, ninth house, acting as the resolution node to the Jupiter skipped steps).

Sara would also be able to find the inner strength to stand up to any authoritarian parent as she embarked on a spiritual path that made sense to her. This spiritual journey would help her relationships evolve. She would understand her parents' social patterns and religious conditioning, and their impact. As Sara learned to love herself more completely (Moon in Cancer, Venus in Capricorn), she would be able to recognize parental imprinting and make efforts to change it whenever a relationship crisis or inequality issue arose.

She would still have deep needs for security (Taurus rising), and would begin to realize that security is not necessarily found in possessions. Sara would begin the search for inner security. As she moved toward finding her own inner knowing, Sara would gravitate toward work that would allow her natural creative talents (fifth-house Pluto Soul) to emerge. She could be a teacher or counselor who helped others to learn how to love themselves better (planets in Sagittarius).

Spiritual-State Interpretation

The beginning stages of the spiritual state would allow Sara to utilize her evolutionary intent to metamorphose her karmic past. Sara would start releasing her ego-based desires and her need to be on center stage (Pluto in the fifth house). Purification of her Soul would be welcomed (Uranus balsamic Pluto in Virgo).

Sara would be getting in touch with her natural leadership abilities and attracting people who appreciated her fairness and humility (eleventh-house Pluto polarity point). She would desire work that allowed her to help humanity on broader and broader levels. She could become a natural teacher (planets in Sagittarius, South Node in the ninth house).

Relative to patriarchal conditioning over the last few thousand years (Piscean Age), Sara could still choose parents who instilled a strong religious upbringing. Now it would serve as the vehicle that allowed Sara to see the limitations of her beliefs.

As crises in her beliefs arose (Jupiter square the nodal axis), Sara would continually evolve toward a more complete understanding of natural laws versus human-made religions and conditioning (South Node in Capricorn, ninth house, acting as the resolution node to the Jupiter skipped steps). She would express her ability to understand natural spiritual principles and how to live them on a practical, day-to-day basis. She would strive to see the largest philosophical picture possible. Sara would search for a philosophical belief system that would support her emotionally (Jupiter square North Node in Cancer).

Her instinctual need to be secure (Taurus rising) would teach her how to replace outer security with inner security. Sara would simplify her material needs, and live in an environment that supported her instead of collecting more stuff to feel secure. Every experience that asked her to let go in some way would be utilized to understand her inner nature better.

There could be early karmic relationships (Scorpio Descendant, eighth-house planets) that taught her to deepen her relationship with herself and a higher power. Even in the spiritual evolutionary states, Sara could experience sexual pain and wounding. Now her Soul would detach (eleventh-house Pluto polarity point) and deeply question how she had attracted those experiences to herself. She would learn to love herself as completely as possible (North Node and its ruler the Moon in Cancer), and to honor her emotional needs from moment to moment. Sara would minimize her dependency upon others.

Sara could evolve to the level where she would attract a Soul-mate partner, someone who was searching to understand relationships in a spiritual context (Scorpio Descendant). She would learn to trust her instincts in relationships (Mars in Sagittarius, eighth house, Scorpio Descendant) and give deeply when she was given to as well (Venus in Capricorn).

In the middle stages of the spiritual state, Sara could be instrumental in initiating more natural spiritual laws and helping others understand and live those principles. If Sara still harbored separating desires to be the center of attention, she could experience humiliations in understanding the separating nature of those desires by losing her leadership role. Alternatively, Sara could understand the need to naturally exhaust the desire by walking through the leadership position and refusing to play the pedestal role. She could be the example of Divine Will regardless of what others wanted.

As Sara's Soul evolved into more and more spiritual states, the same chart pattern could lead her to live the simplest of material existences. She would be simply inspirational in her spiritual messages (planets in Sagittarius). Her relationship with the Source would be all-consuming (Neptune in Scorpio). Her aura would naturally spread unconditional love with every person she encountered (fifth-house Pluto Soul).

As a Soul exhausts separating desires, any and all planetary archetypes are expressed in their highest form. There are many paths back to the Source, and any chart could be the example of a Soul that exhausts its separating desires. One of the most accepted examples of Jesus' chart is full of oppositions in Virgo and Pisces,[1] when one might expect the chart of an evolved Soul to have trines and sextiles.

It is not the specific chart configuration or aspects that matter at this point. It is the evolutionary state of the Soul itself bringing the essence of any planetary archetypes into their highest and best expressions.

Meeting the Client's Needs

These different interpretations of the same chart show that understanding different evolutionary states can provide a wealth of information, as well as a deep understanding of how to best meet a client's needs.

The archetypal meanings of astrological symbols come alive in such a way that astrologers, students, and clients may know that astrology is natural law. That which is natural law may be suppressed and distorted; however, it cannot be destroyed. Like the spiraling circle it is, it rebirths again and again until it is set free and natural laws simply exist.

Evolutionary astrology seeks to discover and understand natural spiritual laws and principles versus human-made religious conditioning. Evolutionary astrology is based upon the premise that astrology actually is natural law. Natural spiritual laws and principles are observable everywhere, especially in nature herself. With an understanding of the evolutionary states of Souls, an astrologer may support students and clients moving toward experiences more harmonious with natural laws, and therefore living happier, more joyous, and spiritually fulfilling lives. Souls can simply understand what their next evolution-

---

1. Data for birth of Jesus: March 1, 0007 BCE, 1:21 a.m. LMT-2:20:48, Bethlehem, Israel, 31N43, 35E12. Source: Donald Jacobs, *Astrology's Pew in the Church* (San Francisco: Joshua Foundation, 1982).

ary step is and fulfill that lesson. The desire to unite with the Divine can be actualized.

ABOUT KIM MARIE

Kim Marie, director of the Evolutionary Astrology Network, spearheads an evolutionary astrology online course for hundreds of students worldwide, teaches classes on evolutionary astrology, and has produced EA conferences and workshops across North America. A student of evolutionary astrology for twenty-five years, Kim Marie counsels an international clientele and publishes free forecasting podcasts on the StarLady Soul-Reader Network, which are also available on her website and on iTunes. Her background includes experience in alternative healing and environmental politics. Kim Marie is also a facilitator for the Energetic Matrix Church of Consciousness, LLC (EMC^2)—a leading-edge computerized spiritual technology for 24/7 self-healing.

Kim Marie resides in the Black Hills of South Dakota with her husband, son, and three cats.

Please visit her website, at www.evolutionaryastrology.net.

4

Relationships and Sexuality in Astrology

BY MAURICE FERNANDEZ

Throughout the ages different theories have come and gone about sexuality, and despite the considerable amount of experience in the matter it remains a mystical force, feared and venerated at the same time. The human mind continues to be baffled by this extraordinary and yet so important aspect of life. Sexuality overpowers the behavioral pressure to act as controlled and cultivated beings, and exposes personality dimensions that may display as irrational, primal, subconscious, dark, liberating, or ecstatic.

Through sexuality, an often concealed side of emotions is exposed with a partner. This is not an easy thing to do, since nature does not encourage blind trust without discrimination; each being must single out whom to be exposed to in order to filter out potential parasites or predators. In a world of imperfection and danger, one of the most basic survival instincts is to stay guarded. Yet sexuality urges each being to eventually overcome insecurities around trust issues because it leaves one with no choice but to depend on others—be it for procreation purposes or desire fulfillment. Thus, when sexually attracted to a stranger, an individual risks danger and surrenders defenses in order to get to know that person. The sexual attraction bypasses intellectual defenses and incites one to take a chance. Through sexuality, a realization arises that our state of separation cannot be permanent because it cannot answer those inherent needs; consequently, sexuality instinctively draws people together. The challenge remains to establish a securing intimacy for it to unfold productively, because the danger of getting hurt remains.

Sexuality is understood by most to have more than procreation purposes; it is a channel for emotional and sensual expression and serves as one of the most important means to integrate the Soul into the body. Moreover, it allows the intimacy of a couple to deepen in mutual surrendering, promoting in such a way psychological and spiritual growth. However, the road to establish fair play and mutual satisfaction is paved with deviation, as power games between the sexes have generated a great deal of distortion during history's course. The fear of displeasing women and enduring rejection has caused many men to de-legitimize the sexuality of women, and in such a way destabilize the balance of power to their advantage. The patriarchal culture prevalent for centuries across the planet is recognized for rendering women objects of pleasure and depriving them of the enjoyment of pleasure in order to deny their power to choose. On the one hand, women are encouraged to be beautiful and attractive, and are simultaneously perceived as "cheap" when sexually assertive. On the other hand, men are trapped in the projection to either be heroes or losers, continuously at the risk of rejection when they fail to meet expectations. Therefore, despite physical nakedness, emotional defensiveness often remains between couples until efforts are invested to establish a true sense of intimacy through which these power games can naturally dissolve; this type of trust requires time and maturity.

Sexuality is also one of the main sources of power. When a person has strong sex appeal and can satisfy a partner's needs to the full extent, he or she may feel tremendously potent. This power can be seriously corrupting in many ways. A person possessing sexual powers may allow himself or herself to abuse others or disregard the emotional reality of a partner because he or she feels sheltered from rejection. However, a person consumed by sexual needs may betray his or her values and ethics to satisfy these sexual cravings; sexuality can overpower common sense because it touches the deepest hunger—potentially leading to bad judgment. For example, someone may remain in a destructive relationship because he or she has become dependent on the sexual power of the abuser.

Many have blamed religious institutions for having condemned sexuality as a corrupting force, and there is some basis to that. Moral and honest people are subject to destructive behavior when consumed by sexual cravings—doing things they may regret later on. However, religious institutions have usually tried to solve that issue through absolute abstinence and mind control—typically associating corruption and negativity with sexuality instead of trying to better understand its role. These extreme measures were bound to failure and further distortion. On the other extremes, the attempt to promote absolute permissiveness in sexual expression has created its own set of dysfunctions. Excessive openness can engender an overly simplistic approach to sexuality that overrides the emotional integration necessary to establish reliable intimacy. The sense of freedom can be deceptive when the absence of true intimacy is subject to cause emotional violations and corruption instead of genuine growth and liberation. One eventually realizes that legitimizing every immediate gratification when responding to every erupting desire can cause extremely damaging consequences; the person becomes a slave to his or her own senses and is subject to psychic pollution when indiscriminately open.

Sexuality is tightly associated with emotions—sexual desires and attraction are an expression of the emotional nature of a person. Whom one is sexually attracted to reflects one's true emotional nature—this is not necessarily what is exposed outwardly. Sexual expression exposes shadows, needs, weaknesses, ethical standards, values, apprehensions, or, in short, the whole psychological make-up of a person. The fear of shadows may incite a person to attempt to control erupting urges. Conversely, when there is acceptance of one's sexuality—with all its intricacies—sexuality can become a medium of healing. The individual may begin to understand the origins of his or her cravings and analyze the reasons for particular impulses. Associating sexuality with emotions can allow one to heal and develop emotions though sexual expression. Through such an approach, sexuality can become a tool that promotes the Soul's evolution, because through it emotions can be worked on. Using a simple example, the need for sexual submission can be rooted in feelings of guilt that may not be otherwise apparent on a day-to-day basis.

We will now explore the natural sexual inclinations of each astrological archetype. This study can allow us to gain a deeper understanding about the emotional nature and the evolutionary necessities of each of these influences. Mars, Venus, and Pluto by house, sign, and aspects are the main indicators of sexuality in the chart. Their associated houses, signs, and aspects must be considered in this regard. There are usually repeating themes in a chart emphasizing stronger inclinations.

Mars, the first house, and Aries reflect the natural assertion of the self and of primal urges. This archetype represents the uncensored self that bypasses the mind—the raw expression is a way for the individual to get in touch with his or her natural expression and needs.

Venus, the second house, and Taurus symbolize the descent of spirit into matter; hence this archetype represents the sensual self—the response to sensory pleasure. On this basis, it represents the attunement to one's sexual needs and values as well as one's magnetism and appeal. Venus, as a natural ruler of Libra, also represents the ability to adapt to a partner and open up to whatever he or she has to offer.

Pluto, the eighth house, and Scorpio symbolize the aspiration to grow beyond personal limitations; this archetype represents the need to redefine the self continuously through the evolution process. Sexuality under these influences is based on the need for merging with another in order to absorb what the other offers. Ideally, through the sexual and emotional exchange, each side gives and receives something, and both are able to grow into a greater sense of being. Moreover, this archetype represents the necessity for the person's sexual nature to evolve in the course of time. Evolution may, for example, manifest in transforming sexual power from an expression of mere release to an experience of love and transformation.

The following descriptions outline the sexual inclinations of each astrological archetype without being specific about the influence of Mars, Venus, or Pluto, and their related house and sign. These are general inclinations that take neither the person's cultural conditioning nor his or her specific evolutionary stage into consideration. A description of the different evolutionary levels of consciousness can be found in evolutionary astrology literature.

SEXUALITY THROUGH THE ARIES ARCHETYPE

Mars, Venus, Pluto in Aries or in the First House
Venus and Pluto in aspect to Mars

Evolutionarily speaking, the Aries archetype relates to the need to assert one's sense of separation. Under these influences, the challenge is to take charge of one's life and avoid relying on external sources to secure one's well-being. Strength to face challenges alone is developed to eventually find one's personal path to self-realization. Aries follows Pisces and, from this perspective, the individual is moving away from a passive approach to life toward a more active, assertive, and defensive approach. There is a need to learn to take matters into hand instead of blindly trusting life to take care of itself.

On a sexual level, there is a strong need from the Soul's point of view to assert sexual needs as freely as possible. Aries types tune in to their primal desires and emotions, thus bypassing the mind's logic and control centers. There is an evolutionary intent to relinquish past-life orientations in which they may have been too passive or frustrated sexually; there is a desire to avoid stagnation and limitations caused by a lack of initiative. Moreover, Aries types feel the need to take the active side because they want to avoid being dominated and suppressed by partners. A memory of domination may trigger anger on a sexual level; this can cause them to be more direct and sometimes even defensive toward the other sex. This condition may lead to recurrent confrontations or separations from partners who are considered too controlling. The prerogative for freedom of sexual expression is not necessarily innate; the confidence to stand up against external pressure and repression may have to be gradually acquired.

Women under these influences may consequently feel utterly at odds with their conditioned societal roles of being passive desire objects and may opt instead for the initiator role in relationships and intercourse. They are often tired of waiting for shy partners to make their moves. Evolutionarily speaking, they need to express their creativity and desires and tend to rebel against gender roles conditioned by patriarchal societies. Some of them even become activists working toward women's rights and gender equality.

The Aries types are the ones taking action and setting the courting sequence in motion because from their own perspective, the desire is urgent and cannot wait for the rest of the world to have an opinion about it. Although ready to risk rejection when their advances are not answered, they do not initially take rejection into consideration. Insecure men may feel threatened by a woman's sexual assertiveness, and despite being flattered by the advances, they may attempt to tone it down or even suppress it as a defensive instinct.

Under these influences, men are often attracted to powerful and independent women, and women yearn for passionate and willful men. Evolutionarily speaking, this desire relates to a need for partners who are inspiring in their competence at dealing with challenges. Yet despite the attraction to power and strength, they compete with it and test their own might in comparison to their mate. A weak, dispassionate, or indifferent partner reminds them of where they are evolving away from; it is a turnoff.

In other cases, some women under these astral influences may have a strong identification with the male principle, because men are associated with assertiveness and creative freedom. The need to be initiators may cause frustration when, at the crucial moment of sexual penetration, they fulfill the passive role of being penetrated. They may wish to take the active role and may experience frustration when not able to do so. A way to resolve this dilemma is by discovering that the female body is very powerful and potent. The woman must realize she has tremendous power and develop her sexual creativity; when she does, it usually leads to more acceptance of her female body and her sexual role.

As Aries types become increasingly more expressive, there is a great deal of excitement and passion that ensues. They discover themselves, as each step forward shows how far they can go. They become relatively self-absorbed and perceive each passing emotion as absolute. When they have an attraction to another, the identification is total, and so it is with repulsion. Complete emotional involvement manifests itself in a strong focus on the chosen partner. Accordingly, Aries types expect immediate emotional feedback from partners and equal intensity in the passion for the relationship, without which they may feel undermined and unrecognized. When the partner does not resonate exactly to their feelings, it is often translated into a form of adversity. Inwardly, the message is "you are either totally with me or against me," and consequently they may have a hard time accepting the partner for having different desires and needs. This form of possessiveness can be the source of power struggles and accusations.

Libra is the balancing polarity of Aries, and through it there is a crucial evolutionary lesson of accepting the partner's distinct emotional composite and need for freedom, just as the Aries person needs his or her own. In so doing, the feeling of adversity may be overcome with more trust. There is a need to understand that compromises do not necessarily mean self-denial. Yet in order to feel secure about compromises, it has to be mutual. Evolutionarily speaking, a lesson is to realize that emotional and sexual compatibility does not solely rely on mutual relatedness but also on existing differences.

SEXUALITY THROUGH THE TAURUS ARCHETYPE

Mars, Venus, Pluto in Taurus or in the Second House
Mars and Pluto in aspect to Venus

The evolutionary intent through the Taurus archetype is to integrate spirit into form and care for the continuance of the form's existence. In this phase, the individual primarily focuses on a relationship with himself or herself and the cultivation of personal resources. Following Aries, Taurus types tire from conquering external goals and concentrate more specifically on self-sufficiency in order to solidify, stabilize, and guarantee continuity.

On the sexual dimension, the descent of spirit into body generates an emphasis on the role of the senses. The need for harmonious touch, feeling, smell, and sight are important for the sexual experience. There may consequently be a tendency within these influences to emphasize the purely physical aspect of sexuality as a means of connection to the dimension of earth. If taken to an extreme, this orientation can lead to negative consequences: in one way, Taurus types could end up ignoring the psychological aspect of a relationship and focus solely on meeting material and physical needs. The couple may live in artificial bliss without having a deeper understanding of each other's actual motives and needs. In further extremes, this dynamic can lead to sexual abuse as a result of perceiving others as beautiful sexual objects or being perceived themselves as such, as if dealing in a meat market. Women are essentially liable to measure their worth according to their "sexiness" and surrender to the image of the sexual object. In extreme cases, this may lead to sexual obsessions and addictions that may upset emotional stability.

Sex can be a sensual experience of pleasure without necessarily strong emotional involvement; nevertheless, there is an evolutionary need for mutual agreement and equality in respect to reducing the chances of abuse and manipulation in these circumstances.

Individuals under Taurus's influence are naturally very territorial and independent. Very few manage to penetrate their fortress and conquer their spirit. Even when in a committed and loving relationship, they will require a lot of time on their own during which they do not want to be distracted. They need partners who have a rich inner life and who are strong enough to occupy themselves as well. In some cases, they may even opt for separate rooms or refrain from moving in with a partner. This does not necessarily undermine the care and affection they may have for the partner—for despite needing their time and space, they may paradoxically be very attached and possessive, emotionally speaking.

Sexually speaking, Taurus types have a strong inclination for masturbation, which reflects the combination of their strong sexual drive and their autonomy. The need for masturbation reflects the fact that they are very faithful to and in tune with their bodily needs and do not wish to compromise, adjust, or wait for the goodwill of another to fulfill them.

The evolutionary lesson is to learn to improve the quality of their intimacy with their partner in order to add new dimensions to their sexual expression. Scorpio being the balancing polarity of Taurus indicates there is a need to learn to include others in one's territory and open up emotionally through the sexual act. The lesson is in risking potential pain or rejection when becoming attached to others. This requires daring to change personal habits and convictions if necessary and deepen the bond, without losing one's own independence.

SEXUALITY THROUGH THE GEMINI ARCHETYPE

Mars, Venus, Pluto in Gemini or in the Third House
Mars, Venus, and Pluto in aspect to Mercury

The Gemini archetype relates evolutionarily speaking to the need to decode the logic of existence in order to be able to better integrate and navigate through it. The individual is pressured under these influences to tune in to the external rhythm of the environment and, while immersed in the simultaneous crosscurrents of life, figure out the way things work. Following Taurus, Gemini influences expose the limitations of isolation as it becomes clear that the need to stay attentive to what goes on in the world is not a matter of convenience but a matter of survival. Therefore, efforts are invested to improve communication skills in order to learn about life.

Sexually speaking, Gemini types may feel the need to intellectually understand sexuality and desires. They aspire to learn about the right ways and meanings of sexuality and therefore do not want to get carried away by sheer impulse. Already in childhood they may develop a strong curiosity about sex, picking up information from what goes on in their environment. Despite not being biologically ripe to perform, they are often well informed about sexual practices and intrigues. This intellectual awareness provides a feeling of security. However, crises may derive from a gap between knowing about sex and actual performance confidence; sex may end up being theoretical and not experienced. Knowing so much so soon, these individuals may present a very cool and confident attitude, while in fact they fear embarrassment, sarcasm, and incompetence. Sometimes, these insecurities are projected onto the partner, and Gemini types can become sarcastic about their partner's insecurities or lack of experience.

The need for assessment can lead to various forms of voyeurism. They may, for example, be intellectually interested in the sexual stories of people or, in a different way, be drawn to pornography; the visual as well as intellectual stimulus can be sexually compelling. The evolutionary lesson is, however, to be able to create an atmosphere of security and intimacy with another and overcome the fear of embarrassment. This may be done through honest communication with the partner about sexual needs and apprehensions. Feeling secure that the other person is on the same wavelength, tensions and fear of criticism may decrease, allowing the Gemini types to gradually surrender their defense mechanisms.

In another way, the intellectual approach to sex may lead to a strong emotional void that is compensated by a need for excessive stimulation. The more the mind is stimulated, the more the sexual drive increases, generating a need to find ever more "interesting" stimulations. They may consequently indulge in experimental sex and become more attracted to the extremes and hardcore experiences. Because emotions are not involved in this case, emptiness remains—despite the strong stimulation.

Evolution occurs when finding the right balance between security and mental stimulation, keeping the Gemini types open-minded about sex without compromising on caring and mutual expression of appreciation. They can be very good listeners and use their mental perspective to find solutions for possible emotional hang-ups. Having honest and insightful discussions about sexuality or emotional needs dissolves insecurities and defensive mechanisms, helping to create a better intimacy in such a way.

Sagittarius being the balancing polarity of Gemini implies there is a need to experience sex in natural ways, and go beyond the mind.

It inspires more spontaneity, playfulness, and authenticity. Sagittarius inspires the Gemini types to transcend fear of shame and embarrassment and to accept themselves for who they naturally are, relinquishing in such a way the need to fit environmental standards.

SEXUALITY THROUGH THE CANCER ARCHETYPE

Mars, Venus, Pluto in Cancer or in the Fourth House
Mars, Venus, and Pluto in aspect to the Moon

The Cancer archetype relates to the evolutionary need to process life through the emotional body. Following Gemini, there is a need in this phase to withdraw from external exposure and stimulation in order to digest life experiences in intimacy at one's own pace. The need in this process is to tune in to the personal inner rhythm and neutralize external pressures. Emotional assimilation serves maturation and growth processes.

In this context, sexual expression and desires are enmeshed with the person's emotions; the sexual act can literally serve as a direct channel for emotional expression and processing. Affection, fear, jealousy, or attachment may each manifest in turn through sex in accordance with the person's present mood. As a result, the person is emotionally attentive and very present when engaged with a partner. There is a strong nurturing inclination and patience with needs and vulnerabilities that the partner may express.

Because of the need for security and intimacy, some Cancer types are able to immediately generate warmth and dissolve defenses when meeting people. They may break all barriers with relative haste in order to waste no time and dwell in the comforting coziness as soon as possible. Partners are usually selected on the basis of strong feelings of identification; once chosen, they are usually considered family relatively quickly despite having been strangers not long ago. Such haste may result in skipped steps when creating an intimacy, and it can consequently be superficial and unfounded. As a result, the partner may feel like family one moment and then be considered a stranger the next; these Cancer types manifest fluctuating moods whereby they are warm and inviting in one moment, and unavailable the next. In order to balance these mood swings and avoid double messages, it is important not to rush the intimacy process and to allow it to be gradual, consistent, and natural.

In other circumstances, Cancer types remain extremely shy in the presence of strangers and feel comfortable only in the company of individuals with whom they are well acquainted. As a result of the need for familiarity, they may create relationships within close circles only, sometimes even between family members. The deep sense of insecurity may lead to slow sexual development and result in late bloomers.

Under these influences there is a need to be nurtured, protected, and, in some cases, dominated by the partner on a sexual level. Having possibly experienced emotional deprivation during childhood, they may project the parental role onto their partner and expect them to be caretakers. This dynamic may go as far as manipulating the partner in capricious ways and pressuring him or her take the lead. In extreme cases, the individual may become sexually and emotionally dependent on the partner and regress into states of infantilism, in which all emotions are unleashed to a point of losing sense and perspective. This may manifest in literally behaving like an infant, having tantrums, competing for care and attention, and needing absolute attention all the time. The roles may be reversed, and Cancer types may themselves attract partners that are emotionally charged in such a way.

Incestuous relationships are possible in extreme cases, but they are not necessarily sexualized; emotional interplays between family members may transgress boundaries in unhealthy ways. Males may unconsciously identify so strongly with their mothers that besides projecting her image onto their partners, they may have a desire to cross-dress. These strong identifications may be more pronounced at a younger age and dissipate as one's personality develops. However, if these needs are repressed and unprocessed during childhood, cross-dressing urges may emerge in adulthood, sometimes to the point of disassociating with the male body. Females may also go through intense emotional phases in this regard, whereby they experience alternating periods of total symbiosis with the mother and times of strife or estrangement.

The balancing Capricorn polarity points to the necessity to establish healthy boundaries in order for emotional processes to be healthy and not overly indulged in. The individual needs to develop an inner authority and ground himself or herself in solid values and principles that can serve as guiding references when engaging in relationships. Taking more responsibility also diminishes unhealthy dependencies and extreme circumstances of dominance and submission; solidifying inner foundations allows the person to be affectionate and nurturing in a consistent way without mood swings.

SEXUALITY THROUGH THE LEO ARCHETYPE

Mars, Venus, Pluto in Leo or in the Fifth House
Mars, Venus, and Pluto in aspect to the Sun

The Leo archetype relates to the need to participate in the process of life and explore ways to enhance it through creativity. Following Cancer, Leo is emotionally involved in every endeavor, emphasizing the importance of life. There is a feeling of being ripe, which generates an inclination to invest personal resources in creative endeavors and take a leading role in life.

On this note, there is a strong need for self-expression and self-validation in relationships and sexuality. Individuals with this configuration often need strong partners who can inspire them and with whom they can explore and enjoy life. Sexuality plays an important role because sexuality is in itself creativity . . . Leo types consequently enjoy a strong libido. Nonetheless, their tendency to overuse or misuse their potency can cause a decrease of sexual vitality with age, especially for males.

Moreover, relationship commitments often clash with a need for creative freedom, and therefore one may feel the need to control the relationship in order to have an upper hand in the way the relationship unfolds—conducting dynamics on one's own terms. When taken to an extreme, they can become dictator-like and expect their partner to submit to their cause. Yet, such a "totalitarian" attitude is often camouflaged by their generosity and playfulness; they may be called "benevolent dictators"! This dynamic is not played out without setbacks, though, because Leo types need to respect and admire their partner just as much, and may not be truly satisfied with an obedient admirer, despite the comfort of such a position.

This dynamic may be reversed with the Leo types falling for a very inspiring and powerful partner who possesses a strong personality; consequently, they can also become the blind devotee and surrender to leading figures. In this scenario, the Leo type puts the partner on a pedestal and expects to be continuously inspired by him or her. If the partner fails to fulfill these expectations, he or she is then abruptly taken off the pedestal. This dynamic can have a castrating effect psychologically.

There is often a conscious or unconscious incestuous sexual attraction with this archetype, especially with reference to the father. Either daughters or sons may be subliminally attracted to the father, or the father may be attracted to one of his children. In other cases, it is the mother who is attracted to her son. The root of this complex is based on strong expectations from one generation to the other to carry the family heritage with honor—hence the projection of admiration from one generation to the other. These emotional dynamics can transpire onto the sexual dimension, even if subliminally so. For example, the child may yearn for a partner, male or female, that captures the energy of that parent. In extreme circumstances, these dynamics can lead to a child being sexually abused by the parent, usually the father. This may occur through intercourse or, more covertly, through sexual innuendos and harassment.

Interestingly, this archetype is particularly related to homosexuality for both sexes. Leo types may feel the need to further grow into who they are, and therefore have an attraction to same-sex partners in order to further "infuse" themselves with their own energy, so to speak—this need derives from a sense of lack. As a result, the homosexual male is attracted to virile men on the basis of needing an additional "infusion" of maleness. The homosexual female glorifies the powerful "alpha female" image and is often attracted to women with strong personalities and a proud spirit.

In other cases, women with this signature may have an obsession with the male principle, and similar to the Aries signature, may fail to identify with their female body, sometimes to a point of suffering from penis envy. This can translate into totally submitting themselves to a strong male, elevating him to the highest pedestal and living through him. In more common circumstances, this emotional dynamic expresses itself in the female being more of a tomboy and being drawn to the company of men rather than women. These women may come from past lives where the female principle was weak and submissive, and therefore they feel alienated from that association—from childhood they tend to identify more strongly with their fathers than their mothers. Only when recognizing themselves as potent creators can they move beyond this projection and fully integrate into their female body.

Generally speaking, the Leo types know how to give personal attention; they can be very encouraging and empower their partners. When in love, passion possesses them and they only think about giving to their partner and making their partner happy. They often radiate warmth and are dramatic in their declarations.

Aquarius is the balancing polarity of Leo and represents the lesson of perspective. The Leo types must learn that it is not enough to be generous according to their own subjective view; rather, there is a need to learn to provide what the other truly needs and to learn to listen in that context. The Aquarian polarity is about mentally reflecting on the emotional dynamics in order to eliminate exaggerated dramas and create a better sense of equality in the relationship dynamics. When these concepts are integrated emotionally, creativity within the relationship and within sexuality can boost and generate growth and maturation.

SEXUALITY THROUGH THE VIRGO ARCHETYPE

Mars, Venus, Pluto in Virgo or in the Sixth House
Mars, Venus, and Pluto in aspect to Mercury

The Virgo archetype relates to the evolutionary need to actively manage and refine resources so that general function may improve. There is a lesson about maintenance and improvement to avoid decline or waste. Through the Virgo archetype, the individual is concerned with having more control over life in order to optimize production and overcome potential dysfunction.

On a sexual level, there is often a paradox within the sexual orientation. On the one hand, sexual impulses and needs are very strong, and on the other hand, a tendency to overanalyze natural urges can neutralize natural sexual expression. Nonetheless, the keen awareness for details may render the Virgo types real sex experts, developing techniques to enhance stimulation. Many of them can become the perfect lovers as a result of constantly improving their performance.

Virgo types often know what they want and how to get there; thus, they have specific taste for the types of partners they want. In most cases, attention to the physical appearance is prominent, causing Virgo types to sometimes fall in love with people for their physical beauty.

Accordingly, they may lose interest when beauty fades—whether it is caused by weight gains, pimples, or age. An overly strong attachment to perfection can render them intolerant to weakness or flaws. Accordingly, they become strongly aware of their body and tend to be self-conscious. In extreme cases, eating disorders often emerge.

As mentioned before, the ability for control can be the Virgo types' forte but also the source of numerous problems. These individuals are very skilled, knowledgeable, and refined, but they often have difficulty surrendering completely to the sexual experience. The aspiration for perfection may sometimes manifest on a moral level; Virgo types may perceive sexuality as impure and coarse. This orientation is often rooted in conservative religious conditioning and can limit their sexual experience to a bare minimum. One may not necessarily go as far as total abstinence but might condemn any behavior that is not considered "normal" according to one's puritanical standards. This approach may, for example, lead to demonizing homosexuality, masturbation, or oral sex.

In certain cases, while feeling trapped by the inability to surrender to the sexual act, Virgo types may be consumed by wild fantasies through which they completely lose control. Accordingly, they may have a strong desire to be overpowered, sometimes going as far as having rape fantasies. Similarly, the need to counterbalance their puritanical conditioning can engender fantasies about dirty sex. They may consequently be trapped in the dichotomy of the saint versus the prostitute. Sometimes males with Virgo influences can live this dichotomy by marrying a dutiful and prudish woman, and sooner or later have an affair with a sexually liberated woman.

In other ways, circumstances may pressure Virgo types to work on their sexuality. Erectile dysfunction, a lack of stimulation, or even a physical handicap may require learning about new ways to approach sexuality. In certain cases the solution lies in specific techniques to improve the purely physical aspect of sex. In other cases, a psychological issue may require therapy to help the person improve the quality of sexual and emotional intimacy.

The balancing polarity of Virgo is Pisces, indicating that an important lesson is to learn acceptance and flexibility. Learning to relax, going more with the flow, and being less critical can help release pressure. The need to let go relies on trusting that, despite possible imperfections, sexual dynamics are most likely to go fine. From this perspective, the motivation for improvement and refinement can be better balanced and less compulsive. Accordingly, the Pisces polarity inspires one to associate more spiritual meanings to sexuality and, in such a way, decrease the focus on the purely physical aspect of it.

SEXUALITY THROUGH THE LIBRA ARCHETYPE

Mars, Venus, Pluto in Libra or in the Seventh House
Mars and Pluto in aspect to Venus

The Libra archetype relates to the evolutionary need to join forces with others in order to accomplish greater tasks together. The lesson is in unifying extremes and eventually dissolving adversities. The Libra archetype consequently encourages the formation of relationships in order to unite polarities. The challenge remains to establish a fair trade in relationships so that all sides may benefit from the union.

Individuals under Libra influences are consequently drawn to people who are inspiring by nature, in order to learn from who they are and what they have. Other people's reality is a whole new world and perspective to discover. This tendency renders Libra types attentive listeners who see validity and value in diversity. It usually generates an adaptable nature that makes them relatively passive and open on a sexual level. Openness may manifest in coming without prejudice and pre-formulated desires to the act. They can consequently become the typical students that surrender to the experience, or the pleasers who are fully attentive to their partners' needs and vicariously experience personal pleasure in satisfying them. However, despite wanting to learn everything about the other, Libra types seldom expose themselves emotionally or sexually and remain elusive as to who they are intimately. This condition may be rooted in a reluctance to reveal their weaknesses because they fear disappointing. In other circumstances, it is simply the result of their own uncertainty about who they are and what they truly want. This situation can lead to imbalances in the giving-and-receiving dynamic, setting the stage for the Libra types to be taken for granted and expected to adjust to the partner's needs.

A sense of inner lack may generate a recurring feeling of emptiness that is projected onto partners. Sometimes, in idealizing others they may constantly feel that they are missing something. It can occur even when being in a relationship—a need to diversify experience can lead to new sexual attractions. As a result, some of them may have difficulties with settling for monogamy. However, this inclination may not necessarily lead to numerous sexual relationships at once; they may remain loyal to a partner and eventually move on to a new one when the relationship is completed. When breaking up, conscious communication and fair compromises often keep things amicable.

In some cases, polygamy is accepted by both sides and results in open relationships. The lesson remains to examine the motivation for this need for variety. It can be a valid need to keep an open mind in order to diversify emotional exchange and sexual experimentation. Yet, in other cases, polygamy may be rooted in the pathology of seeing the grass as ever-greener elsewhere and never feeling satisfied—the latter resulting in a constant feeling of inner void.

On a sexual level, experiencing polarities may manifest in going through phases in which they move from mild sexual experiences to more hardcore ones, from passivity to activity, or, again, from dominance to submission. The length of these phases may vary from years to days. The attraction to the experience of polarities can generate in particular cases a desire to cross-dress in order to experience the reality of the opposite sex more intimately.

The balancing polarity of Libra is Aries, in this case pointing to the evolutionary lesson to stay connected to one's own authenticity while in a relationship. The individual losing himself or herself in others may experience abuse in order to learn about boundaries and to learn to defend his or her position. Partners can be equally frustrated by this behavior when not knowing what the Libra types really want or need; hence, through Aries, the necessity is to better define themselves. The Aries polarity reflects the need to take action and think independently.

SEXUALITY THROUGH THE SCORPIO ARCHETYPE

Mars, Venus, Pluto in Scorpio or in the Eighth House
Mars and Venus in aspect to Pluto

The Scorpio archetype relates to the evolutionary need to outgrow personal limitations through transformation. Consequently, vulnerabilities have to be exposed so that these may be worked on and overcome. Moreover, the transformative process can occur through forming intimate relationships with others and gaining strength through the emotional exchange. Any form of resource trade can support the growth process.

On this basis, there is an aspiration to form relationships that are deeply intimate or even symbiotic. Similar to the Libra influence, one may have deep feelings of inner lack that stimulate the strong need for relationships; yet the desire for trust and deep intimacy usually makes one selective when choosing a partner.

There is a very strong sexual drive under these influences, because sex is used as a means to penetrate another's Soul. The individual may feel that the body itself is an obstruction between core essences. Nevertheless, Scorpio types often face rejection and are denied access to the heart and Soul of another. Rejections may occur on sexual grounds as a result of not being good enough or appealing enough for the other, reducing Scorpio types to face personal limitations and low self-esteem. As a result, Scorpio types may remain reluctantly single or stay in relationships but feel unloved. Abandonment fears can at times generate misplaced emotions and induce possessiveness, jealousy, and emotional manipulations. Roles may be reversed, and it may be that the Scorpio types are the ones to attract insecure partners. As they face these limitations, Scorpio types learn to re-empower themselves through inner and outer changes. There is a strong need to heal emotional wounds once they are exposed.

When more emotionally conscious, Scorpio types use the experience of rejection as a learning experience. They learn self-sufficiency, solidify personal foundations, redefine priorities, and work on ways to enhance their attraction power. In such a way, they work on defying the odds of rejection and come out of the crisis stronger. From a position of defeat, they manage to ascend to new heights. Gaining more confidence, Scorpio types may open up only to relationships that have a potential to be meaningful. Sexual power in this case is not necessarily manifesting in purely sensual experience but also in the depth of intimacy.

Sexuality can serve as a medium through which one's personal nature and emotional complexities are mirrored. Stimulated to transform themselves and grow into a greater sense of being, Scorpio types may feel compelled to redefine their approach to sexuality. The trigger for transformation may be a sense of meaninglessness or experiences of inadequacy. They may consequently learn to address sexuality with more depth, growing beyond mere immediate gratification.

Scorpio types often have the ability to generate sexual intensity and fuse with their partners in ways that are emotionally conquering. While they often take action and initiatives, they yearn to lose themselves in the experience and dissolve separations between them and their partner. The need for merging is very strong—it can deepen their love and commitment in the relationship, paving the way for growing into a greater sense of being.

The Taurus polarity to Scorpio implies the individual has to begin relationships with strong inner foundations for a healthy exchange to occur. Taurus relates to establishing a sense of self-worth outside the relationship before entering it. It points to the necessity to reduce dependence in learning self-sufficiency in order to avoid obsessive attachment and emotional abuse.

SEXUALITY THROUGH THE SAGITTARIUS ARCHETYPE

Mars, Venus, Pluto in Sagittarius or in the Ninth House
Mars, Venus, and Pluto in aspect to Jupiter

The Sagittarius archetype relates to the evolutionary need to realize there is more to the truth than what is exposed in the current reality. Sagittarius follows Scorpio, and from this standpoint it symbolizes the need to free oneself from past experiences of emotional stress. It reflects the need to adopt a philosophical approach to life in order to put emotional struggles in the perspective of higher meanings and, in such a way, better cope with them. This dynamic fosters intuition, faith, and optimism, encouraging one to search for higher meanings and live a more direct and authentic life experience.

The orientation to truth-seeking manifests in a need for authenticity and open expression in relationships and sexuality. Sagittarius types usually prefer a direct and natural attitude, decreasing in such a way the fear of shame or criticism in relationships. They can be quite explicit when defining their feelings, sometimes getting carried away with enthusiasm when being passionate or excited. In the latter case, they may come on too strong and skip introductory phases to form intimacy. This dynamic may manifest in disregarding boundaries of privacy and potentially being too invasive.

Moreover, their belief in the potential of the relationship can induce idealizations and take them too high too fast without consistent foundations. The excitement is usually conveyed through their sexuality as well, generating phases in which they can overindulge, sometimes to the point of losing perspective. They may also reveal themselves too fast to new encounters and feel embarrassed afterward.

In a different way, their naturalness can generate a tendency for exhibitionism; from standing naked in front of open windows to uncensored conversations about their sexuality, they feel free about who they are and what they do, sometimes having a taste for provoking "prudes."

Men with these signatures are usually attracted to women who have more of a wild spirit and do not obsess on physical appearances; such women might not wear make-up or high heels. Authenticity and simplicity is better appreciated by both sexes. It can go as far as having a fascination for the bestial instinct and a need to reconnect to the primal and unconditioned nature through sex. They may strip themselves completely on an emotional and instinctual level and become animal-like as a way of getting in touch with the source of sexual instinct. When lacking the consciousness to express this tendency in a healthy way, it may come out in vulgar ways.

In a different fashion, there is a tendency to be sexually attracted to partners from different cultures and races. Usually the attraction is to the more primal, emotional, or natural cultures, for these represent the warmth and naturalness they yearn for. For example, many people influenced by this archetype coming from predominately white, northern, Western cultures may feel attracted to darker races or Mediterranean temperaments. These "exotic" experiences may at times result in difficult cultural conflicts as the religion or culture of one is imposed on the other. The evolutionary lesson intrinsic to cross-cultural encounters is also rooted in the instinct to explore different ways of addressing relationships and life in general.

On another level, there is a need under these influences to associate personal belief systems with sexuality and relationships. Sagittarius types may conduct everything in their relationship and sexual expression according to a philosophy, a religion, or spiritual concepts. This dynamic reflects their need to give meaning to everything and to try and find the truth in everything. They may, for example, attribute a spiritual context to different sexual phenomena, including female menstruation, commitment issues, or pre- and post-marital sex. They may consequently have strong opinions on these issues rooted in their belief system.

The balancing polarity of Sagittarius is Gemini, which describes a lesson in communication skills. In this regard, Sagittarius types learn to take their environment into consideration and make efforts to adapt to other people and circumstances, decreasing in such a way the tendency to come on too strong. Gemini teaches a lesson in measure and openness, in order to create a true dialogue and for both sides to actually learn from each other through being attentive to sexual and emotional inclinations and needs.

SEXUALITY THROUGH THE CAPRICORN ARCHETYPE

Mars, Venus, Pluto in Capricorn or in the Tenth House
Mars, Venus, and Pluto in aspect to Saturn

The Capricorn archetype relates to the evolutionary need to structure what is believed to be the truth in order to establish a model of rightness by which all people may live. Through this phase, the orientation to life shifts from being personal to being more collective; there is a need to cooperate and integrate into the larger structure from which one can learn how to live more productively. There is a need to be guided under these influences and learn from the wisdom of elders. Accordingly, the person matures to become in turn an authority figure for those seeking guidance.

On the relationship and sexual level, there is a strong need under these influences to find the right way to be with a partner. Impulses and passion are often controlled in order to channel emotions and energies more constructively. These individuals tend to gravitate toward partners who are more serious, reliable, and mature.

Capricorn types often create relationship circumstances in which one partner guides the other, with roles changing from relationship to relationship. One may have more authority than the other, sometimes escalating to dominance-and-submission themes. On these bases, Capricorn types are often attracted to teacher-type personalities or people with social status. Consequently, they tend to give tremendous power to the partner, expecting the partner to be some sort of father figure they can follow. Sexual attraction to employers is not uncommon in this context. They often experience disappointment when the partner fails to meet their expectation and is revealed to be weaker than expected.

Similarly, they can be attracted to intergenerational relationships—either attracting much younger partners with whom they fulfill a mentoring role and initiate into sexuality, or much older partners they feel they can surrender to. When unbalanced, there may be a sexual attraction to teenagers or children. This inclination reflects a need to vicariously regain their own lost childhood through the youngster. However, in the great majority of cases, the intergenerational relationships are between consenting adults where the experience factor plays an important part in the initial attraction.

Given that they feel the need to find the right way to address sexual matters, many Capricorn types can adhere to conservative values, often dictated by religious texts. They can be heavily conditioned by established codes of conduct and therefore repress sexual needs when they appear too self-indulgent. They may feel guilty for having certain fantasies and consequently hide their true nature under a presentable persona. Sexual repression causes emotional distortions and can generate a wide range of misplaced emotions, including anger outbursts, harsh attitudes, and self-effacement. In further extremes, they may publicly condemn sexual behavior they consider decadent, and perform these same sexual activities behind the scenes. These double standards reflect their own failure to accept their sexual nature.

Capricorn types have a strong sexual nature, and their desire for strength may generate attraction to intense sexual experiences. An inclination for dominance-and-submission themes reflects the mentor-apprentice dynamic they associate with. This tendency can go as far as sado-masochistic interplay. Similarly, an attraction to anal sex reflects their need to lose control as the anal muscle is psychologically associated with control tendencies.

When centered in solid values, Capricorn types express their strong sexual nature in a conscious way; their maturity comes across through deeper values and reluctance to follow superficial immediate gratifications in relationships. Relationships are led with maturity, patience, and a nurturing approach.

The Cancer polarity implies there is an evolutionary lesson to accept vulnerabilities, for only in such a way can the maturation processes unfold in a genuine way. Otherwise, the tendency is to swing between the extremes of external demonstration of strength and infantilism. The Cancer influence inspires one to accept the inner child within all people, regardless of how mature they are. More grace, tenderness, and forgiveness resulting from the balance generates more harmonious and fulfilling relationships.

SEXUALITY THROUGH THE AQUARIUS ARCHETYPE

Mars, Venus, Pluto in Aquarius or in the Eleventh House
Mars, Venus, and Pluto in aspect to Uranus

The Aquarius archetype relates, evolutionarily speaking, to the concept of progress. Following Capricorn, there is a need now to allow existing structures to grow so that civilization may continue its course. The need for progress incites one to develop an attitude that is detached from immediate emotions in order to be able to gain greater perspective on processes. There is a need to free oneself from expectations and explore new dimensions of being that promote progress toward self-realization and collective betterment.

On a sexual level, this approach may manifest in a sense of alienation from common expectations to perform according to social norms. The person may, for example, perceive traditional gender roles—in which men have to act macho and women play passive roles—as obsolete and uninspiring. Aquarius types tend to be more androgynous in their approach, and they approach others for who they are inwardly, not who they are racially and physically. Accordingly, Aquarius types yearn to gain greater perspective on sexuality in order to address it in more conscious and progressive ways. There is an attempt to grow beyond the primitive side into a more refined and civilized expression of sexuality.

If no avenue to take sexuality to more advanced levels is discovered, Aquarius types may lose their libido, as the thoughtless motion of intercourse may seem foreign, unappealing, and "stupid." When this occurs, these individuals may feel there is something wrong with them for not liking sex like "everybody" does.

The need to be more conscious of sexual expression may render the Aquarius types more critical in general and very discriminating when choosing partners. They yearn for someone who is mature, interesting, and self-reflective. They cannot relate to people who act foolishly when consumed by their sexual appetite. They wish to have reason lead impulsive drives rather than the other way around. However, when taken to an extreme, Aquarius types may remain too much in their heads and become detached from instinctive urges. They may fear embarrassment if they lose control and become sarcastic toward their partner's wilder sexual expression. Such an approach can be "castrating," as it deflates sexual fervor. They must learn that being more aware of sexuality should not be at the expense of the act itself.

In some cases, the lack of identification with traditional sex roles can manifest in bisexuality. Attraction to another is based on *who* he or she is rather than *what* he or she is. As long as chemistry exists, the person sees beyond the biological "casting," and so the attraction to a partner will be purely for the companionship rather than biased by procreative needs.

In other cases, these influences may point to a clear homosexual orientation. Evolutionarily speaking, this inclination can result from a conscious or unconscious drive to challenge the existing logic of things and the *apparent* biological order of the universe, again as an instinctive urge to challenge an existence that would be purely rooted in biological identification. This reason may appear too intellectual to be authentic, but for the Aquarius types it manifests into a deep-seated emotional need. Other reasons for homosexual inclinations include a need to process emotional complexes relating to one's teenage experiences, whereby same-sex friendships were not adequately processed during adolescence. As a result, same-sex sexual attraction becomes a way to emotionally process these unresolved dynamics.

The aspiration to explore and develop sexuality generates a need to break free from expectations and judgment in order to see for themselves what works. For example, the Aquarius types may be open to including an additional partner in a relationship, and thus legitimize living a love life with two partners. The lesson, however, is to avoid living this pluralism in a double life through cheating, but rather to express that in honest and open ways with mutual agreement. Aquarius types are not primarily jealous and possessive, as long as integrity and fair play are maintained. However, this type of lifestyle may end up very appealing on a mental level but ineffective when emotional security and nurturing are needed—one may have an open mind but fail to understand emotional sensitivity. For example, the individual may appear to be cool with, and supportive of, the partner's idea of including an additional lover in the intimacy, while hiding feelings of threat and insecurity about it.

In another fashion, the desire to understand the science of sex may direct these individuals to the practice of tantric sex (in its diverse versions nowadays) or other philosophical systems that aim at cultivating sexuality in order to take it to new dimensions, possibly to use it as a spiritualizing tool, moving away from using sex as mere release.

Aquarius types may disengage from their bodies and "stay in their head" as a way to feel safe from wounding. Because they have high standards, they are also self-conscious and fear inadequacy. In extreme cases, disengagement results from previous and severe emotional traumas that they choose not to deal with. The need to re-engage into their bodies may result in becoming attracted to extreme sexual stimulation. This dynamic may include an attraction to physical pain in order to stimulate the nervous system. The challenge, however, is to re-engage in the body through tenderness rather than intense stimulation, because overstimulation is likely to cause further numbness of the senses. If emotions are not integrated into the experience, sexual stimulation is bound to remain unfulfilling.

Leo is the balancing polarity of Aquarius, and in this regard it symbolizes the need to legitimize passion and emotional excitement in sexual expression. The Leo influence encourages the person to be more playful, creative, and expressive in sexuality instead of remaining a distant spectator who hides fears of embarrassment behind knotty theories or snobbery. When integrating the polarities, the Aquarius types may live a fulfilling sexuality that encompasses love, fun, and openness, with high awareness.

SEXUALITY THROUGH THE PISCES ARCHETYPE

Mars, Venus, Pluto in Pisces or in the Twelfth House
Mars, Venus, and Pluto in aspect to Neptune

The Pisces archetype relates to the evolutionary need to realize that every form of life originates from the same Source and that all are unified beyond their individuality under this universal umbrella. Pisces follows Aquarius, and from this perspective it makes one aware that the human mind, however sophisticated it may be, cannot fully control life. Consequently, the Pisces archetype refers to the need to accept the unknown and trust there is a higher meaning to everything—it brings one back to innocence, making one feel as a child of the universe.

On a sexual level, this influence may manifest in a completely innocent approach to relationships and intercourse. In one way, innocence may manifest in unresponsiveness to the sexual instinct, as if not knowing in the first place that such a thing exists. The Pisces types may consequently be very late bloomers who may remain virgins until advanced adulthood. Interestingly, just as they may proceed with life without a developed sexual life, the moment sexuality is discovered and starts to bloom they can become consumed by it as if having found a new candy!

In another way, innocence may take the form of naïve trust in sexual matters and manifest in a total lack of shame, boundaries, or morals when addressing it. This may be, for example, the case of a teenager who masturbates publicly, not realizing it is an intimate thing to do. The individual may also lack a sense of discrimination and become sexually available to every stranger. This naïve openness is challenged at a certain point when being taken advantage of or when possibly contracting a sexually transmissible disease. In extreme case, the Pisces types may in their innocence attract sexual predators and fall prey to overpowering experiences such as rape. Following these shocking occurrences, the lesson of discrimination and self-protection becomes a central concern.

In extreme cases, the lack of boundaries may go as far as compulsive exhibitionism, orgies, prostitution, or bestiality, raising controversy. The lack of boundaries may originate from childhood experiences in which the parents had sex either in front of or with their children. Exaggerated permissiveness may have blurred the parents' capacity for mature judgment, paving the way for potentially inappropriate behavior, abuse, and depravity.

Awakening from innocent openness, the individual may swing to the other extreme of fear, limitation, and abstinence. The overexposure to sex may traumatize the Soul and generate revulsion. This dynamic often requires an undefined period of healing, away from any stimulation. The challenge is to eventually regain one's center and learn to balance between surrendering to sexual desires wherever they may lead, and finding the boundaries necessary to filter out unhealthy and damaging experiences.

Concerns about commitment are common with these influences. The Pisces types may fear being trapped in relationships as a result of past experiences in which they lost control and were controlled by their partners. Commitment may scare them, because they may not trust their own ability to get out of a destructive relationship and, therefore, they may feel safer when uncommitted. Moreover, they have a strong need to maintain their free spirit and keep "all options" open. Pisces types feel oneness with everyone and may consequently postpone committing to a single partner.

The sexual act can be an opportunity to lose control totally and surrender. Pisces types may consequently be more passive in the act and give all powers of decision to their partner. Passivity may at times be rooted in not knowing exactly what they want and having a hard time formulating desires for themselves—they can feel more comfortable adapting to others. The lesson becomes to get in touch with their sense of self and explore their desire nature in order to find deeper satisfaction. When better in touch with themselves, they are usually soft, nurturing, and compassionate with others while incorporating romanticism and fantasy in the emotional and sexual interplay.

The balancing polarity of Pisces is Virgo, pointing to the fact that relationships and sexuality require work, maintenance, and awareness in order to remain healthy and functional. The lesson is to realize that it is not enough to have chemistry and passively wait for everything to fall into place—personal engagement is a key to keeping relationships alive. Moreover, the Virgo polarity points to the necessity to discriminate and to analyze dynamics, instead of blindly going through the motions.

ABOUT MAURICE FERNANDEZ

Maurice Fernandez took his first professional steps into astrology in 1990. His dedication and research quickly earned him worldwide acclaim. Today, he teaches and lectures in the United States, Canada, Europe, South Africa, and Israel, enriching the study of astrology with spiritual essence. He is an organizer of the River of Stars Astrology conference, and is the author of two self-published books: *Neptune, the 12th House and Pisces* and *Astrology and the Evolution of Consciousness, Volume One: Astrology Fundamentals.*

Please visit his website, www.mauricefernandez.com.

5

Twins: Similar Charts, Worlds Apart!

BY KRISTIN FONTANA

Early on in my study of astrology, I often asked known experts in the field to explain the scenario of twins. The charts appear to look the same, yet each twin would typically manifest such different realities. One response to this question was that each twin would take on a different expression of the same aspect. In other words, twins would express different sides of the same coin, or one might express the light and the other the shadow of any given aspect. So much is wrapped up in a single signature where various dynamics can potentially play out. The key is to know in full what a certain symbol represents. Although I found that twins do play out different sides or expressions of an aspect, I needed more—something more specific and complete.

I understood free choice to be an obvious indicator of various differences between the lives of twins, and clearly their environment is a factor. An example of this is when twins enter school. In most cases, the two are separated and given different teachers, thus different environments. But it was the discovery of evolutionary astrology that ultimately satisfied my quest in finding a method of interpretation to decipher the unique individual expressions of twins. In many cases, even a few minutes of separation can create enough of a shift in the chart, although visibly subtle, to uncover the potential realities for each twin.

Because astrology is a natural science based on observation and correlation, one must observe the very nature of each twin in order to gain a clearer understanding of what is seen in the chart. If this is not possible, asking simple questions will allow greater clarity of the observed symbols.

Equally important to understand is that, although the charts of twins appear to look the same, one is dealing with two different Souls. This fact means two Souls with different past-life dynamics, evolutionary intentions, and, in many cases, different stages of evolution.

As Carl Jung shared in his teachings, an essential role of the counselor is to objectively validate the subjective reality of the client. With that said, much information is gleaned by simply observing each twin, asking questions, and adjusting accordingly.

The method for understanding the significant symbols for interpretation will be explained in the following pages using two case studies. The first case study is a set of fraternal twin girls, and the second is a set of identical twin boys. Fraternal twins are more common than identical twins and account for about two-thirds of twin pregnancies.

In my study of twins, I have seen cases in which as much as forty minutes of separation in birth times exist and in some a difference as little as two minutes. Those two minutes make for a more challenging analysis, but I have yet to see two charts where a difference could not be measured.

So where do we begin? We start with Pluto, the Soul. Why? Because a Soul is timeless. The Soul is pure energy. Energy can never die; it can only change form. Pluto in the birth chart represents where the Soul has traveled from a past-life perspective. It not only explains what has come before, but it also symbolizes the current-life evolutionary intentions—the next chapter in the growth of the Soul.

Due to Pluto's slow movement, Pluto in a certain sign reflects what a generation of Souls may encounter. One will not see this planet changing signs in twins. However, there is a possibility that Pluto could end up in a different house. If this is seen in twins, the difference is monumental. I personally have seen a handful of cases in which the time separation resulted in Pluto landing in two different houses. If the twins both have Pluto in the same house, the next place to look would be the sign on the house cusp where Pluto stands. This vital piece of information can make the difference in the interpretation. In my experience, I have not observed many astrologers emphasizing the house cusp where Pluto or the nodes exist. This is one of the most important tools that I learned in studying evolutionary astrology. The symbol on the house cusp signifies the foundation of the operating planet(s) in that house. It is as if the foundation of the house were built with the energy of the sign on that cusp.

If Pluto is in Leo in the ninth house and Cancer is on the cusp, Cancer energy is the foundation for this Soul. Even though Pluto is in Leo and in the ninth house, which defines the structure of the Soul, the fact that Cancer is on the cusp of the ninth house means the foundation of that structure is conditioned by the Cancer archetype.

Any Soul that has a ninth-house Pluto will have had, and still has coming into this life, an underlying desire to understand the nature of phenomenal reality, what the nature of reality is, and the origins of life itself. Thus, that Soul comes into this life with the desire to understand life philosophically, which can also manifest as various religious understandings of life. As a result, many of these Souls will have a desire to teach others or be taught by others. This need and desire can also cause a fundamental restlessness within the Soul, for the desire to *know* never stops. For many Souls with a ninth-house Pluto, this can also manifest as a related desire to travel through other lands in order to collect and experience the knowledge or understandings of other cultures. This desire can also cause the Soul to read extensively for the same reasons. As a result of gaining vast knowledge, this can also create a desire in the Soul to teach others about what it knows and believes.

Cancer on the cusp reflects possible scenarios in which the desire to teach others may result in the individual experiencing encounters forcing the Soul back into his or her emotional body. This is because the existing philosophy of the Soul is tied up in, or just bound by, its emotional body and thus its sense of security. The water sign of Cancer is a yin quality, energy moving in, which causes the emotional body to be highly sensitive to the point that much of the Soul's journey, apart from teaching others, is to uncover the Pluto complexities of one's own emotions. This will also allow the Soul to pick up on the emotions of others whether the Soul wants to or not, feeling with greater intensity than most. Conversely, such a Soul can attract external teachers or others who have different philosophies of life that can also trigger a deep sense of emotional insecurity. This is the nature of Cancer.

If this Soul had a twin whose chart showed Leo on the ninth cusp, instead of Cancer, the twin would be more self-centered. Like its ruler the Sun, which is the center of our solar system, the Soul typically considers itself to be the center of its universe. Leo represents yang energy, energy moving out from the center—a Leo being quite certain that its existing philosophy is correct. As a result, the Soul will tend to "prove" to others the rightness of its philosophy and way of looking at life. Additionally, the philosophy of life that such a Soul orients to is directly linked to the underlying sense of purpose for the life being lived. As a result, whatever the philosophy is tends to be fixed, whereas the Pluto in Leo coming through a Cancer cusp is more open to change and an evolving philosophy because of the specific link to its emotional body and underlying sense of emotional security. With Leo energy, there is an insatiable desire for more, and one of the intentions and needs of this Soul is to move from a subjective perspective to a more objective focus. Of course the entire chart must be taken into consideration, but this is an example of how much can be uncovered simply by using Pluto's house, sign, and sign on the house cusp.

The polarity point of Pluto correlates to where the Soul is going. In evolutionary terms, this is the bottom line intent for the life. The nodes of the Moon follow the position of Pluto. The North and South Nodes of the Moon, as well as the Moon itself, all correlate to what we call the subjective ego. The ego allows the Soul to have a distinct self-image in any given life. The Soul creates the type of ego necessary in any given life, for the ego is structured in such a way that its very nature allows for the underlying evolutionary intentions of the Soul to be actualized. The natal position of Pluto correlates to where the Soul has already been in its evolutionary past, and its polarity point, by house and sign, correlates to the next step in its ongoing evolution: the "why" of the current life.

The South Node of the Moon correlates to the prior-life egocentric structure that the Soul created that allowed for its prior evolutionary intentions to occur, and the location of the South Node's planetary ruler correlates to how it was done. The North Node of the Moon correlates to the evolving egocentric structure in the current life that allows the current evolutionary intent to be actualized, and the location of its planetary ruler correlates to how it will be accomplished. The natal Moon in the birth chart correlates to the current-life egocentric structure that the Soul uses for the entire life. This allows for not only the current life's evolutionary lessons and intentions to be given a personal form, ego, but also for the ongoing need to integrate the continuous transition between our past, the South Node of the Moon, and our future, the North Node of the Moon.

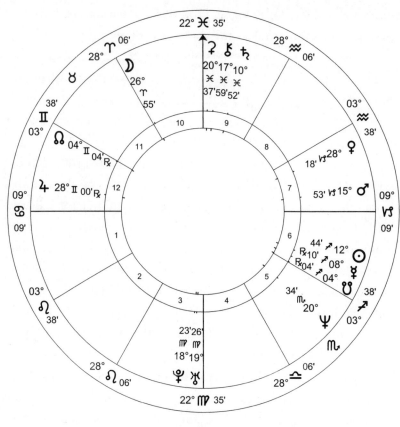

Twin 1

December 4, 1965 / 6:31 p.m. / Los Angeles, California

CASE STUDY #1—FRATERNAL TWIN GIRLS

Mutual theme: Break free and recover your voice

On these pages we will be looking at the charts of two fraternal twin girls who did not look very much like twins when they were growing up. On many occasions, they were even mistaken for brother and sister rather than twin girls. In their younger years, up until puberty, one of the twins appeared to be more feminine and the other more masculine. It would not be a stretch to say that the tomboy twin may be experiencing a gender switch, either with this life or in recent lives. A female expressing strong male energy, or a male expressing strong

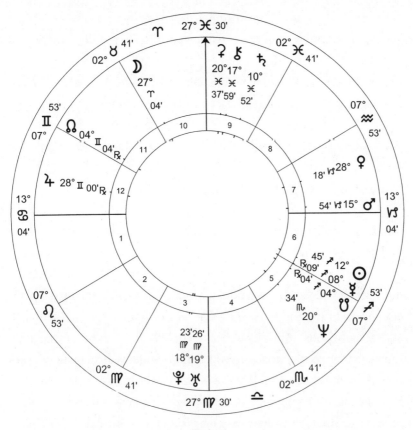

Twin 2
December 4, 1965 / 6:49 p.m. / Los Angeles, California

female energy, can often indicate that the Soul is in the process of switching gender and coming through to integrate the opposite vibration in order to balance the energy of the Soul.

One's observation of the mannerisms and desire natures of the two different Souls, along with the supporting data of the strong signatures supporting gender switch that will be discussed below, suggests the tomboy has been in the process of switching gender in recent lives. With this being said, the desire structure and orientation to life of the tomboy will play out quite differently from her twin. Twin 1 is the "girlie girl," and Twin 2 is the tomboy. Twin 2 wanted to be a boy when she was young. She wore her older brother's Levi's and Hang Ten shirts whenever she could get away with it. She demanded that her hair be cut short. She asked for the Big Ken Jeep and Camper set for Christmas while her twin preferred the fashion Barbie. Twin 2 was given a drum set one Christmas, and her twin a tambourine.

It is a natural progression of a Soul's evolution to integrate the yin and the yang, male as well as female. More validation of this can occur when you interface with a highly evolved Soul. They will tend to look male and female at the same time.

So, where does one look to validate a signature of gender switch? Cancer and Capricorn connect to gender. Cancer, the fourth house, and the Moon connect to the female. Capricorn, the tenth house, and Saturn connect to the male. We are looking for the placement and sign of Pluto, the nodes, the Ascendant, Moon, Saturn, and the sexual planets—Mars and Venus in the signs Cancer or Capricorn, or in the fourth and/or tenth house. Another indicator could be Saturn and/or the Moon squaring Pluto or the nodes. In addition to gender switch, these symbols can also connect to a Soul that has been suppressing the other half of its inner gender, remembering that all Souls are equally male and female—in other words, when a female is suppressing her inner male and when a male is suppressing his inner female. Thus, the symbols in either case demand that the evolutionary intent is to actualize the other half of their inner gender in order to be whole. However, according the teachings of Jeffrey Green, Souls predominantly manifest in one gender over the other throughout their evolutionary history. Please refer to the charts of this case study to uncover a possible gender-switch scenario.

Moon, Cancer's ruler, is in the tenth house
Mars in Capricorn
Venus in Capricorn
Cancer Ascendant
Saturn squaring the nodes

Thus, the Aries Moon is ruled by Mars, which is in Capricorn, which is then ruled by Saturn, which is squaring the nodes: gender switch. It is true that both twins share the above information, and it may also be true that the more feminine twin has had a gender switch at one time.

Considering the idea that we pick up where we left off and we are here either to continue or culminate relationships from the past, there is little doubt in my mind that these two Souls were in relationship as male and female in their last life together. With Moon in the tenth house, Cancer rising, Saturn squaring the nodes, and Mars/Venus in Capricorn, it is clear they have been in family together. With Mars and Venus in Capricorn in the seventh house, this tells me they have also been married. Simply having Mars and Venus in the seventh house would not suggest marriage. It is the Capricorn piece, linking relationship with family, that implies marriage. In addition, they share a tenth-house Moon, reflecting family. The Moon, reflecting mother, in the tenth house, reflecting father, supports the signature of marriage in the past. Tenth house and Capricorn also connects to contracts, thus the contract of marriage.

So why did these Souls choose to come into this life together? This question can truly only be answered by also observing the nature of the two in relationship together. Twin 1 is what Jeffrey Green calls a "trailer" Soul, meaning Twin 1 attached herself to Twin 2 on the way into the womb. As early as they both can remember, Twin 2 wanted to be totally independent and create her own sense of identity: this is seen by the North Node in the eleventh house, relative to the South Node in the fifth, a Leo house. Twin 1's sense of identity had much to do with the approval of others—the approval of the father, the brothers, but, most importantly, her twin. This desperate need for approval is symbolized by Leo on the cusp of the house where Pluto stands in combination with her South Node in the sixth house and is magnified by the Sun/Mercury conjunction, also in the sixth house.

With Twin 2's South Node in the fifth house, she has already been developing self-actualization before this life, and thus, self-validation. Twin 2 never allowed Twin 1 the luxury to totally attach in this life, seen with the North Node in the eleventh and Pluto conjunct Uranus in the third house of siblings/twins; therefore the relationship between the two has been heavy, Saturn opposing Pluto in the third house, and strained at times. Because of Twin 2's detachment, North Node in the eleventh house, Twin 1 had to look elsewhere for more attention and validation, and tended to come from a place of lack. She felt a lack of acceptance, a lack of love, and a lack of understanding. This is seen with her South Node in the sixth house, and re-emphasized with the ruler of the North Node, Mercury, conjunct that South Node. She searched churches and met with counselors, North Node in the twelfth, but continued to feel emotional lack and wounding. Her Cancer rising supports this fact as well. The Cancer rising reflects the need to create one's own emotional security, not depending on external sources for validation. It is vitally important in this life for Twin 1 to disengage from Twin 2 and to actualize her inner male, so that her need to develop independence can occur. This will then allow the two to experience more harmony in relationship together.

Another important piece to observe is the possible stages of evolution. Just because two Souls come into this life as twins does not mean they share the same place on the evolutionary wheel. Based on observation, Twin 1 is the third-stage consensus and approaching first-stage individuated, and Twin 2 is in the third-stage individuated approaching first-stage spiritual.[2] Both appear to have had one foot in one world and one entering another, implying some ambiguity about what lies ahead. Souls often re-create what is familiar, not necessarily what is good for them. Thus it takes a heavy-duty transit from an outer planet, such as Pluto, Neptune, Uranus, or Saturn, to facilitate real growth. Transiting

---

2. For additional information on the stages of evolution, please refer to chapter 1 by Jeffrey Wolf Green and chapter 3 by Kim Marie.

aspects from outer planets can create opportunities for deep change, because their influence lingers long due to their slow movement, allowing us to understand more clearly the lessons the universe is attempting to teach us. The degree of the pain linked with this growth is often determined by how much the Soul resists necessary change. By the twins' Saturn return, at the age of twenty-nine, they were each finally ready for Soul growth. It took a *big* transit such as the return of Saturn for them to be serious about making real change. At the same time, Pluto was approaching their South Node, the past; as well as Mercury, their means of expression; and the Sun, their creative life force. This life represents immense growth for them both and thus a long-awaited progression of their Soul evolutions.

With both twins having Pluto in Virgo in the third house, reflecting the energy of Gemini, there is a natural restlessness and intellectual curiosity in these women. They have a strong need to experience as many circumstances as possible of their own making, in order to better understand their place in the world. This has allowed them to expand their ideas and conceptions of who and what they are in relation to their physical environment—and also, as is so typical of Souls with Pluto in the third house, to own countless books, some of which are half-read and many of which have never been opened. They both exhibit a restless intake of information and an incessant desire to learn. With Pluto in Virgo and Sun/Mercury in the sixth house, they are very methodical about how they learn and must be in an uncluttered space when doing so. With Pluto in the third house, they are easily distracted. The Virgo energy described creates a feeling of not being smart enough, focusing on what knowledge is lacking, so never "feeling ready" to act out their Soul's deepest desires.

In the past, they have found it difficult to communicate what emanates from their Soul, and it is typical for them to feel as if they are at "a loss for words." This has created much frustration because they have so much to express. A mutual theme for these twins is to "recover their voice." This evolutionary desire and need is symbolized and reflected in the fact that the ruler of the North Node, Mercury, also known as the voice, is conjunct the South Node for each twin. The frustration is re-emphasized with Uranus conjunct Pluto—communication breakdown. They experienced lifetimes of trauma, Uranus, as a result of what was not expressed. They also experienced persecution for their ideas and beliefs by those in authority if those ideas opposed or conflicted with the prevailing authority of the consensus of whatever societies or cultures they were born into. This dynamic also occurred in the context of their family of origins, typically manifesting as conflicts with the parents. This includes father figures, churches, and teachers. This is seen with Pluto conjunct Uranus in the third house, opposing Saturn in Pisces in the ninth house.

They have also feared that what they express might be criticized. This can be seen in Pluto squaring its ruler Mercury in the sixth house. In this case, this suggests the Souls experiencing crisis and humiliation as a result of what was communicated. The ruler, Mercury, is in Sagittarius. The sixth-house constant self-analysis that occurs is given a break at times with the vision and insight, Sagittarius, to understand the big picture and to know there must be a reason for it all. Mercury in Sagittarius also allows for a keen intuition along with the knowledge, and when they learn to trust this, and integrate the right brain as well as the left brain, natural expression can begin to occur.

Mercury in Sagittarius as well as its ruler, Jupiter, is retrograde, meaning these Souls can only take in what is relevant to them, making this knowledge inwardly realized and unique. The famous example is the child who is at the top of the class when the subject has deep personal meaning and relevance, but barely passes the class if the subject does not. The retrograde also represents another statement about what has come before, and what must be done again: the lessons in communication and the importance to trust their intuition and their way of knowing what they know without knowing why. A natural intuition!

The aspect of Pluto's conjunction to Uranus, opposing Saturn and Chiron in Pisces in the ninth house, signifies intense trauma, Uranus, and persecution for their beliefs in many prior lives. Much of the persecution involved the patriarchy, Saturn, forcing their beliefs, ninth house, upon them. They experienced total disillusionment, Pisces, and deep wounds, Chiron, ultimately not knowing whom to trust. As a result, in a few recent lifetimes, Twin 2 went into hiding literally and figuratively because of the persecution that occurred. This is seen with Pisces on the ninth-house cusp. The ruler Neptune is in the fifth house in Scorpio, re-emphasizing the fear to self-actualize and own her own power.

Twin 1 has Aquarius on the ninth-house cusp, so compensation of one's natural identity would be the theme—this being a result of the heavy conditioning. Uranus, the ruler, is opposing Saturn. The goal for these twins is to use all of that information-gathering and life experience of their Pluto in the third house, coming up with their own truth but still embracing all truths and understanding that many paths lead to one.

The next step would be to see if any planets are squaring the nodal axis. This will tell you that a theme is being repeated, suggesting there is more to uncover and address specific to the planet making the square. Saturn in the ninth house is squaring the nodal axis. There are skipped steps because of the hiding and compensation. The term *skipped steps* means that the two Souls did not resolve the pertinent Saturn issues in recent lives, and so this must be a focus in this life in order for the two to evolve. The skipped steps of Saturn must be resolved first before the North Node can be fully accessed and actualized. These two Souls individually have the opportunity to recover those in this life. This will be determined by the choices made by each Soul.

Saturn also squares the ruler of Pluto as well as the twins' Sagittarius Sun. This is not easy energy for a fun-loving Sagittarius. It forces them to be real, dig deep, and fight the fight. Saturn also connects to judgment. There existed a great fear of being judged by the father, the church, and society, so inevitably each twin experienced resistance in expressing their inner voice and natural way of being. Over time, whatever is repressed becomes distorted, and so a deep anger manifested in both of the twins.

Even though a Cancer rising indicates for some schools of thought in astrology that the Moon is the planetary ruler of both charts, it is clear that the archetype of Saturn is the dominant planetary archetype that has affected both of these Souls. This is symbolized by the fact that the Moon for each is in a Capricorn house as well as Saturn, forming all the aspects that it does to other planets, including Pluto and the nodes. The Moon is one's own personal identity, which has been opposed or crushed by external authority in general, the father figure specifically, which when combined has been the cause of the inner compensation for their personal identities. Thus the karma in this life and the skipped steps needing to be worked through for both twins is about the father and the restrictions they both felt by society, religion, or anything that placed limitations on them.

These Souls set up this life in such a way that it would be nearly impossible to ignore the Saturn issues that have needed to be embraced and worked through. One simply cannot hide and compensate for long when taskmaster Saturn shows up to deliver repeated tests—tests meant to help each Soul sustain the deep change that is so necessary for the desired evolution to occur. Two aspects fueling the growth of these twins' Souls are Pluto and Uranus trining Mars: "It's breakdown or break through."

These twins' Aries Moon in the tenth house would never allow breakdown. The inner rage of the past and the desire to express their individuality in society, Aries Moon in the tenth house, will pave the way for the intense metamorphoses that are bound to take place. It was necessary for the Souls to set up a Saturn extreme life so the feeling of incongruence about who they naturally are would trigger a response to remove the mask and take the leap of faith. But this time it will be a faith of their own making, not a faith force-fed by another.

These twins were raised by a father and mother who expressed the essence of conservative religious values and morality. The father ran a tight ship and was not afraid to use discipline. He was the music director at a large evangelical church. In my evolutionary astrology training, we were taught that Saturn in Pisces in the ninth house can be called the "Billy Graham archetype," meaning the need to convince and convert in a charismatic way. This was spot-on for these twins, as not only did their father exemplify this religious charisma but also they found themselves in Sunday school and church every Sunday in front of one of the most well-known evangelists in the world. Choir rehearsal and piano lessons also took place during the week. Sagittarius, Jupiter, and the ninth house connect to exaggeration or an abundance of something. The responsibility, Saturn, to attend and be present for countless religious events, Saturn in Pisces in the ninth house, was in abundant form.

The two girls sang duets on national television at an early age. Twin 1 reveled in the spotlight. Twin 2 thought it was some kind of torture treatment having to perform in front of thousands, let alone having to wear a dress and her hair in curls. Twin 1 has Leo on the third-house cusp, and Twin 2 has Virgo on the house cusp where Pluto stands. Twin 2 did not feel worthy singing to thousands of people. She knew her voice was not "TV quality," so she preferred to sing backup to her twin. The fifth house represents entertainment and creative self-expression. Twin 1 has Libra, ruled by Venus, the planet of beauty, on the fifth-house cusp. She has a beautiful voice. Twin 2 has Scorpio there, so she experienced an intense fear of humiliation and of being exposed. She would rather sing in the shower.

The mother was a stay-at-home mom; she sang in the church choir and was the hostess for countless church gatherings. She brought breakfast in bed to her husband every day of their marriage. This is seen with Virgo on the fourth-house cusp, service/servant to the family, with Libra intercepted. It was peace at all cost. She was a consummate giver.

Twin 1 has Aquarius on the house cusp where Saturn stands. She had a unique and special relationship with her father. He was an Aquarius, and she adored him. Twin 2 has Pisces on the ninth-house cusp. She wanted to disappear from it all and talk to God in her own way. She would have been happier climbing trees. She felt a deep inner conflict with her father. Twin 2 felt powerless when it came to him. Notice Scorpio, the archetype of power versus powerlessness, on the fifth-house cusp. Her resolution node for the skipped step of Saturn is the South Node in the fifth house. To uncover which node is the resolution node, look to the node that Saturn is applying to or the node that most recently crossed Saturn, taking into account that the mean motion of the nodes is retrograde, thus clockwise on the wheel. So with Scorpio on the cusp, one of her Soul's evolutionary intentions as it relates to her father is re-empowerment of the self. With Scorpio on the fifth house cusp, Twin 2 could also see right through her father, as the energy of Scorpio can penetrate to the essence of anything, seeing him for who he really was. Her South Node in Sagittarius in the fifth house allowed for a sixth sense. Twin 2 knew that a loving God would never induce guilt, Saturn, and instill so much fear as the church and the father seemed to do. You can see this re-emphasized: the ruler of Saturn in Pisces is Neptune in the fifth, Twin 2's inner knowledge of a loving God.

Twin 1 was an adorable little girl and was often told so by family and friends. Her need for doting feedback attracted a sexual predator from the extended family by the time she was three years of age. An uncle by marriage sexually abused Twin 1 at family gatherings for several years up until she turned ten. Twin 1 has Aquarius, the uncle, on the ninth-house cusp where Saturn stands. Note that some schools of thought look to the sixth house for extended family. However, in the teachings of evolutionary astrology, Uranus, Aquarius, eleventh house is the extended family—thus the uncle. The ruler of the ninth cusp, Uranus in the third house, opposes Saturn and Chiron. Uranus can also represent trauma. Notice Aries on the eleventh-house cusp. The ruler of Aries is Mars, which is in Capricorn and resides in the seventh house. Saturn is in the ninth house opposing Uranus and Pluto. In this context, this represents sexual abuse by the uncle. In an attempt to gain more acceptance and attention, Twin 1 created a crisis for herself, South Node in the sixth house. Her Soul instinctually transmitted a more vulnerable vibration than her sister, thus making her an easier target for the uncle. One of the lessons of the sixth house is learning discrimination. The crisis was created as an attempt to establish appropriate boundaries. Thus she was thrown back on herself for her own emotional survival. Twin 2 has Pisces on the ninth house cusp and managed to escape most of the abuse. The ruler of Pisces is Neptune, which falls in Twin 2's fifth house. Neptune sextiles Uranus and trines Saturn; God saved her.

By the time Twin 1 turned twenty-five, she confronted her uncle with courage and clarity, fearing for the lives of other innocent Souls. Transiting Uranus was in Capricorn, and it was making a conjunction to her Mars in the seventh house. Capricorn's ruler, Saturn, was in Aquarius in her eighth house. The twin's deep, dark secrets surrounding the trauma were exposed along with her uncle, Uranus in the eighth house, and her Saturn walls were finally coming down. These aspects served as critical triggers for the truth to be known and for a little girl to reclaim her power once more.

There have been many differences shared in these charts; however, the most significant symbol for this case study is the South Node. Because Saturn is squaring the nodes, and Saturn is clearly their emphasis and hurdle this life, we look to the resolution node for how this Saturn issue can be resolved. The resolution node is the last node that crossed the planet making the square, remembering that the mean motion of the nodes is retrograde. Thus the South Node is the resolution node, with Twin 1 needing to express this resolution through the vehicle of the sixth house, while her twin will need to embrace the fifth house.

It also makes perfect sense that the inevitable Saturn transits they experience will be the universe's way of saying, "Now is your chance to break free, to re-remember your natural self." But this will take maturity, Saturn, and time. This has proven to be the case.

In the formative years, it could be observed that Twin 1 needed much validation, constant reminding of how pretty she was, although when she received the compliment, she found it hard to believe. She also made excuses for dropping out of college, claiming she was not smart enough. This is an example of a sixth-house nature coming through from the past.

Twin 2 was "full of herself," South Node in the fifth house, when in her natural environment. She had many goals and visions at a young age. School was very important to her. She was on the honor roll and voted Queen of her junior high school by her peers. With Virgo on the third-house cusp and her Sun and Mercury in the sixth house, she had a natural humility around her accomplishments and never settled for second best, South Node in the fifth house. Although Twin 1 was full of fire and as feisty as they come, she always looked up to Twin 2. More so than Twin 2, Twin 1 was forever her own worst critic, South Node in the sixth house. The twins competed in sports. Twin 2 was usually voted MVP, South Node in the fifth house, while Twin 1 was often voted "most improved," South Node in the sixth house.

Even marriage, however, did not allow a natural emotional separation to occur for Twin 1. She admitted that if it ever came down to her making a choice between her husband and her twin, she would choose her twin. The attachment to the twin was still strong and outwardly evident as the years passed, even in what appeared to be a happy, loving marriage between Twin 1 and her husband. Within a year or two of getting married, Twin 1 and her husband became open to starting a family and they actively put their energy into making that happen. One early miscarriage and years of trying to have children found them tens of thousands of dollars out of pocket due to infertility costs—and childless.

In the meantime, Twin 2 and her husband had two children of their own relatively quickly and painlessly. This only fueled Twin 1's desire for the same experience, as she could not understand how her very own twin had not endured the same life challenges as she had. To look at the astrological signature for this, one can look at the cusp of the fifth house, the house of children. Twin 1 has Libra on the cusp, the ruler being Venus in Capricorn in the seventh house. Libra is an air sign, and the symbol of the scales suggests the need to establish balance. Venus, the ruler, is in Capricorn, which suggests there can be a block or a delay in having the child. Capricorn reflects the need to be mature, to come of age before the desired result can manifest. The need for balance is re-stated with Venus being in the house it naturally rules, a Libra house. Typically one would look to the position of the Moon and the fourth house, which rules the mother and the womb, but both twins have the same sign there and the ruler of that sign is in the same house, so we must look further, to the fifth house, the house of children.

Twin 2 has Scorpio on the fifth-house cusp. Scorpio is a very fertile water sign compared to airy Libra. Conception is dependent on water for the "swimming sperm" to reach the egg. The ruler of Scorpio is Pluto, which makes a trine to Mars, another fertile signature.

In my opinion, it is vital that Twin 1 establish Capricorn, relative balance, Libra, in her family relationships—in this specific case with the twin—in order for a baby to come through.

After years of desperate and costly attempts to conceive, Twin 1 was left with five frozen embryos, and specialists were unable to explain or find a reason for her inability to conceive. On two prior occasions she had attempted in vitro fertilization, a surgically performed procedure whereby a fertilized egg is placed in the uterus to encourage pregnancy, and both times five fertilized eggs were implanted and the results were negative. Twin 1 believed she could not conceive on her own, that she may need the eggs of her twin in order to hope for a viable pregnancy, so she approached her sister. Twin 2 felt instinctual resistance.

The transits around this request are fascinating. Transiting Mars, connecting with instinct and desire, was conjunct the twins' Moon in the tenth house. Twin 1 had a desire for her sister's eggs. Twin 2's instinct, Mars, was to resist, tenth house. Transiting Mars also was squaring their Venus in Capricorn in the seventh. This suggests a confrontation, transiting Mars, and a difference in needs, squaring Venus in the seventh house. Twin 2's eggs, mixed with her sister's husband's sperm, then placed in the uterus of her twin, would only continue to encourage the Soul attachment, delaying what she felt inevitably needed to occur for herself and the Soul of her sister. A reminder: Twin 2 has her North Node in the eleventh house in Gemini. This Soul needs to individuate, eleventh house, from her twin, Gemini.

Twin 2 did not take to the news in the way Twin 1 had hoped. Twin 2 felt that it was a last-ditch effort for Twin 1 to continue the theme of attachment. As much as Twin 2 wanted to help her sister, this was further than she was willing to go to support her and so her response to Twin 1's request was an emphatic no, leaving no room for compromise. This proved to serve as a critical evolutionary shift in the nature of these two Souls' connection. Finally, Twin 1 painfully understood Twin 2's need for autonomy and independence. She realized in that moment that she could not depend on her sister to save her any longer. The dependency must cease.

After weeks of processing the reality of her sister's words, Twin 1 came to a place of peaceful resolution within herself and apologized to her twin for laying such a heavy burden on her, sharing that the issue at hand was the responsibility of her and her husband. Twin 2 felt a release within her Soul as if the weight of lifetimes had lifted. Twin 1 got pregnant the following month, just as her sister had predicted, after ten years of trying. Transiting Mars had moved into Taurus in her eleventh house, and was conjunct the transiting North Node in Taurus when the conception occurred. The eleventh-house energy connects to something unique, special, or progressive—thus, in combination with Mars, this would explain the in vitro–fertilization form of conception versus natural conception. Mars served as a trigger for change and new beginnings relative to Twin 1's own need to individuate. Mars in Taurus can create an incredibly fertile energy, and in Twin 1's case it proved to be exactly what she needed to give her the result she had been seeking for years. Transiting Mars was also forming a grand trine with the Twins' Pluto, the Soul, in Virgo in the third house of siblings, and their natal Mars in Capricorn in the seventh house. This is a strong signature of Soul progress. And, clearly, it was.

Both Souls continue to embrace the Pluto polarity, ninth house. Ultimately, both Souls need to intuitively realize the whole truth and the essential unity of all paths leading to the truth. They will establish a bottom line to all they embrace in this life and must not judge what others find as truth. Once the evolutionary lessons are developed, these Souls will have natural communicative skills that can inspire, motivate, enthrall, hypnotize, and metamorphose other people's intellectual patterns and opinions by sheer contact with them. With Mercury and Jupiter in the gibbous phase, they will both continue to be the eternal student due to their heightened awareness of what they are not. This will allow the opportunity for continued growth and expansion of their ideas. In Twin 1's case, this would occur in a more traditional setting because of her observed stage of evolution. With North Node in the twelfth house in Gemini, ruler in the sixth house, she earned a master's degree and is counseling those in crisis. Twin 2 will challenge the consensus with her

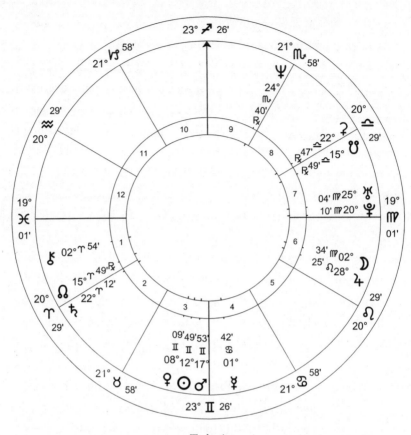

Twin A

June 3, 1968 / 1:37 a.m. / Glendale, California

ideas, North Node in the eleventh house. Because of the eleventh-house placement of her North Node, it indicates radio or broadcasting as one possible medium to express her Aquarian nature. This has become her reality. She will test the limits of society and share with others the idea of a natural world, a world that embraces and accepts all truths.

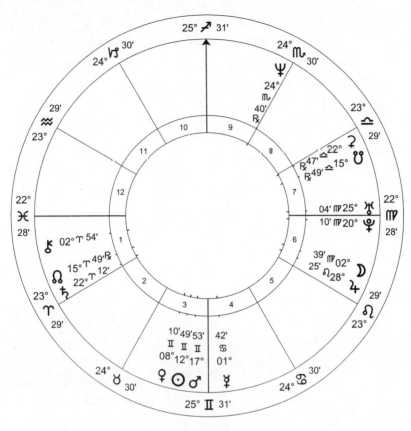

Twin B
June 3, 1968 / 1:46 a.m. / Glendale, California

CASE STUDY #2—IDENTICAL TWIN BOYS

Mutual theme: Establish your own authority, gain the respect you deserve, and allow individuation to begin to take place

Noting that the North and South Nodes are in the Aries/Libra axis, the connection between these twin boys can be correlated back to the times of ancient Rome, when Judea, the historic region of southern Palestine, was under Roman rule. This forceful takeover is seen with Pisces and Aries in combination. As was typical of the time, males were rounded up by Rome's authorities to be gladiators. These gladiators were expected to fight to the death for the amusement of the authorities. It is not hard to see how these life-and-death conditions created a total bonding with one another. In such critical times as these, it is not hard to see how such intense bonding would lead individuals to make promises to protect one another.

As the emotions are integrated into the subconscious, they remain as deep imprints within the Soul. Through such deep commonality and self-preservation bonding, two Souls can become completely reliant on their understandings to the point of exclusion of all others. As such, we can surmise that these two Souls made a pact to protect one another from future persecutions and attacks. Notice the Sun in Gemini wedged between Mars and Venus in Gemini in the third house. This is a powerful statement validating the twin connection over numerous lifetimes. The South Node in Libra trines the lineup of planets in Gemini, the ruler Venus among them. The two twins have both stated that the most significant relationship in their life is with each other, even before their spouse. One twin in conversation referred to his brother as his Soul mate. The evolutionary intention now is to begin an individuation from each other in which each learns to become self-empowered and self-sustaining—North Node in Aries in the first conjunct Saturn in Aries. Saturn is in the second house in Twin A's case.

My observation of the twins' stage of evolution is third-stage consensus, but they are fascinated with and beginning to integrate first-stage individuated ideas. The twins both find themselves in corporate America. Both wear the badge of vice-president, drive a BMW and a Mercedes, and present themselves as "clean cut," wearing highly conservative apparel.

The two Souls are so busy that it was challenging to meet with them to engage about their twin experience. But when I changed my e-mail salutation from addressing them by name to "Dear Mr. President," I could almost hear the bellows of laughter come in with their response to my e-mails. They must have been waiting to see the signs of respect. My addressing them as Mr. President was music to their ears. Another fascinating astrological correlation is the quote that each uses at the end of an e-mail correspondence.

Twin A: "You will become as small as your controlling desire, as great as your dominant aspiration." Saturn conjunct North Node in Aries. This quote is from the book *As a Man Thinketh*, by James Allen.

Twin B: "As a man thinketh, so shall he become." This quote, the inspiration for the same book, *As a Man Thinketh*, is adapted from a biblical passage (Proverbs 23:7). It displays the workings of a driven Gemini mind and the desire to make something of oneself, Saturn, allowing the mere thought of success to reproduce itself and make it a Saturn reality.

The two twins share a mutual desire to create the greatest sense of security possible (Saturn), for themselves and for their families. They were the first in their extended family to attend and graduate from college. They both have an incredible work ethic and carry positions demanding long, arduous hours, including travel—although the travel involves short day trips as opposed to extended time away from home. The hard work combined with the freedom to explore is once again a reflection of the North Node in the first house conjunct Saturn. The short trips connect to the Sun and Mars in Gemini in the third. The ruler, Mercury, is in Cancer in the fourth, so there is also a strong desire to return to the nest.

Their energy appears boundless: Jupiter conjunct the Moon and Mars conjunct the Sun. Their optimism is unparalleled. With a Moon in Virgo in the sixth house, a Soul has a never-ending desire to self-improve, and with Jupiter there, this tendency is exaggerated. But Jupiter does induce a sense of perspective, allowing the twins to laugh at themselves and at each other. Jupiter in Leo shines brilliantly and injects a self-confidence rarely found in a Soul with the Moon in Virgo.

As long as they are doing the work, Virgo, and moving in the direction of their dreams, the twins' confidence is undeniably present.

It is fascinating to observe these two in action. On one hand, one would witness the serious and strong Saturn influence, Saturn /North Node conjunction, but on the other hand, they display immense fire and enthusiasm about life; even life's greatest challenges are taken head-on with a positive outlook, as if life were simply a game with the idea "may the best man win." This can be seen in three combinations: North Node in Aries in the first house; Mars, ruler of Aries, is conjunct their Sun; and Jupiter is in Leo conjunct their Moon. The charts reveal two strong, contradictory influences between Saturn, the need to control, and Jupiter, a desire for freedom.

However, the phasal relationship between these two planets is ideal for what these Souls intend to create for themselves in this life. Saturn and Jupiter are in a first-quarter trine at 126 degrees, which represents a Leonian energy and an emphasis on one's subjective development. This is very supportive energy as it relates to their career success and creative self-actualization. This is not surprising due to their mutual track record of success in business. It has been grand like Jupiter, but the build has been gradual and sustaining, Saturn. Also, although Saturn suggests heavy demands, it pays dividends to those who follow through and do the necessary work.

The twins grew up with very little. Saturn on the North Node can indicate limited resources, but with Saturn in Aries and the North Node in Aries in the first house, a desire to make more of what they have is almost guaranteed. Their father left the boys and their mother by their first Mars return, shortly after their second birthday. The ruler of Saturn in Aries and the North Node in Aries is Mars in Gemini. The father leaving can been seen by Saturn in Aries, the ruler Mars in Gemini conjunct the Sun. Saturn also connects to the family unit and with Saturn in Aries, the ruler Mars can be the destroyer with its need for independence. Also, on the fifth-house cusp of children is Cancer. This is then ruled by the Moon in Virgo in the sixth house. This in and of itself will reflect the emotional needs not being met, and there being a lack, Virgo, sixth house, of emotional nurturing. This Virgo Moon is also squaring Venus, the boys' needs, and is conjunct Jupiter in Leo, which exaggerates this fact. Jupiter in Leo is trining Saturn in Aries, thus a self-centered, essentially narcissistic, father who was unable to supply the emotional needs of the boys.

The fourth-house cusp could explain the emotional influence in early years and the connection to the mother, which reveals the sign of Gemini. The mother remarried. Her new husband became the stand-in father for these two boys. Gemini also connects to the boys, who provide emotional support to each other, and the ruler Mercury is in Cancer in the fourth house. The twins were like puzzle pieces, the yin and the yang. This is also represented when observing the most significant difference astrologically in these two charts, the position of Pluto. Twin A has Pluto in the seventh house, a yang/Libra house, and Twin B has Pluto in the sixth house, a yin/Virgo house.

I spoke with each twin separately about their childhood. Twin A, with Pluto in the seventh house, said nothing of an upbringing of struggle, but Twin B, with Pluto in the sixth house, focused on the struggle and the ensuing crisis that followed the abandonment by their father. As much as they are alike and few can tell them apart physically, there are also many differences. Twin A, with Pluto in the seventh, was the social director from very early on and had many friends. His brother, with Pluto in the sixth, was and is more reserved and conservative and preferred a few close friends. Twin A used to be somewhat of a "ladies man," while his twin was a "one-lady man." Twin A is free-spirited, and his twin has a more serious nature.

When the boys were ten years of age, they decided they wanted to dress differently. In a photo of them together from this period, Twin A has chosen bright red Ocean Pacific shorts while his brother opted for a safe navy blue pair. As they worked their way through their school years, Twin A was a bit mischievous and Twin B was very responsible. He would check on his brother frequently to make sure he was on track. Twin B was more disciplined than his brother. He worked harder, Pluto in the sixth, and thus received better grades. Also, Twin B with his Virgo influence was a math whiz, expressing his Pluto in the sixth house, while math was more of a challenge for his twin.

Twin A has been known to call his brother the "good twin," because he seemed to keep himself out of trouble quite often during college. Twin A would already be planning the following weekend's social activities on Monday of that week, while Twin B had his nose in the books. Following college, both twins jumped right into corporate America, both receiving their first opportunity in medical sales with established companies. Surprised? The Sun, Mars, and Venus in Gemini in the third house would make sales an obvious profession; and with a Virgo Moon in the sixth house conjunct Jupiter in Leo, the medical field would feel like a natural place to shine. They both excelled immediately and began creating the structures of their life that in many ways still stand.

Twin B has an even greater inner sense of urgency than his twin to provide as much security as possible for himself and his family. In fact, he has created a world with greater responsibility. His Saturn in the first house in Aries created an instinctual desire to have a family, so instinctual that three of his wife's pregnancies were unplanned. By the time Twin B's Saturn return was over, he had married and fathered four children. Twin B had four children in less than four years: two boys and two girls, and the two youngest are twins. With Mars in Gemini conjunct the Sun in Gemini in the third house and the ruler of the South Node in Libra, Venus also in Gemini, it appears obvious that one of these boys would have his own set of twins.

Typically, Saturn conjunct the North Node can represent a delay in having a family, perhaps when the Soul is older and more mature, Saturn. But when you see Saturn in Aries conjunct the North Node in

Aries in the first house, the family emerges without forethought. Twin A has Saturn in the second house and is taking his own sweet Taurus time in starting a family. Twin B has an instinctual desire to be the kind of father that he had always dreamed of having as a child.

Twin B harbored great resentment toward his natural father. In fact, his natural father had recently heard about his four grandchildren and felt he "deserved" to see them. Twin B wanted nothing to do with his father. Twin A, with Pluto in the seventh, played the mediator, Libra, and wrote his father saying when and if the twins chose to reunite in any way with him it will be on their terms, and in the meantime to please "honor our needs." This was a sign he was establishing his own authority with his father. Twin A also used very Saturn-on-the-North-Node and Pluto-in-the-seventh-house language: "honor our needs." The archetype of Libra connects to the importance of being clear about one's needs and, in this case, learning to conduct this relationship in a "new" way, mirroring those needs. This is an example of embracing the Pluto polarity. What is also occurring for Twin A is a reflection of his Saturn in the second house, creating a structure in which to get his needs met, as long as he is calling the shots. Twin A hoped to understand his father better and create a sense of harmony, Pluto in the seventh house, meeting halfway at some point. But that day never came, as the father died suddenly at the age of fifty-four. He never did see his grandchildren. Nor did he mend his fractured relationships with his only children, the sons he left at the tender age of two. That single event served to signify as the catalyst, which allowed their fierce determination and sense of independence to unfold.

The boys did attend their father's funeral and were given some of their father's belongings, one of which was a workbook journal. At the top of the first page it read: "Nov. 3rd, 1984—Guiding yourself into a spiritual reality." The workbook was used for creating a vision for the future. The father then wrote, "secure, dynamic, and harmony with my children." He died in late 2002. Eighteen years had passed since he had written that vision, but the harmony with his sons never came. But in order to be in harmony with something, pure intended actions reflecting co-equal amounts of giving and receiving by all parties must occur. Being secure and dynamic must have overshadowed the father's desire to be in harmony with his sons. It took his passing from this planet in order for any semblance of harmony to exist.

The twins have a Pisces Ascendant, and so they strive to resolve their father issues with him spiritually, now that he is "on the other side." Twin B, with Pluto in the sixth house, has embraced the polarity, Pisces in the twelfth, "dissolving old mental and emotional barriers," which have prevented a clear understanding of the big picture. A sense of forgiveness has taken place, and it has in turn released many of the demons and sadness that Twin B carried regarding his father.

The very reason these twins chose this father to begin with was to encourage their Soul's evolutionary need to establish their own authority, Saturn conjunct the North Node in Aries in the first house. The trigger came early, and anger, Aries, from centuries past, Saturn, flooded their world. Their Saturn authority figure was nowhere to be found. This does not come as a surprise if you look more deeply into the chart. This father was also one of the Roman authorities responsible for rounding up the two boys to fight to the death as gladiators for his own amusement and entertainment. His needs always came before the needs of the boys, so much so in this life that he abandoned his own family when the boys were only two, and did not contact them for years. Note that the natal Mars in the chart of the father is 16 degrees of Libra, connecting to Rome, and exactly conjuncts the boys' South Node. This same Mars opposes the boys' natal Saturn, which symbolizes the forced fighting in Rome, the separation from the family then and now, and the anger that ensued as a result.

The ruler of the boys' South Node in Libra is Venus. Venus is in a balsamic phase to Mars as well as the Sun. A balsamic phase indicates a culmination of themes relative to the planets involved. Venus and Mars in a balsamic phase represent the culminating relationship with the father. The Sun and Mars in a balsamic phase provide more evidence that a current life purpose, the Sun, is to culminate this theme with the father. If you take it a step further, Mars is the ruler of their Saturn in Aries, authority figure, which is sitting on their North Node, their future, thus they came through this father in order to culminate lifetimes of this Saturn/Mars dynamic with this father in particular but also any other authority figures attempting to control or limit them in any way. Saturn on the North Node tells us these boys have been working on culminating this connection to the father in recent lives. The abandonment by the father left them no other choice but to establish their own authority, which is exactly what they have done.

Before sharing past-life themes with Twin A, we were discussing his need for freedom. "Give me freedom or let me die" were his words. Even a simple statement such as this could support the idea that the gladiator experience was his own. Twin B validated this to an even greater extent. A therapist once told him he is like a samurai warrior before battle, preparing for death. He faces life challenges with the idea that if he prepares to "die," he will be fearless going into challenging situations.

"What's the worst that can happen? Would I die as a result? Done it before," Twin B said.

Every story of twins is a unique and vivid example of how we as Souls in the human form can manifest such extraordinary attachments to one another. The twin connection often originates from lifetimes back, traveling through the ages in many different forms. As discussed in the case studies, the bond may have been formed initially in intimacy or in battle when survival was on the line. In any case, there exists an undeniable emotional attachment by one or both Souls. So, in alignment with one of the founding philosophies of evolutionary astrology, regarding the thought that Souls have two co-equal desires—the first of which is to separate from the Source or that which created us, and the second of which is to return and merge back to the Source—there is an inherent need for all Souls to act out their individual desires, separate from one another. Although the universe granted the twins entrance into this world together, the ultimate intention will be for each Soul to find its own unique expression here on Earth.

ABOUT KRISTIN FONTANA

Kristin Fontana graduated from UCLA with a degree in kinesiology. She studied with Jeffrey Wolf Green and is a certified graduate of his School of Evolutionary Astrology. Kristin has been a mainstay speaker at the Jeffrey Wolf Green Evolutionary Astrology conferences and has also lectured for the NORWAC conferences in Seattle.

She provides a weekly astrological-forecast column for the *Beach Reporter* in Southern California, which is also posted on her website, www .kristinfontana.com. Kristin is listened to worldwide on her weekly EA radio show, *Guiding Stars*, online at www.healthylife.net.

6

When Planets Square the Nodal Axis:

Insights from a Past-Life Therapist

BY PATRICIA L. WALSH

For several years I have been using the paradigm of evolutionary astrology (EA) in conjunction with past-life regression work with clients. I have found that the unique rules in evolutionary astrology that modify the understanding of the nodal axis are reflected in people's own past-life recall, and can be seen clearly in the chart. By sharing clients' own past-life stories and how they relate to their natal charts, this chapter will explore the issues that arise when planets square the nodal axis.

A square to the nodes is understood to mean that the squaring planet also becomes a part of the karmic axis. In fact, in almost all the cases of regression I have done, when the nodes are squared the squaring planet becomes a significant force in past-life wounds and also subsequent healing. The North Node also becomes a part of the past-life experience, which is where evolutionary astrology's understanding of the nodal axis makes a dramatic departure from traditional karmic astrology.

Start simply by looking at the fact that the T-square is both square(s) and an opposition. The tension inherent in both those aspects, when it involves the nodal axis, implies that the Soul's usual struggle between the South Node and North Node opposition is amplified by the presence of a third pull, causing a tense triangle of forces seeking equal integration. What has happened in the Soul's history is that *none* of these forces has been able to be fully integrated, and so the tension continues. The reasons for the inability to integrate each of these factors is different in every case, but mainly there is a simple division, resistance to evolution, or extenuating circumstances beyond the control of the individual, making it impossible to embrace the archetypes represented in a healthy way. For any of these reasons, the squaring planet is referred to as a *skipped step*, as it represents an aspect of the Soul's growth that has been missed and thus becomes a highly focused point of tension in the current life so it can be worked on.

In order for that skipped step to be integrated in the current life, in evolutionary terms, it needs to be focused through the node that formed the last conjunction. The easiest way to figure out which node that is, is to pretend you are standing on the planet making the square, facing the center of the chart, and look to the node on the left. This is the node that made the last conjunction, and these archetypes, by house and sign and aspects, are what need to be worked on consistently to integrate the squared planet. This node can be either the North Node or South Node. This rule does not change the understanding of the North Node as the direction that needs to be developed for evolution.

Before we look at all of these dynamics, it's important to look first at karma imprints and how they are carried from life to life.

THE SQUARING PLANET AS A FOCAL POINT

In our first session together, Kara started to tell me about her childhood. Since I was preparing to work with her in regression therapy,

I was listening to what she was saying in a way that would illuminate what past-life story might be behind her current problems. In other words, what imprints from past lives is she carrying today? She started to tell me about her troubled childhood, one during which her mother was very verbally abusive to her. This impacted her, of course, on many levels. I looked down at her chart and noticed a prominent karmic signature around anger; her Sun was in Aries in the twelfth house squaring the South and North Nodes. Chiron was also in Aries in the twelfth, not squaring the nodes but within orb of a conjunction with the Sun. The nodes were placed in the fourth (South Node Leo) and the tenth houses (North Node Aquarius). The Sun being the ruler of the South Node, and squaring the nodal axis along with its contact to Chiron, was what caught my attention. This indicated to me a karmic wound with the archetypes of the twelfth house, Aries, and the Sun itself.

If you think of the archetype of Mars/Aries, and Pisces/twelfth house combined, in a person's current life, this type of signature might indicate an inability to express anger directly. Or in psychological language, this person might display what is commonly called passive-aggressive behavior. Again, the question would be, why did this Soul carry this into the current life as a prominent karmic wound? These thoughts then prompted me to ask Kara, "What about the anger?"

She said she hadn't realized she was angry, until she went into counseling in her later teen years. She was now in her late twenties, so this self-awareness had not been too far in the past. Further discussion revealed that this was not a resolved issue. She experienced frequent feelings of rage (Aries) that would seem to surface out of nowhere. Noting that this is a deep Soul issue, I asked her if she would be prepared to work with the anger that day, and while this frightened her, she courageously agreed to do so.

We started the session by exploring the emotions that had arisen in childhood, when her mother was abusive to her. She instantly went into the position of clenching her fists and jaw. In her memory, she went back to being a small child while her mother was berating her. Each muscle in her body progressively tensed, as if bracing against an onslaught, as she tensed to hold in her anger. Had she expressed her anger at the time, as her body and her emotions would have wanted to, certainly the abuse would have gotten worse. She was only a small child, quite powerless in comparison to her mother. She went into the immediate feeling of being overwhelmed. And out of that overwhelm arose a heart-wrenching sense of hopelessness.

At this point, I guided her into the past-life memory that might be the cause of this current-life replay. Immediately, her arms rose over her head and crossed as if they were bound there. Her body was remembering the past-life story. As the associated images arose, she found herself to be a prisoner shackled against the wall in a medieval-type dungeon. She realized she had been imprisoned unjustly and was outraged over this. She struggled furiously against her chains, full of anger and rage (Aries) but unable to free herself. This caused her to collapse in upon herself, into a sense of hopelessness (twelfth house). She fluctuated between fury and giving up, as she hung there in her memory. As time went on, it became obvious she had been left there to die. During each cycle of struggle she was getting weaker, as she was slowly starving to death and losing her strength. Her will, her ability to act (Aries) was slowly being eroded (twelfth house). Eventually she succumbed to a total sense of giving up, as her body and mind weakened. She died this way, and as that past-life self passed to the other side, it remained in this state of "give up" and hopelessness.

From this case, you can see that the wound of this past life was replayed in her current life but in a different scenario. This helps us to understand that the notion of karma as just being a force of retribution, "an eye for an eye," is not the whole story. Quite frequently in Past Life Therapy (PLT), it becomes obvious that past-life traumas are replayed in the current life (often with a lesser intensity) with the divine intention of healing them. Current psychological knowledge of the nature of trauma, and how it repeats, supports this finding, when the understanding of the human psyche can be expanded upon by allowing the timeline to encompass that of past lives also.

In the previous case, we see that the state in which she died in the past is important to how this imprinted upon her. Death and the state of the person at death have long been understood in Eastern and ancient traditions as having a key effect upon how the Soul is able to progress from life to the afterlife and also the kind of imprint that is carried into future lives. This is understood in PLT as well, and the departing consciousness is worked with through the moment of death into the afterlife. Once the consciousness is free from the body, it can and does still carry the imprints from that life. In the previous case, a part of her consciousness stayed trapped in that dungeon, not knowing there was another option for it to move on. The heaviness of the trauma and defeat had been so strong that in essence it weighed the consciousness down.

Again, this is not the totality of the Soul that remains but a traumatized fragment. Even though this part of the Soul is fragmented, it is still connected to the total Soul but remains earthbound, continuing to remain fixated on its "unfinished business." The Tibetans describe in the Tibetan Book of the Dead the many planes, or *bardos*, the Soul must traverse in the afterlife and its propensity to remain attached to the earth plane, weighed down by unfulfilled desires, thoughts, and feelings. The death and after-death rituals of many cultures and traditions point to the knowledge that the journey isn't over at death, nor is safe passage to the other side guaranteed. Thus the teaching presented, in many traditions that embrace the continuity of the life of the Soul after death, is that it is essential to die as untroubled as possible, with one's mind at rest about the life that is being left behind and fixed on the divine, or "higher realms," to fully "ascend."

Quite frequently, it is found in PLT that this is not the case. Soul fragments do remain earthbound, and need to be worked with to be able to be liberated. Traumatic deaths and sudden deaths quite often leave a portion of the consciousness in shock and earthbound, as do other conditions at death. The earthbound Soul fragments affect the present-day incarnation like a state of chronic subconscious PTSD. A part of the total consciousness is still frozen in the past; the effects of this are felt, but the cause is usually unknown. These afterlife "bardos" can be correlated to the archetype of Aquarius and Uranus, reflecting the natural law that thought creates reality. In these "bardos," as the consciousness is unencumbered by the density of a physical body, the creation of reality is instantaneous.

In Kara's case, this defeated, hopeless part of her consciousness was worked with to realize first that it was dead, and that life was over and that it had an opportunity to move on. Through psychodramatization, Kara was encouraged to remove the shackles that bound her, and then pull her arms down away from the wall where she died bound. Progressively reclaiming her freedom, this part of her consciousness was liberated, eventually breaking out of the dungeon and running in an open field in the afterlife remembering the vitality, mobility, and power it had once had. She had died young in that life, full of dreams and unspent youth; this was also worked with in the afterlife, so that the imprint of hopelessness was eventually lifted. Astrologically, we can see this reclaiming process as an empowering of the wounded Aries archetype (youth, vitality, freedom), which was the main karmic signature that we started with (Aries Sun square the nodes).

PLUTO SQUARE THE NODES

Here is another example of a skipped step. Note in chart A that Pluto and Venus square the nodes, and they are the rulers of both the North and South Node. Pluto's square to the nodes indicates a tense current-

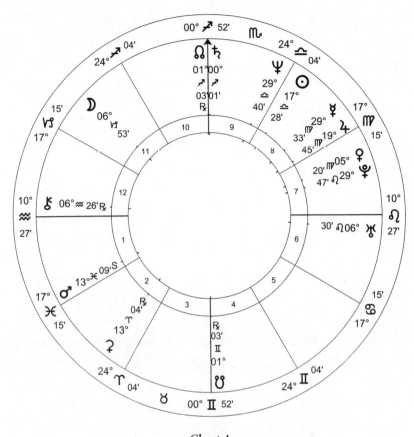

Chart A

October 10, 1956 / 3:32 p.m. / Oceanside, New York

life evolutionary condition where the dynamic of the skipped steps is amplified. The usual struggle between the past and present that exists for everyone is magnified when Pluto squares the nodes. I have noticed with this aspect that there is often a deep level of Soul fear that causes the person to feel internally paralyzed when confronted with choices that involve karmic issues. Moving out of the fear can feel like jumping off a cliff, where the fear of the fall into the unknown is so great that it is often avoided for many lifetimes. The fact that Pluto squares the nodes in the current life means that the person is at a crucial evolutionary juncture, which often has a do-or-die feeling to it, within their psyche.

Unfortunately, this often only increases their fear, and the propensity to dig deeper into the karmic rut can be repeated. But Pluto's presence will bring things to the surface so that they must be worked on. This next story shows us how the fear of "jumping off the cliff" can manifest, and is both literal and metaphoric in this regard.

Chart A, for a client I'll call Ellen, is also an interesting study for the Libra archetype, as on the surface one's attention may be drawn to other archetypes in the chart within the karmic axis, and may miss the preponderance of Libra that is represented by her past-life stories. A quick look at the karmic axis shows us why. Pluto is in the seventh house conjunct Venus. These two planets are the rulers of both the South Node and North Node and square the nodes from the seventh house. Neptune is in Libra quincunx the South Node and sextile Pluto, and the Sun in Libra is semi-square Venus and Pluto.

Ellen's story didn't start with direct exploration of any typical Libran themes, which also makes it a distinct example of how the truth of the archetypes lives within the memories of the Soul and is not limited to our conscious intent in revealing these memories. It also reveals how Pluto, even by house position, lies in the background of the circumstances of each past life, providing an integrating meaning.

Her reason for coming to a session was a classic fear of heights. A phobia of heights can have the underlying fear of being pushed or of accidental falling, or, in some cases, as in this one, it can be due to a past-life suicide. While being interviewed, she recounted that this fear first surfaced when she was about five years old and remained with her all her life. When my client was a young girl, she and her family went to the Swiss Alps on a family vacation. They took a gondola ride, and my client threw herself on the floor of the gondola, screaming and crying. Her mother's rationalization for this behavior was that she was cold, and they had not brought the right clothes. My client, of course, had another, deeper emotional memory of absolute panic and grief.

This phobia persisted all through her adult life and still plagued her at the time of our session. As we explored the fear, immediately the thought "I am going to jump" arose, and she found herself in a past life as a young woman on the edge of a cliff, overcome with grief and progressively going into "automatic pilot" as she was about to commit suicide. Other thoughts arose in the last minutes before jumping: "I've got to find him" and "I've got to see if he's okay." I took her through this quick death (knowing we would revisit it later), and then back earlier into the lifetime to find out who "he" was.

She went back to an earlier memory as a young girl about eight years old, in a field playing with flowers with her younger brother (South Node in the third sibling). It was a simple, prairie type of existence (Taurus South Node), and she was responsible for watching over her little brother (Saturn as part of the nodal axis). She was enjoying playing with him and being a little mother (Moon in Capricorn trine Pluto/Venus), and all seemed fine. Her little brother started to wander away, and some distance came between them before she realized how far away he was. There were also horses in the field, and at the same time something spooked the horses. Everything went black, and her next memory was of people in the field, taking something away.

This is a common Venus/Libran denial defense of "I don't want to see this"/"This isn't really happening," and it protected her psyche from overwhelm in this traumatic situation. It is obvious that the little girl was in shock, and the layers of trauma needed to be reworked progressively for the full memory to come (Chiron is in Aquarius in the twelfth, quincunx Venus—a well-constructed defense of denial, leading to dissociation, fragmentation, and loss of memory). After reworking slowly through these moments, she became aware of her panic and the thoughts of "I've got to get to him" and "He's in danger."

In working with her further, the full recall came and she collapsed as she saw her brother trampled by the horses before she could get to him. She went into shock with thoughts of "It's all my fault" and "I was supposed to be watching him" (Saturn and Venus, ruler of South Node in Virgo), and, most importantly, "I just want to die; it should have been me" (Saturn conjunct Scorpio North Node; because of the square, the North Node is part of the past-life experience). The life-and-death struggle involving a sibling is symbolized by the Taurus/Scorpio axis in the third/ninth houses.

We moved forward through the details of how people came and took her brother's body away, the funeral, and so forth. Her parents did not blame her, but the weight of her own guilt was so deep that their forgiveness and understanding did not reach her at all (Saturn and Virgo—self-recrimination and guilt). From that moment on, she was unable to feel anything but guilt, and that is what drove her to the moment on the cliff where she was about to commit suicide. She was about twelve years old as she perched on the edge of the cliff, telling herself, "It will be okay. I just want to go find him." She fluctuated between sobbing and steeling herself against the emotions so that she could bring herself to the point of jumping. The pre-death thoughts of needing to find him continued in the spirit world after she left her body, as she was saying over and over, "I've got to find him."

Because she had died with such a cloud of despair around her, I suspected that she would not find him on her own, but I gave her the time in the spirit world to look for him. As it turned out, she did not find him, and she started to panic and cry. In actuality, this was the truth of where that Soul fragment remained, which is why it was problematic for her in her current life. Because we were now working on healing it, I then asked some helpful spirit grandmothers to come and bring him to her. They did come, and interestingly he showed up as a full-grown young man, smiling and seemingly radiant with vitality. She was stunned at seeing him and actually quite speechless. It was obvious to me that he was already communicating to her, that just by his appearance he was fine, and she had no reason to feel responsible for him anymore.

She was unable to take in this energy and information (stubborn Taurus South Node in the third) and was still quite caught in her own self-recrimination (Saturn/Virgo). They dialogued for a bit, and eventually even the spirits of her parents from that life came to her, telling her, "It wasn't your fault" and "Look at him, he's fine now." They and the loving grandmothers were are all communicating the same message: "Let it go, it's over, it's not your fault." None of this was breaking through to her, so I asked the grandmothers, and other higher beings there with her, to show her other lives or reasons behind what I was now perceiving as a deeper crystallized pattern that these two Souls had played out before.

Past-life patterns of codependency and fixated attractions are common for the Libra and Scorpio archetypes. Because her Pluto is in the seventh house conjunct Venus, reliving key past-life relationships to find equality or balance where it hasn't been before is an evolutionary intention.

The helper spirits complied, and immediately Ellen was brought into another life where she was a young Native American male. The brother in the previous life was also a brother in this lifetime, but this time he was older. In the first moment of the past-life memory, they were preparing for a war raid (third-house siblings and Mars oppose ruler of the South Node). Native American lives show up most typically in the mutable signs, and the nodes are in the mutable houses. As they were getting closer to the village, the younger brother (Ellen) was aware that he looked up to his older brother, yet didn't really want to be involved in the fighting (Mars in Pisces/oppose Venus on the first/seventh house axis—war and peace). During the heat of the battle, he stayed on the periphery but always with the older brother in sight, this time with a sorrowful sense of wanting to protect him but being unable to. The older brother was full of warrior energy and quite swept up in the battle, but the younger brother just wanted peace and couldn't condone what he perceived as the senselessness of slaughter (Mars in Pisces oppose Venus). Yet he still felt the urge to protect him (Saturn). The older brother was killed suddenly, and he was saddened by this but did not feel totally responsible this time. The rest of that life was spent alone, as he separated himself from the tribe (Chiron in Aquarius) and went away to live in isolation (Taurus South Node and ruler in Virgo). His life was spent dealing with his feelings of grief and trying to come to terms with the stupidity of war (Venus/ Mars).

After death he met his older brother in the spirit world, and again the older brother was quite happy and vital—seemingly untouched by his violent death. Now, deeper realizations started to occur to El-len's current-life self, and she concluded that these are not the only times they have enacted these dramas. She said, "He is the one who just breezes through life, taking risks, living on the edge, and I am the one who is the rock" and "He moves on without a scratch, and I stay stuck." In others words, the dynamic is starting to become clear to her; she carries all the responsibility for him and he carries all the forward-moving, risk-taking impulses.

Her Taurus South Node, its ruler in Virgo, and Saturn's involve-ment aspecting point to her propensity to stay stuck in guilt and re-sponsibility in relation to another person. Also, because the polarity point to Pluto is Aquarius in the first house, part of her evolutionary growth implies gaining detachment and a healthy sense of self (apart from relationship), and this would feel unnatural to her.

I asked her to go back even further, to where this codependent pat-tern began. She found herself in a "planning stage" bardo where they were just balls of light coming to an agreement that they would balance each other out (Pluto/ seventh house/Venus). I asked her to consult with the guides there to find out two things: first, if the agreement they made to "balance each other out" was healthy, and second, if not, is it irreversible? The guides immediately urged her to let him go. She real-ized in that moment that this Soul is her college-age son in her current life. She was sobbing at the idea of letting him go. I assured her that it felt as if the guides were telling her to let go of the pattern, but not the love between them. I asked the guides to show her what "letting go" of him would look like. She immediately saw two paths form, leading away from each other—he is on one, and she is on the other.

He started to walk away on his path, but she was crying, feeling stuck at the beginning of her path (Taurus South Node—Pluto square nodes, fearful resistance to evolution). She waited until he was out of sight and turning to concentrate on her path; she saw it as an uphill, rocky climb. This scared her, and she said, "I don't want my future to be like this uphill difficult climb" (Saturn) and "I don't trust this" (Scorpio—mistrust, in the ninth—fear of the future). I suggested she ask a spirit animal to come to help her as a guide on her path, and she immediately saw a rabbit hopping along her path. I was already struck by the image of the rabbit as an antidote to the way her energy has been so deeply invested in being solid, responsible, and stuck (Taurus and Saturn). I urged her to trust the rabbit and follow; she reluctantly did, as she started on her path, grumbling about how it was straight uphill and difficult to get a foothold. "This is so hard," she was crying.

I see this all as beautifully metaphoric for her breaking a deeply entrenched karmic pattern, and that often going in a new evolutionary direction seems scarier than it actually is; I had full trust in the wisdom of this rabbit guide and urged her onwards. I asked her, "How is rabbit doing on the path in front of you?"

She replied, "Well, he is just hopping along, no problem, but it is such a struggle for me."

This rabbit is very much like the energy of her and this other Soul. The rabbit is just cruising forward while she is resistant. It became even clearer that rabbit was pointing her to a new way that she needed to own in herself, and not project onto another, or else she would remain in a polarized codependent pattern (Pluto polarity point of first house/ also ninth-house North Node—freedom and independence).

All of a sudden, the path started to even out: it became less rocky, and she found herself in a lush, green forest type of grove. The rocks were covered in moss, and she said, "They are soft now, everything is softer here." There was a waterfall and rabbit just laid down by the side of it, quite relaxed and calm. She said, "It's so green here, quite cushy, in fact" (empowered Taurus South Node) and "This place is exciting, like it's filled with a deep healing and wisdom" (North Node in Scorpio in the ninth).

I asked her to revisit the image of the broken body she left behind from jumping off the cliff. We created a healing burial ritual for it in the spirit world, and when the body was finally laid to rest, grass and moss grew over it quickly. She was happy to see this happen, and commented, quite breathlessly, about the deep, lush green and how healing it was.

I noticed her legs twitching a bit, and I asked her what was going on there. She said she was watching the rabbit, which was jumping up and down now. I asked her if that is what her legs wanted to do. I supported her as she stood up on the mat and started to jump in place. She was giggling like a small girl and was filled with a sense of wonderment (empowered South Node in the third). A higher voice was telling her, "You don't have to be afraid anymore. You won't lose your grounding if you hop a little." She said, "This feels so free, like I can just let go and trust" (the empowered side of Libra, ninth house and first house as polarity to Pluto).

Now Ellen started to see that he has represented an energy that she needs to find in herself, that it's okay to take a little risk . . . to jump (first house polarity point to Pluto). We had now returned to the exact energy we started the story with, but on higher turn of the spiral—taking a risk and doing something different did not need to equate to jumping off a cliff anymore in her own psyche. The healing that happened was not only the clearing of a trauma from a single past-life story that became her fear of heights, but also a karmic/psychological pattern that needed to be released for her to grow spiritually.

She did ask me how soon she could try to see if her fear of heights was gone, and I told her to take it slowly. Maybe I was mirroring an old, cautious voice from her past, but she was full of the feeling of newfound freedom (Pluto polarity point and North Node in the ninth) and scrambled onto her roof the next day just to test it out. She found she had no fear. She also told me a few months later that she and her family went to the Space Needle in Seattle (another previous site of a panic attack), and she was just fine going to the top.

The resolution of her nodal squares makes the South Node the resolution point before the North Node can be accessed. From this one session, we can see that she had to revisit her ability to be self-sufficient (make her own path) and reformulate old, stuck ways of thinking (Taurus/third house). Her past security had been found by playing a role (Pluto in Leo) in the way she was in that relationship (seventh house). But in moving forward to her North Node she will be able to participate in deep, meaningful bonding (Scorpio) that allows herself and others the freedom to explore themselves outside of the relationship, and bring out deep self-authenticity (Scorpio/ninth house). The old, codependent pattern of molding herself around someone else's needs (seventh house) kept her in a Taurus rut and away from her own inherent natural abilities.

By this client's request I have not included her son's birth chart, but I can point out that he has a natal Pluto in Scorpio in the eighth house, making his polarity point a double signature of Taurus: slow down, let it be gentle. Quite amazing as she is working toward the Aries energy of risk taking, and he is learning the lessons of slowing down into Taurus!

In their composite chart they have a Pluto in Libra in the eighth house, which is the exact signature of needing to transform past relationships with each other but also is the signature showing how they fell into such a "life or death," fixated codependency. This gives them the polarity point of Aries and the second house as the evolutionary intention. As they each become more self-sufficient (second house), they will each become more of their true selves (Aries).

Seeing how resolution was achieved through the psyche's own direction in this session demonstrates how the tension of the polarities of the karmic axis and squares exist in us as fuel to release greater potential.

SQUARING PLANETS AND THE RELEASE OF KARMA BY TRANSIT

Chart B, for a client I'll call Julie, has a Capricorn South Node in the second house and Pluto in Virgo is in the tenth, so there is a double signature of Capricorn in the karmic axis. The nodes are squared by Jupiter in Aries in the fifth house, so the North Node is also a part of the past-life experiences. The resolution node for the skipped step in this chart is the South Node. This case also demonstrates how transits and current events can act to release karma, as it was the events of September 11, 2001, that brought this woman into a state of a "healing crisis" (Pluto in Virgo).

Julie worked in international finance; during the September 11th attacks, her office building was directly across from the World Trade Center in New York City. She was traveling for business that day so she was not in her office, but her company's building was destroyed from the collapse and several of her co-workers died. Upon learning of what happened, she went into shock. This is termed "vicarious trauma," when one is a witness to another's trauma either as a bystander or as a caregiver but nonetheless is impacted psychologically, sometimes as severely as if the trauma were one's own.

In current-life psychology, it is said that this stems from an empathetic reaction. From the past-life perspective, what is understood is that traumatic events that one witnesses, even in a movie theatre or

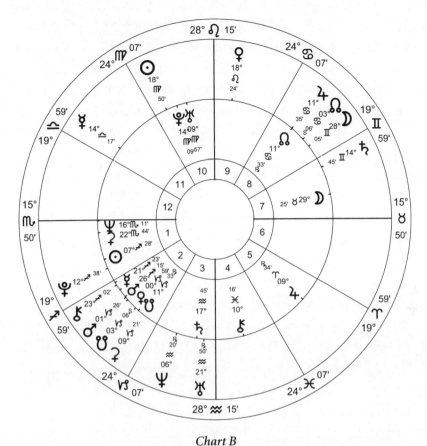

Chart B

November 30, 1963 / 5:20 a.m. / Colchester, Vermont

Transit chart as outer wheel to natal chart

September 11, 2001 / 8:48 a.m. / New York City

on the news, can trigger deeply personal, buried past-life traumas. In her case, she went into "soldier mode" for several years and then had a near-complete breakdown. The combined signature of Capricorn and Aries is the primary indicator for warrior/soldier karma, as her stories will further illustrate.

The transits for September 11th show that Julie had already had her nodal return and Jupiter was exactly conjunct her North Node. Jupiter's importance comes from the fact it is the squaring planet to her natal nodal axis. Mars was also just coming into orb of a conjunction with the South Node. It took her several years of standard therapy before she was able to even approach the depths of past-life therapy, but when she did start it was in early 2008, when Jupiter had traveled halfway across her natal chart and was exactly conjunct her South Node. As these stories will also show, the traumas that were awakened within her, and their subsequent resolution, changed the course of her life and initiated her into the possibility of manifesting her North Node.

After September 11th, when her company was nearly destroyed, the remaining staff rallied together to "save the company." She took much more responsibility (Capricorn) than her role dictated, but this was driven by her subconscious need to "save" the company (Jupiter). Note that Jupiter is square the nodes, which, combined with the Capricorn signatures, indicate the Hero and Savior are deeply active in her consciousness. Her Jupiter in Aries in the fifth house fueled her exaggerated response and her drive to accomplish her goal, basically putting her into overdrive. She worked day and night under tremendous pressure but also with a nagging guilt that no matter what she did, it wasn't enough (also Pluto in Virgo). Furthermore, she was exhibiting classic signs of PTSD, but she attempted to override them through sheer will, emotional shutdown, and hyper-focus on her duty (Aries, second house South Node, and other planets there and Capricorn). After about four years of this, she neared breakdown and left the company for a hiatus. A few years later, when Jupiter was exactly conjunct her South Node, she started to work with her past lives.

The first past life she explored found her in charge (Aries/Capricorn) of a unit of about three hundred soldiers in World War II. They had landed on a beach in the early morning (presumably D-Day), and the mission was to cut a safe swath through to a fence line to allow them, and others depending on them, safe passage during intense bombardment. My client reported, "I was stunned by the noise

and the carnage, but I had a mission and I just focused on the goal"
(Aries/Jupiter).

As is often reported by soldiers, there is no training that can prepare them for the reality of war (Capricorn). Accomplishing this
mission (Aries) was not easy, as there was chaos on the beach. This
commander was immediately presented with the reality that the majority of his men and others relying on them to make the way safe
would not make the passage, if he made the approach as was origi-
nally planned. The only way to accomplish the mission was to split
them into two units, sending one out as a "decoy." He struggled with
this decision, but battlefields are not places for long thought, and "in
a moment that felt like a lifetime, I ordered the second-in-command
to lead a portion of the troops to the left. I was desperate to find another way; we both knew what was happening, but we also knew what
needed to be done" (duty, honor—Capricorn).

That group of men was quickly slaughtered, and unfortunately it
did not stem the tide as he had calculated, as his group came under
direct fire. He not only had to watch the first group of men die, but
now his remaining men were in danger of failing the mission and losing their lives. In the midst of this, he was shot and became paralyzed.
In many charts, Saturn/Uranus/eleventh house contacts often indicate
past-life paralysis. My client has this karmic signature, as Saturn is
ruler of the South Node and is in Aquarius; also Pluto is conjunct
Uranus in the tenth house. Despite his injury, his men tried to carry
him, and their courage and devotion in doing this made him feel even
more the failure (Capricorn). He died as they tried to save him, feeling "They trusted me and I let them down," "I got them all killed for
nothing," "It's all my fault," and "What a waste."

All of these are Capricorn futility, guilt, and failure imprints. Because he died in this state, this commander never left that beach and
was activated in Julie today when her company was nearly destroyed.
She made the current-life connections quite easily: "I felt the whole

company was my responsibility. I felt those who died were my responsibility, and no matter what I did, it would never be enough."

The Soul fragment that remained in that state was worked with in the afterlife, and a pivotal moment happened for him when he met the spirit of a soldier who also remained on that beach but for different reasons. This soldier had a message for him: "I am standing sentinel here today, to guard the freedom you bought with your blood." This brought waves of tears, of both grief and relief, to the commander. Some of his own soldiers came to him in spirit form to let him know they won; it was not in vain. He had died not knowing the outcome of the battle or the war. Now that he was feeling lighter, he was also able to help other spirits of soldiers that were still stuck on the beach in shock. After "dismissing the troops," they were all happy to ascend to higher planes into the light.

As this story shows, even soldiers who have fought an "honorable" war can die feeling dishonorable. As it related to my client, resolving this past-life commander opened the door to her own emotions again and helped her evolutionary process of movement to her Cancer North Node. During the time of her hiatus and therapy, she changed her life direction to work in professional coaching. She said that because this past-life commander was unresolved in her, she had been "unable to let people in," as she felt "I can't be trusted" (North Node in the eighth). His guilt had kept a protective barrier around her, because subconsciously she feared she would only get people killed. The South Node as the resolution to the square showed she needed to revisit and heal the isolating barrier of guilt (second house, Capricorn South Node), which then naturally opened up the North Node potential. Other connections she felt related to this particular past life were "an inability to really feel" (South Node in Capricorn in the second) and "feeling everything is my fault," as well as an inability to be around loud explosive noises. "It's all my fault" is one of the most classic Capricorn karmic scripts.

She found that her "limits of responsibility became clearer" and that it was a liberating feeling for her to realize how "out of control" the events of September 11th were for her personally, since she had internalized so much of the responsibility (Pluto in Virgo in the tenth). The vicarious traumatic reaction from September 11th also eased for her as this commander was laid to rest. She had been unable to watch any footage from that day, and although such footage is still disturbing, as it is for anyone with compassion, it does not have the charge it did for her before. The fact that the Cancer North Node is also a part of her past-life consciousness is clear when she describes herself as afraid to care or get close to others, but her actions do not reflect that.

This past-life commander clearly did care, but with the squared North Node in the eight house, caring, which is the essence of Cancer, in the past had been a "larger than life" issue. For her, letting someone be close in her current life carried the gravity of personal responsibility over life and death (Cancer North Node in the eighth—caring equals death). When she felt the pain of the loss of her co-workers on September 11th, and how that affected her company, she was deeply moved, because her Soul had already experienced the caring of the Cancer archetype. Transforming the way she cares is one potential of the Cancer North Node in the eighth. The healing of her emotional body and its transformation is represented not only by the North Node, but also the polarity point of Pluto's house and sign is the fourth house and Pisces (with Chiron there).

Another past life of this client shows another imprint that is familiar to Capricorn: the feeling of being a fraud. Because the ruler of the South Node is in the third house, this brings the Gemini archetype into focus as well. Both these archetypes as well as her Jupiter contain various facets of truth/truth-telling and honor versus dishonor. In this relatively recent past life, she was a young boy. In the first memory of this young boy's past life, he was on a stage about to receive an award. He felt sick to his stomach, as inside he felt "it was all a lie" (third house and Jupiter). What had happened was that he and another young boy were running after a puppy in the street. He pushed the boy out of the way of an oncoming vehicle and ended up saving his life. Several adults saw this and hailed him as a hero (Capricorn and Jupiter). What he described was different: "I pushed him 'cause I wanted the puppy. I didn't even see the vehicle" (wound of impulsive selfishness—Aries). His dad was so proud of him, and he was unable to tell anyone what had really happened. He kept the truth to himself and went on stage to receive the award in front of his whole school. What he didn't know was that the other boy had already told a band of his friends what happened, and they blurted this out while he was on stage (public humiliation/Pluto in Virgo and tenth house). His father took him home and beat him.

This young man never recovered and grew up feeling so ashamed that he became a "loser and alcoholic," eventually drinking himself to death (Neptune square ruler of the South Node also trine the North Node—the easy way out). The imprint of dishonor is present, but also this sort of event points out that when we don't live up to our own ideals, have unresolved guilt, or feel we have "copped out" on ourselves in past lives, it can leave a subtle imprint of fraudulence. This can make all forms of accomplishment tainted, and sets the stage for the Capricorn self-saboteur to dismantle achievements sometimes before they even manifest. The self-saboteur is not exclusive to Capricorn, because ultimately the self-saboteur lies behind a broader fear of owning one's power, which relates to other archetypes as well. The work in healing this self-saboteur is to align oneself with intrinsic integrity, which is a higher octave of Capricorn and Jupiter/Sagittarius.

Jupiter in Aries is also about the ability to accomplish goals. This client was able to do so in her life (her Sun is in Sagittarius in the first house), but she also had the unresolved feelings of fraudulence and shame tainting everything she achieved. She felt she constantly needed to prove herself (Jupiter in Aries), as a way to avoid the discomfort of feeling internally fraudulent and undeserving (Capricorn/second house). Clearing the shame that tainted her self-worth (second house) allowed her to feel a deeper sense of authenticity (Jupiter/Sagittarius) that opened the way for her to truly accept others' applause and appreciation (fifth-house Leo).

OVERVIEW OF ARCHETYPES
SQUARING THE NODAL AXIS

When a planet squares the nodal axis, the archetypes of the planet, house, and sign are all involved in the past-life experiences. These archetypes need to be synthesized to understand how they have become a karmic issue. Archetypes squaring the nodes are looked at from the same perspective from which one views the South Node; there are both strengths and wounds that have been a part of the past-life experiences that these archetypes reflect. The North Node also by sign and house is a part of the karmic axis when it is squared. To understand the complications of the square, it is possible to reflect on a positive quality of the archetype(s) and then ask, what could go wrong? For example, the positive side of relatedness of Venus/Libra can become unbalanced codependency, as we saw in the first case in this chapter.

Each archetype has a spectrum of meaning as well as a diversity of natural qualities. The diversity is often reflected in different karmic themes that the Soul is working out in the current life, as we saw in the second case. One of her past-life themes was resolving the feeling of responsibility that came from the deaths of others, and the other theme was fraudulence and truth. The following listing is a compilation of past-life issues by archetype, which can be used to help understand possible karmic imprints for the North Node and South Node, squares to the nodes, and Pluto.

Aries/Mars/First House

Unhealed battle trauma from warrior-type lives (combativeness/ competition/paranoia/PTSD); aloneness as a leader or someone special; being either invaded or an invader; pioneer; anger/rage; death because of violence or premature death (life cut short); failed initiations causing either fear of starting things or excessive need to initiate action but fear of following through; wounded instinctual nature; impulsiveness; excessive willful nature or shutting down of willpower; identity crisis or narcissism; tendency to go "too far too fast" or fear of limitations; inability to act on freedom or fear of it.

Taurus/Venus/Second House

Shutdown of feeling nature; poverty and issues around survival; wounded or excessive self-reliance; feeling unworthy or deserving; clinging to possessions because of fear of poverty/overemphasis of what is needed for security; simple lives/farmer/peasant /shepherd; hoarding; stagnation/feeling stuck; isolation/self-withdrawal; fertility complications/stubbornness born of fear of exposure.

Gemini/Mercury/Third House

Having been an inquisitor or victim of an inquisition; being the messenger; inability to get the message out and frustration because of it; limitations in knowledge or learning or needing too much information; inability to communicate effectively or doing it excessively; taking in too many opinions/revolving viewpoints; inability to reach a goal; living only by reactions; fear of making mistakes/looking foolish; duality, such as living a double life; internal splits; indecisiveness; inability to manifest ideas; living only in thoughts; thievery and lies/mistruths or half-truths.

Cancer/Moon/Fourth House

Wounds to early development; emotional needs not met or excessive neediness; orphan; dependency/helplessness; lack or fear of nurturing; issues of mothering or being a mother; overwhelmed by family needs; limitations of family conditioning/imprinting; discomfort in gender role; vulnerability; oversensitivity; cocooning; isolation; death in childbirth or as a child.

Leo/Sun/Fifth House

Overly dramatic reactions; caught in others' drama; need for approval; starving-artist syndrome; being singled out as special/expected to perform; performance anxiety or feeling need to always perform; inability to bring gifts/talents out; wounds to the giving and receiving of love; joylessness; need for applause/approval or never able to get it; royalty; creative mania; fear or blocks to creativity; inability, or excessive need, to have fun and play; romance/affairs.

Virgo/Mercury/Sixth House

Humility/humiliation; servant/slave; masochism; inferiority complex; neurosis/nervous disorder; crisis-oriented; panic/anxiety; fear of "coming out" or being seen; not feeling ready or good enough (inadequacy); apprenticeship; persecution/victim; self-sacrifice; overburdened/psychological burnout; depravation; doubt/fear of taking action; pessimistic; critical or being criticized.

Libra/Venus/Seventh House

Codependency; inequity in relationship; mistress/Casanova/love triangles; flirtatious; being prized only for looks/charm; vanity; masks/persona inability to be self; conforming to social or others' needs only; societal role and classes; arranged marriages; being devalued; damaged trust; wounds to heart; conditional love; projected expectations caused by inability to express own needs; desire for harmony causing denial of reality; romanticism/fantasy; going to extremes to find balance; pleasantries/shallow relating.

Scorpio/Pluto/Eight House

Fear of, or wounds due to, vulnerability and intimacy; fear of exposure; marriages of convenience—mutual misuse; power struggles; inability to own power or fear of it; loss; being manipulated or betrayed; misuse of, or victim of, power; covert actions/spy; interrogation; hiding/secrecy; addiction to intensity; magic/curses; abandonment; destruction/annihilation; "Armageddon consciousness"; paranoia; mind games/psychological torture; entrapment; prostitution; sexual abuse/misuse.

Sagittarius/Jupiter/Ninth House

Loss of faith or overly trusting; immigration and trauma of displacement; nomadic/homeless; running away; limitations to freedom causing fear of it; overabstraction; dogma/dogmatic; religion; persecuted because of own truth or persecuting others; missionary; living in ideas; overenthusiasm and exaggeration; being the savior/hero; gullibility with teachers/gurus; intuition; withheld knowledge or denied learning; charmer; naïveté.

Capricorn/Saturn/Tenth House

Conformity; limitations/slavery/imprisonment; repression and suppression; politics/politician; wounds to authority or suppression by authority; over-responsibly; burdened; feelings of failure; inner saboteur; soldier; guilt; loss of position or authority; father/fathering; immobility/paralysis; traditions; limited by societal and familial conditioning; leadership/responsibility; discipline/punishment; rigidity/fear; totalitarianism/nationalism; depression; old before one's time; bitterness; loneliness.

Aquarius/Uranus/Eleventh House

Psychological shock and trauma; fragmentation and splitting; loss of hope/ideals; inability to manifest, or thwarted in manifesting, ideas/ideals; bizarre; loner; alienation; fear of being different or overprotective of individuality; being singled out; tribal lives; cast out of, or limited because of, tribes; antisocial; rebellion/rebel; anarchist; insanity/

mental illness; persecution because of difference or ingenuity; group or mass traumas; fear of the future; being ahead of one's time; secret or fringe societies; elitism/aristocracy; class systems.

Pisces/Neptune/Twelfth House

Naïveté; misplaced/wounded trust; burnout; helplessness; victim/ martyr; savior; overwhelmed with others' needs; losing oneself in others; mystic; inability to "be in the world"; escapism; drug/alcohol addiction or codependency with addicts; misused because of, or misuse of, psychism; delusions/illusions; disillusionment; death by failed drug initiations; avoidance; confusion and dissociation; psychic wounding, including Soul loss/theft; Loss of self/identity; mirroring others; projected onto by others; persecuted; insanity/madness; getting or feeling lost; spirituality; astral glamour.

ABOUT PATRICIA L. WALSH

Patricia L. Walsh is a graduate of the Jeffrey Wolf Green School of Evolutionary Astrology and is a certified evolutionary astrologer. She is also a certified Deep Memory Process (DMP) regression practitioner and is the chief U.S. trainer for Dr. Roger Woolger's school of Deep Memory Process.

She is the author of *Understanding Karmic Complexes: Evolutionary Astrology and Regression Therapy*, published in December 2009 by The Wessex Astrologer Ltd.

Along with astrology, she specializes in multidimensional healing work based in Shamanic principles, including soul retrieval/fragmentation and spirit releasement (ancestral and earthbound spirit work). Her focus is in healing present-life and past-life trauma, synthesizing intuitive hands-on healing and therapeutic approaches.

Please visit Patricia's website, www.HealThePast.com.

7

Time's Arrow:

The Nature and Function of the Planetary Nodes in Evolutionary Astrology

BY MARK JONES

Time present and time past
Are both perhaps present in time future,
And time future contained in time past.

—T. S. ELIOT, *FOUR QUARTETS*

In many forms of astrology we have become familiar with the roles of the Moon's nodes, and yet very few astrological approaches recognize and work with the fact that all of the planets in astrology have nodes. The nodes are simply abstract points in space where the planetary body crosses the line of the ecliptic, which, as astrologers, we posit as the baseline for the constellations and our measurements. If we take the familiar example of the Moon, we find as the Moon rises above the ecliptic, we have the creation of the North, or Ascending, Node of the Moon (the dragon's head), and as the Moon falls beneath the ecliptic we have the Descending, or South, Node of the Moon (the dragon's tail). This principle works with every other planet as well, so that Pluto crosses this plane, albeit at a much slower pace and therefore has an Ascending and Descending Node also.

What is the purpose of these points? Exploring the uses that planetary nodes have for us, as astrologers, is the purpose of this chapter. To initiate this process I will begin with a brief examination of the nature of the Moon's nodes within evolutionary astrology in order to both consolidate what we might already know and provide a blueprint, in principle at least, for how we might explore the unknown— the unfolding in time of the planetary archetypes.

The trinity of the water signs (Cancer, Scorpio, and Pisces) encapsulates in miniature the key principles of evolutionary astrology— with Neptune/Pisces we find the collective unconscious, the ground of being that we might see metaphorically as the primordial ocean. In Pluto/Scorpio we have the fixed point of intensity we call the Soul, the wave upon the ocean. A wave formed within the dual desires implicit in the Soul: to be ever more truly itself and separate as a wave and to dissolve once more back into the ocean, its origin. In Cancer/Moon we find the lens of ego awareness, the tip of the wave, that part of consciousness that brings a particularized awareness to the Soul: this life, this name, my personal identity.

As evolutionary astrologers, once we have identified and analyzed the nature of the Soul's desires through the Pluto placement, we can move to the South Node of the Moon as a window through which to view the histories of the multiple egos or personalities that the Soul has manifested and lived through, with regard to its purpose and desires. The Moon represents the ego; therefore, the South Node represents the multiple forms the ego has taken within the past, always with regard to the types of desire emanating from the Soul (Pluto). An incredible tool to be sure, but how many of us are aware that we can also seek out the same historical evolution through every one of the planetary archetypes—for example, the history of the Soul itself on some level in the South Node of Pluto, or even the larger currents of the primordial ocean through the South Node of Neptune?

It is this more esoteric dimension within the chart that I will be focusing on here. Rather like a hidden vault in an old building that allows one access to the plans and maps of ancient foundations, the planetary nodes open up dialogue with the dimension of time ever more comprehensively in the chart. Some of these foundations are collective in nature: the nodes of Jupiter, Saturn, Uranus, Pluto, and Neptune move very slowly over long periods of time, often linking every one of us on the planet at any one time to certain ancient principles and lineages. The planetary nodes of Mars, Venus, Mercury, and the Moon move much more quickly within generations or just a few years, enabling these foundations to allow another dimension to our personal evolutionary journey, the stories carried in our Soul and in our cellular memory. As a result of this quicker movement alongside the angles that the planetary orbits make to the ecliptic, the difference between the Ascending and Descending Nodes of the planets from Mars inward does not correspond to 180 degrees as with the lunar nodes and the nodes of Jupiter outward to Neptune. So the South Node of Venus, for example, is not necessarily opposite the North Node of Venus.

To explore the collective picture, even the very word *history* used with regard to both our personal and our collective experience can be deconstructed from the perspective of the South Node of Pluto, which occupies a position between 18 and 21 degrees Capricorn, a position with very little change over time. This is the story of the evolution of patriarchy over the last seven or eight thousand years. Interestingly, the South Nodes of both Saturn (17–29 degrees Capricorn) and Jupiter (0–21 degrees Capricorn) back up alongside that of Pluto.

The *Astrological Ages* is the name given for the transition of the procession of the Equinox throughout time—a reminder that even the relatively "fixed" points of the zodiac are themselves evolving through time. As a consequence of the nature of the earth's axial tilt and the wobble caused on that axis by the deformation of the Equator—where the earth bulges due to the gravitational influence of the Sun and Moon—the earth, over time, changes its alignment with the fixed stars. If you draw a perpendicular line through the poles of the earth in the Pisces Age, that point would appear to land in the constellation of Pisces on the day of the Spring Equinox. Draw that same line 2,500 years earlier, and the Sun is "seen" to land in the constellation of Aries on the Equinox—just as it is now slowly changing to the constellation of Aquarius. This central point of revolution is referred to as the "pole of the ecliptic."

If we trace back through the astrological ages from the perspective of evolutionary astrology, an interesting picture begins to emerge. The Age of Pisces began with Christ as sacrificed god carrying a message of love, which then evolved through the Virgo sub-age of the Pisces age (a sub-age's influence beginning roughly halfway through the age) in 1200 AD, as seen, for example, with the great European cathedrals built at this time and the effacement of man before God. In the Age of Aries begins the story of the chosen people, the Old Testament, Abraham, and the flowering of the warrior state in Rome and Greece, and through these states in the Libra sub-age the flowering of the arts, politics, and philosophy. In the Age of Taurus, we find the Egyptian culture develop with the goddess Hathor and the increasing emphasis on agriculture and possession and ownership of land. Through the Scorpio sub-age we see the increasing obsession with the rites of passage after death, the underworld, and the nature of the Soul. In this time period, early Minoan cultures and Mithraic influences are present. In the Age of Gemini we see the flowering of language and trade in early Sumerian culture, the city at Uruk, the story of Gilgamesh (its first king), the first written record of the time, and the migration of such cultures and their influence in the sub-age of Sagittarius.

In the Age of Cancer we have a time when civilization was still primarily focused in a matriarchal fashion, with all-inclusive tribal and familial units the central cultural power. In the sub-age of Capricorn, around 6500 BCE, the shift toward patriarchy begins. Jeffrey Wolf Green has written, in his book *Pluto, Volume II: The Soul's Evolution Through Relationships*, about the increasing recognition in men for their part in making babies and how this leads to the debate of ownership of women and children that becomes a prevailing theme of patriarchy. Riane Eisler, in her seminal books *The Chalice and the Blade* and *Sacred Pleasure,* has written extensively on the increase of the "dominator" mode of consciousness growing at this time through the rise of the "Kurgan" tribes sweeping across Europe and Asia, bringing an increasing struggle for power amongst key men and an increasing awareness of the need for warfare and power over others.

Through the planetary nodes of Pluto, Saturn, and Jupiter as a collective, our attention, should it seek out our own history, is being brought to bear upon this critical moment in the evolution of humankind. Why? What is the purpose of this collective link to this event or timeline?

Astrologically, we can locate the need to understand the nature of our Soul (Pluto), the structure of our consciousness and civilization (Saturn), the nature of our beliefs (Jupiter), and how all of these have been shaped by the impact of patriarchy (the South Nodes of Pluto, Saturn, and Jupiter in Capricorn). We could say that it is being pointed out to us that this time period and what occurred really matters; the story of the past still concerns present and future evolution.

Saturn, Capricorn, the tenth house correspond to the very nature of conditioning as the bedrock of society and civilization. This conditioning can operate on a familial and societal level, from parents who force us to eat everything on our plate because they grew up on war rations to a society that rewards celebrity status over those who teach our children. The examples are endless and will vary from family to

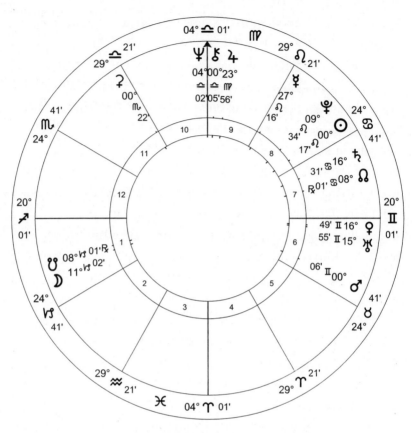

Chart 1: Alison
July 23, 1945 / 4:00 p.m. BAT / Basra, Iraq

family and from country to country. Yet the South Nodes of Pluto, Saturn, and Jupiter are pointing to the archetypal role that conditioning plays in our lives, how it covertly influences and corrupts, and how its very origins lie in profound shifts in our collective paradigms, stemming back many thousands of years.

In chart 1, of a woman I'll call Alison, who is in her sixties and came to me for a reading recently, we can clearly see that the Capricorn dynamic is emphasized; the South Node of the Moon is in Capricorn in the first house conjunct the Moon (the ruler of the lunar North Node), and Saturn (the ruler of the lunar South Node) is conjunct the North

Table 1: Planetary Nodes		
Mercury	Ascending Node	15°Cn10
Mercury	Descending Node	26°Le23
Venus	Ascending Node	12°Cn11
Venus	Descending Node	15°Vi55
Mars	Ascending Node	17°Ge14
Mars	Descending Node	10°Li56
Jupiter	Ascending Node	13°Cn12
Jupiter	Descending Node	05°Cp09 R
Saturn	Ascending Node	23°Cn54
Saturn	Descending Node	22°Cp24 R
Uranus	Ascending Node	15°Ge50
Uranus	Descending Node	11°Sg25 R
Neptune	Ascending Node	10°Le49
Neptune	Descending Node	11°Aq34 R
Pluto	Ascending Node	19°Cn50
Pluto	Descending Node	19°Cp13 R
Chiron	Ascending Node	21°Li59
Chiron	Descending Node	02°Ta22

Node in the seventh house in Cancer. Neptune squares the nodal axis in Libra in the tenth house (Capricorn) and is therefore expressing the nature of a skipped step in evolutionary development. With the ruler of the South Node on the North Node and the ruler of the North Node on the South Node, we clearly have a situation of reliving prior-life dynamics, in part simply through a karmic necessity (North Node ruler conjunct South Node) and in part to reorientate the being, through remembrance of such experiences, to the intended future direction (South Node ruler conjunct the North Node). We must place all this structural knowledge of her karmic need to re-experience the past in order to move forward (Neptune as a skipped step resolves through the North Node) within the context of the eighth-house Pluto in Leo, which conjuncts the Sun, and expresses the energy of the current life to embody the Soul's purpose—of exploring themes of power and powerlessness in order to understand the truly creative nature of the Soul's structure.

The nature of the past that needs to be re-experienced becomes much clearer when we add the information that the planetary nodes can offer: the South Node of the Moon and the Moon conjunct the South Node of Jupiter link the present and prior-life ego structures to the nature of personal and collective beliefs. Then the ruler of the South Node of the Moon and the North Node of the Moon conjunct between them the North Nodes of Mercury, Venus, Jupiter, Saturn, and Pluto—linking the past-life conditioning to the future purpose of the ego (Moon's North Node), which in turn is linked to the evolutionary direction of five other major planetary archetypes!

Clearly, this is a situation wherein prior-life patriarchal conditioning, and experiences of the evolution of patriarchy from its inception, are something that this Soul needs to uncover and re-experience in order to reintegrate in the current life, taking in a great deal of Soul knowledge of how power is experienced in the process (the natal Pluto placement, eighth house, Leo).

When we locate Alison as an Iraqi native living in a British culture that she has embraced in later life to move beyond the restrictions of her upbringing, a culture that still had soldiers stationed in her birthplace, some of the complexities of this situation emerge. In her upbringing, she experienced the rule of the father within her family and bowed to his view; she then transferred this experience to her husband (Saturn, ruling South Node conjunct North Node in Cancer the seventh house), from whom she would eventually separate and move to England, where she has undertaken a variety of healing paths and procedures (Pluto in Leo in the eighth house is conjunct the North Node of Neptune, which we will go on to explore). However, it has remained very hard for her to feel inside that she is free from the level of conditioning in her past and resultant inner judgment that she has felt, corresponding with the inner emptiness she felt in her family (Neptune in the tenth house as a skipped step), which paradoxically has seen her become through such experiences a de facto counselor with the many young people from all sorts of backgrounds with whom she works.

In working with this client (before I knew about her history), I helped in a process of self-validation. I wrote about the memories of multiple prior lives under the influence of patriarchy (the destructive aspect in the Saturn rulership of the second house, Venus with Uranus in the sixth house both square Jupiter, having her life threatened or claimed through being judged inadequate or wrong through her sexuality and innate feelings) and the way she may have struggled against her own gender through the inequality, through memories of being outcast or disempowered as a result of her sex. The imprint of slavery haunts the Neptune skipped step; in Roman and Greek times (the Libra imprint), many tribes and cultures (Cancer North Node, Moon on the South Node) were raided for slaves and also treated many women within their culture as if they were slaves. Many women were left with the dichotomy of institutionalized slavery through marriage, or the risk of independence and a possible education as a courtesan with the resultant difficulties implicit in that position (not naturally desired sexual contact, the risk of betrayal from one's client/ lovers, etc.) and the guilt that could then accrue.

Furthermore, once in slavery a young woman may have very little capacity to resist any unwanted sexual advances, being made to feel guilty, to carry the secret of her rape even from her own family (Pluto eighth ruling twelfth house, Aquarius on the third house Venus and Uranus conjunct, the Capricorn emphasis). Such secrets, potentially including an incest motif, indicated by Venus conjunct Uranus, ruling the third house, would have been interpreted or judged very differently within earlier goddess-centered or matriarchal cultures, and later patriarchal systems in which the taboos around sexuality, the threat of the feminine as temptress of the male, and the association of sexuality with lineage began to incur the potential for tremendous guilt. This internalized guilt is shown in the South Node in Capricorn in the first house and Neptune in the tenth house as a skipped step or square to the nodal axis. Everything in this chart resolves around the Cancer lunar North Node, the skipped step, the North Nodes of Mercury, Venus, Jupiter, and through the Saturn conjunction to the lunar North Node on to both the North Nodes of Saturn and Pluto. To remind Alison of her own innate matriarchal memory knowledge, that she has to some extent survived her reliving of the past and that her own emotional integration as a woman is a completely valid experience that she can be with at this point in her life, was very helpful to her, as she expressed. She was enabled to do some follow-up work, with new awareness.

This chart serves as a clear example of how the archetypal story (the nodes of the outer planets) can intertwine with a personal story through interconnections between the personal planets, the nodes of the Moon, and the planetary nodes. Interestingly, the example of the Venus placement and its nodes in this chart illustrate clearly the potential for the story of a person's life to interact with archetypal themes. We can see that the South Node of Venus is at 15 Virgo in a wide conjunction to Jupiter, and that the natal Venus placement at 16 Gemini, conjunct Uranus, is therefore square its own node. The square to its own node shows the unresolved issues around Venus coming into this life. That the North Node of Venus is at 12 Cancer, widely conjunct both the North Node of the Moon and the natal Saturn, shows the intention in this life to take responsibility for the Venus function, the personal needs and way of relating. Personal planets or the nodes of personal planets intersecting the planetary nodes of the outer planets can reveal ways in which the personal unconscious or experience intersects with the collective experience or significant archetypal themes. In this case, this is the intermingling of one person's exploration of sexuality and feelings, and the larger story of the experience of the feminine in our culture.

With the South Node of Venus in the ninth house in Virgo, we see that through the Virgo archetype that the past is shaped by a crisis in Alison's sense of values that has come about through negative messages from others that she has internalized. Jupiter is also with Venus in Virgo, and we see that limiting beliefs about the nature of the feminine and what is a natural or godly mode of self-expression have created an ongoing crisis about how she relates to herself and others. The natal Venus placement and its conjunction to Uranus, a signature of traumatic experience, emphasizes this insight. However, both Venus and Uranus conjunct the North Node of Uranus, and clearly hold the key to an awakening—a potential for liberation from certain conditioning.

In this client's own life she experimented sexually, enjoying lesbian affairs and multiple encounters to break free of her own chains; her response to my analysis of her sexuality led to some increase in understanding and awareness of why her life had happened the way it did. All of these are experiences serving to illuminate (following the Uranus and its North Node intention) an enlightening process that integrates with the conscious new direction held in the Venus North Node in Cancer in the seventh house—that through reintegrating the damage to the ego, through remembering the matriarchal consciousness free of judgment, she might form relationships with people based on an equal footing of emotional and psychological weight instead of succumbing to the dictates of the past, whereby she must always be subservient to a man.

If these powerful signatures in Capricorn (South Nodes of Jupiter, Saturn, and Pluto) really do hold open a door to our patriarchal heritage, then we might assume that they would crop up—with some larger than purely statistical weight—with a special prominence, within charts of war, invasion, and domination. I owe my initial thoughts on this subject to the promptings of Theodor Landscheidt, an astrologer who pioneered work on the planetary nodes in the sixties and seventies. Of course, as he first reflected, these nodes do show up with significant emphasis with quite alarming regularity. If we take as an example the chart for the invasion of Poland by the Nazis, the start of the Second World War (1 September 1939, 04:40 CET, Wielun, Poland), we discover that Mars is in Capricorn in the fifth house, conjunct the South Nodes of Saturn and Pluto, and that it furthermore squares the nodal axis of the Moon (South Node 0 Taurus, North Node 0 Scorpio), as does Pluto from the twelfth house in Leo—a fixed cross of evolutionary intensity, the crossfire of powerful skipped steps that through the South Nodes of Pluto and Saturn take us right back into the power and structures of our very civilization. Ominous portents indeed.

If we examine the chart of Baghdad, the base of Saddam Hussein at the start of the first Gulf War (17 January 1991, 02:38 BAT, Baghdad), we encounter a phenomenal conjunction of Mercury with Uranus, Neptune, the Sun, Saturn, and the North Node of the Moon in the second house. Uranus and Neptune are closely conjunct the South Node of Jupiter and the Sun; Saturn and the North Node of the Moon are closely conjunct the South Nodes of Pluto and Saturn. With Chiron conjunct the South Node of the Moon and both conjunct the North Nodes of Pluto and Saturn in the eighth house, Pluto is again in the twelfth house, this time in Scorpio, brooding over collective issues of power and how resources (oil) are to be shared.

Again the archetypal influence of the planetary nodes overwhelm us. How many of our wars still reek of early shifts of paradigm in our prehistory, how much do we know ourselves and our deeper motivations for our collective actions when placed in these contexts? I do not intend to fully attempt answers to these vast questions, but as astrologers beginning to utilize these planetary nodes, and as concerned human beings, they are surely interesting. In the chart for the start of Operation "Iraqi Freedom," the planetary South Nodes of Pluto, Saturn, and Jupiter step up again in the form of a Chiron-Mars conjunction in Capricorn in the tenth house, a placement receiving the end of a yod formation from Jupiter and the North Node. The Pluto-Saturn opposition crosses the planetary nodes of Uranus—we shall begin to explore the significance of that now.

Uranus as an archetype challenges us to liberate ourselves from conditioning; it is in an archetypal struggle with Saturn, which represents conditioning. Uranus encapsulates paradox, and as such runs the whole range of possibilities within itself—from the most terrible trauma or shock to the greatest blueprint of our potential, stored within us like a butterfly within a grub. As such, when we examine the South Node of Uranus, which lies between 10 and 17 degrees Sagittarius for almost all of us, we are looking into the history of that which can potentially destroy us or liberate us; in short, we are playing with fire.

Sagittarius as an archetype then contains the blueprint of the evolution of Uranus as an archetype, and in this knowledge we become keyed in to the powerful role that the nature of our beliefs holds within the process of conditioning, and, indeed, de-conditioning. At the very heart of the Sagittarian archetype is nature, the natural laws that underpin all of life, the laws that hold the growth of a lotus from a seed to the birth of a supernova in space. In Sagittarius, the archer combines both the human and animal in the one shape of the centaur. The transpersonal psychologist Ken Wilber named the process of the fusion of the consciousness and form into the body-mind the *Centauric stage*, the formation of a single consciousness that can appropriate different states without restriction. This is Sagittarian knowledge: intuitive, single-pointed consciousness able to investigate the nature of forms by becoming one with them. This is the history of our liberation, if you will; this is time's arrow, for in this oneness the normal barriers of Saturn—for example, time and space—are less stringent, less demanding, and we can capture glimpses of what it is to remember ourselves deeply, to remember our heritage. Indeed, at its core Uranus holds the archetype of memory in its most far-reaching consequences: remembering prior lives, remembering our birth, the things we would rather forget . . . The history of this remembering (South Node of Uranus) is in nature and its laws (Sagittarius).

As part of the natural law, humans have set themselves, like Prometheus, in the joyous and dangerous position of wrestling illumination from the forces of creation. It is within this project, the creation of meaning, our search for truth, that many of the traumatic memories within the South Node of Uranus originate; for one person's truth is another's heresy, as the extremity of opinions surrounding the latest war in the Persian Gulf (Pluto, M.C. conjunct the South Node of Uranus, Saturn, I.C. in Gemini on the North Node . . .) suggests. One person's liberating philosophy is another's prison. The strictures of man-made laws grow alongside the uprising of patriarchal awareness within the picture we have already explored through the Capricorn archetype, yet our very liberation (Uranus) from such conditioning is implicated in the same struggle.

It is too simple to go back to nature like a Rousseau; at the same time, if we don't in some fashion, we may not have a world left. It is too egalitarian to suggest every point of view is equally valid (the Taliban cleric may struggle at the naturist disco), and yet if we do not create a vision of freedom, we risk imprisonment in our Souls. These are the dilemmas we face as we explore the evolution of Uranus through its South Node.

If we move on to the South Node of Neptune, at between 9 and 13 degrees Aquarius, we move further back again into our collective past; the future movement of the Equinoxes from Pisces to Aquarius that is in a transition at the turn of the twenty-first century is only in part a New Age, as we are carried through the South Node of Neptune in to the memory of the spiritual heritage of our race back in the last Aquarian age some 25,000 years ago. What is in part a movement into

Table 2: Planetary Nodes		
Mercury	Ascending Node	19°Sg24
Mercury	Descending Node	02°Sg52
Venus	Ascending Node	23°Sc05
Venus	Descending Node	12°Sg29
Mars	Ascending Node	16°Ar54 R
Mars	Descending Node	27°Sc08
Jupiter	Ascending Node	16°Cn28 R
Jupiter	Descending Node	05°Cp14
Saturn	Ascending Node	27°Cn51 R
Saturn	Descending Node	19°Cp35
Uranus	Ascending Node	13°Ge57 R
Uranus	Descending Node	13°Sg31
Neptune	Ascending Node	12°Le52 R
Neptune	Descending Node	09°Aq34
Pluto	Ascending Node	20°Cn30 R
Pluto	Descending Node	18°Cp27
Chiron	Ascending Node	02°Sc40
Chiron	Descending Node	26°Ar37 R

the future is also a stepping-back into the harmonics of the past, a paradox in time's function similar to our archer's gaze as it is fixed into the heavens, staring backwards into the history of the evolution of our universe—a universe still travelling toward the centaur at the speed of light.

This prior Aquarian age preceded the transition to patriarchy that we have explored with the nodes of Jupiter, Saturn, and Pluto, and which holds a place at the center of the prior matriarchy. In light of the sextile between the South Node of Uranus in Sagittarius and the South Node of Neptune in Aquarius, we can see the mutual interpenetration of this ancient matriarchy within the laws of nature, free from the suppressive or dominating aspects of patriarchy's relationship with the body and nature. In a sense, our goal in moving forward to another Aquarian age is to remember this wisdom:

"In essence, we will become aligned with the original and true self-image that has always been there since the beginning of time . . . Spirit and flesh will no longer be interpreted as mutually antagonistic. As a result, the patriarchal beliefs leading to suppression of all that is natural will be removed . . . the causal factors leading to all kinds of displaced rage and anger will no longer exist." (Jeffrey Wolf Green, in chapter 11, "Pluto in Sagittarius," in *Pluto, Volume II: The Soul's Evolution Through Relationships*, p. 388.)

Jeffrey's own chart is a fascinating example of the relevance of the planetary nodes of Uranus and Neptune (December 2, 1946, 4:52 a.m., Hollywood, California). With his lunar nodes conjunct the Nodes of Uranus, we can clearly see his own prior-life incarnations within natural environments and tribal realities, whereby a sense of nature and of personal freedom was paramount. With Mars and the Sun on the South Node of the Moon, we see also a need to relive these experiences, and an anger or righteous indignation about such experiences coming into this life, stemming in part from a violent death within one of these lifetimes (Mars on the lunar South Node, Mars in the second house opposite Uranus in the eighth house).

With Jupiter in Scorpio in the twelfth house on the Ascendant, the ruler of the South Node of the Moon (with the South Node of Uranus), we can clearly see the internal memory and awareness of these lifetimes coming through in the birth process and the very early instinctual self (Ascendant)—here is a person who remembers such experiences (Uranus-memory) even as he comes into this life, struggling in this lifetime to make sense of what had come before. When the lunar South Node intersects with another planetary node, we can posit that the personal memory of prior incarnations touches the archetypal issue held in the planetary archetype whose node is in aspect. In this example, the South Node of the Moon conjuncts the

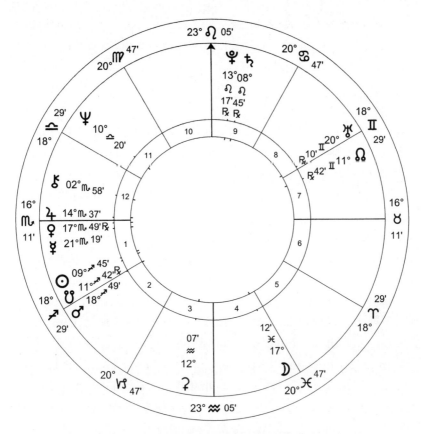

Chart 2: Jeffrey Wolf Green
December 2, 1946 / 04:52 a.m. / Hollywood, California

South Node of Uranus; the archetype of memory infuses the personal awareness, in a man whose vivid memories of prior lives has informed his astrological teachings with a radical (Uranus) depth. Such memories involve the trauma of the disintegration of natural and tribal life (South Node of Uranus in Sagittarius, Mars opposite Uranus, Uranus on its own North Node), the struggle of such peoples to survive (Sagittarius on the second-house cusp), and the difference between forced and chosen nomadism.

With Pluto and Saturn in the ninth house, we can clearly picture a Soul for whom freedom and cosmological laws and principles are the very essence of the way this consciousness is structured. With Saturn in balsamic conjunction with Pluto, we can see that a whole cycle of the way that this Soul has related to authority is coming to an end, and that a culmination is sought through being a teacher himself (Wolf medicine). We see in this Saturn-Pluto meeting the previous struggles with authority, the echo of the violent death at the hands of an oppressor, and also the healing intention. Through the conjunction of Pluto-Saturn to the North Node of Aquarius, the polarity point of Pluto is therefore the South Node of Aquarius, showing the need for the healing of these old wounds, and that as a teacher his intuitive truth will point toward the spiritual heritage of humanity, for which we have already seen evidence in the quotation on the previous page. Healing through the dynamic of the primordial wisdom of Neptune, his own evolutionary needs (polarity point of Pluto) lead back into the spiritual roots of the humanity on Earth at this time (polarity point of Pluto conjunct the South Node of Neptune).

In this fashion, the North Node of the Moon conjunct the North Node of Uranus clearly signifies that both personal and collective healing can occur through this man, recording what he has himself lived, and intuitively discovered and received, through his writing and teaching—the outcome of which is the reason behind this book. In this way we can name the greatest potential of the Pluto-in-Leo generation to become seed people for the paradigms and teachings that will help inspire the new old age as their Pluto can resonate with the North Node of Neptune. Showing creativity, the individual rising to his subjective fullness, as the essential way that group dynamics can be truly realized, a unity in diversity, a humanity that celebrates and includes difference as the only way forward for the spiritual vision implicit in the planetary nodes of Neptune.

Even within the selfishness and excess of the Pluto-in-Leo generation, glimpses of a new future have been found, particularly in the flowering of consciousness in the late-1960s artistic and countercul-

Table 3: Planetary Nodes		
Mercury	Ascending Node	01°Ta59
Mercury	Descending Node	11°Ar26
Venus	Ascending Node	17°Ta25
Venus	Descending Node	10°Pi58
Mars	Ascending Node	10°Ta20
Mars	Descending Node	20°Sg55 R
Jupiter	Ascending Node	00°Cn15
Jupiter	Descending Node	21°Cp17 R
Saturn	Ascending Node	17°Cn11
Saturn	Descending Node	29°Cp11
Uranus	Ascending Node	11°Ge47
Uranus	Descending Node	16°Sg10 R
Neptune	Ascending Node	09°Le40 R
Neptune	Descending Node	13°Aq21
Pluto	Ascending Node	18°Cn36
Pluto	Descending Node	21°Cp55 R
Chiron	Ascending Node	29°Li21 R
Chiron	Descending Node	28°Ar53

tural revival, which in all its naïveté and preponderance still holds much of value as a first effort toward visioning a new world. It becomes the role of the Pluto-in-Virgo generation (now gaining maturity in the world) to confront their own crises and continue the movement through the cleanup of health, and through promoting the ethical work functions that this world is crying out for.

Both of the previous example charts I have used, through their involvement between the lunar nodal axis and the planetary nodes, have obviously served as great examples of how the personal and the archetypal intersect with the utilization of the planetary nodes. I chose them that way! Yet to qualify that statement, the client of chart 1 was a recent one, and with reference to the example of Jeffrey, my teacher, this material only emerged in the writing of this . . . What I am trying to say is

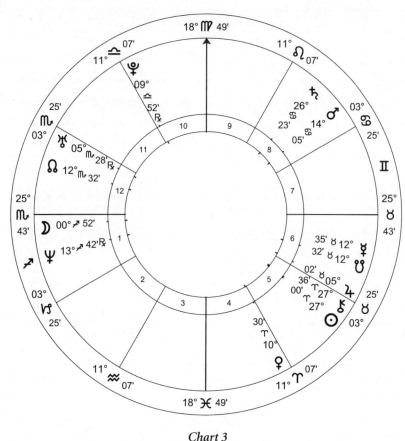

Chart 3
April 16, 1976 / 10:40 p.m. BST / Luton, England

that planetary nodes are not just relevant in a few select charts (good examples), but rather they can give valuable information within any chart. To illustrate this principle, I have selected a chart at random from the clients I have worked with in the last two weeks. Chart 3 is that of a young English woman.

With Pluto in the tenth house in the cardinal sign of Libra, we clearly have a Soul who is closing a chapter of evolutionary development, who is seeking to sum up this process, take responsibility for it, and move on. With Pluto in the tenth house opposite Venus in the fourth house, with Mars in Cancer in the eighth house T-squaring both, we can clearly see that family dynamics and the experiences within families of origin have played a huge part in the prior developmental story. We can see the enormous transformation (Pluto-Venus) required to fulfill the evolutionary potential of fulfillment within society (Pluto tenth house) that must include a radical upheaval within the emotional body (Venus in the fourth house) and in the way that her desires exist and are fulfilled (Mars T-square Pluto-Venus). In part, these desires (Pluto-Venus) have been expressed within a codependent fashion with her family of origin in this and in other lives, families that may not have always had her best interests at heart—an issue that corresponds to the challenging aspects Pluto makes to Venus and Mars.

With Saturn in the eighth in Cancer square the Sun, ruling the second house, in this context, we can see difficult family experiences through judgment, suppression, possible abuse (with Pluto-Mars-Venus and the eighth-house Cancer), and a struggle with her gender (Pluto tenth house, Venus fourth house, square Mars in Cancer), perhaps including memories of a destruction as an infant or young girl for being "useless" or a burden (eighth-house Saturn Cancer square the Sun in the fifth house, ruling the second house "survival"). We can see the potential for such scenarios playing out within classical cultures (Pluto in Libra), perhaps including the dichotomy facing many women in those times between the suppression of marriage (Pluto Libra tenth house) and the relative freedom of the courtesan (Venus Aries, square Mars). Certainly with the dynamic stress of a T-square from Pluto-Venus on to Mars in Cancer in the eighth house, Mars ruling the fifth house, we can see the painful loss of a child, the judgment of family or society within that process (Pluto tenth house), possibly their involvement, or the involvement of someone very close in the taking of a child (Mars conjunct Saturn in the eighth house in Cancer, the link back to Pluto-Venus in the tenth and fourth houses respectively). Whichever way it happened, the link of Sun with Chiron in the fifth house, and the difficult conjunction of the rulers of the fifth and second houses, reveal the massive impact on this Soul. The loss for her was simply too much to bear.

With the South Node of the Moon conjunct Mercury and Jupiter in the sixth house in Taurus, we see a fundamentally honest Soul (South Node of the Moon conjunct Jupiter) coming into this life with strong thoughts (Mercury) and beliefs (Jupiter) shaped around the issue of surviving (Taurus) strong persecution and humiliation (Virgo). The crisis is around how best to serve; memories of serving without feedback, reward, or response are paramount, though. Even in this life, the story will be repeated (planets conjunct the South Node), as this young woman spent her teens nursing her sick mother after her father had left; her older sister (Mercury on South Node), despising her in the process, left as soon as she could, abandoning her to do the work alone. The whole time her father lived just a few streets away but did nothing to help; occasionally he would call her on the phone, but when he did so he was very verbally and psychologically abusive. Later she would collapse herself with a variant of myalgic encephalopathy, an autoimmune-triggered condition that leads to prolonged fatigue. This condition lasted for three years in her late teens. Somehow she completed her education; she is very bright (Mercury-Jupiter on South Node).

How can the planetary nodes add to this picture, to a concise evolutionary perspective on the chart? Well, Sun-Chiron on Chiron's own South Node speaks powerfully of the history of wounding that desires integration within the current life (the Sun) and how the loss of children mirrors the loss of her own childhood, and shows the crisis within her own creative self—how to ever feel validated for what she does. At college, even when graduating with her first-class degree, she was unable to feel her own gifts, and when I first worked with her she was working at a local café as a waitress. This of course echoes the powerful Saturn signature that rules the second house. Mars with Saturn in the eighth house in Cancer is conjunct the North Nodes of Saturn and Pluto, revealing both corroboration of the psychologically abusive relationship with her father (echoes of other abusive relationships with men over many lives) and also a deeper theme: that of the role of the feminine within patriarchy, that of the re-emergence of a more matriarchal awareness within herself as a woman, the true girl power.

This is the backdrop of true femininity within her desire body (Mars) and structuring her consciousness (the proximity of the North Node of Pluto to natal Saturn also)—and this gives us an increased insight into the intended transformation within the Pluto-Venus opposition, which places Venus in the fourth house in Aries as a key integration point of the whole chart, as this point is the polarity point of Pluto (the opposition to natal Pluto indicating the point that the Soul or Pluto intends itself to evolve toward). This insight places the intended transformation of Venus to include the integration of the matriarchal consciousness that has also survived within the Taurus South Node that Venus rules, which has not been completely eradicated through the persecutory haze of her experience (the sixth-house South Node). In this way, Neptune in Sagittarius in the first house, as the focal point of a yod from the South Node-Mercury-Jupiter and Mars, comes into its own when we add that this focal point is conjunct the South Node of Uranus, intending the integration of trauma in this life (supporting the natal Uranus placement with the node), and that this will take place through a relationship with nature, through the healing that will bring.

As I am a psychosynthesis therapist as well as an astrologer, I sometimes work with people in a more ongoing fashion rather than just for a one-off chart reading. This is the case with this client, who has, since working with me, met a producer of wildlife films for the BBC who has invited her to personally oversee the publicity for the project and who wishes her to work for him on several projects. His role is not just as a program-maker but also as a conservationist—a role that sees him struggle with the Establishment at many points. He sensed my client's sensitivity (Neptune) and her radicalism (Uranus with North Node in Scorpio in the twelfth house), which he felt could help him with his film projects. The planetary nodes may seem like an esoteric approach to astrology, but it is my hope we are all beginning to see how they can help expand the picture of a chart so that the astrology itself begins to live in people's lives, helping us all to understand in the most authentic fashion the nature of our lives on this earth.

Part of the healing we have explored occurred as Pluto transited Neptune and the South Node of Uranus, and my client undertook a past-life regression whereby she vividly recalled the complexities of a prior-life scenario in which her child was abducted, probably by a family member, and in which she was later stabbed by the same man. In the same regression she went back to being a forty-year-old monk in red robes giving out blessings, yet retreating slightly lonely to his temple, having been forced to leave his family. When we locate the South Node of Venus in Pisces, we can see the sincere desire for service (linked to the South Node with Jupiter in the sixth house) this young woman had coming into this life, where she would literally enact it in her youth to the extent of having little "life" herself. The recollection of the lifetime as a monk seems almost a fulfillment of the North Node with Uranus in Scorpio in the twelfth house (the red robes reminiscent of Tibetan cultures); perhaps prior-life memories shape the possibility of the North Node of the Moon also, or this "recollection" is as much a future possibility.

The Ascending or North Node of Venus is in Taurus, conjunct the South Node-Mercury-Jupiter; in reliving the past experiences with her family in this life and surviving, her heart is reminded of her potential now. This survival theme is evident with the North Nodes of Mercury and Mars also being in Taurus. With the South Node of Mercury conjunct Venus, we see the history with the sister, the need for change (Pluto-Venus) in that old relationship (Mercury-South Node of Moon), and the South Node of Venus in Pisces shows the essential forgiveness that my client is already beginning to be able to surrender to with her sister even whilst some very painful memories persist. As Pluto moves to conjunct her South Node of Mars in the first house in Sagittarius, this young woman is able to begin acting in such a way that validates her own desires that for so long were held in abeyance for the sake of others.

The inclusion of the planetary nodes in the reading of a chart can deepen perception both through the introduction of the archetypal sphere through the South Nodes of the outer planets and through the personal memories contained in personal planets. Additionally, they can provide a context (including elements of why any of us are here at all in this world) and a way of helping us to understand the types of experience we may have personally had—experiences that shape both our personality and our destiny.

___

ABOUT MARK JONES

Mark Jones is a psychosynthesis therapist, evolutionary astrologer, and hypnotherapist living and working in private practice in Bristol, England. Mark teaches the U.K. branch of the Jeffrey Wolf Green School of Evolutionary Astrology. He is a regular speaker/workshop facilitator at the NORWAC astrology conferences and the evolutionary astrology conferences (since 2005), and has published articles in both *Major Sky* and *The Synthesist* magazines. He is a member of the Council of Evolutionary Astrologers.

Please visit his website, www.plutoschool.com.

8

The Evolutionary Astrology Perspective of the Archetype of Capricorn

BY ROSE MARCUS

THE CAPRICORN PSYCHOLOGY

The sign of Capricorn is positioned at the zenith of the zodiacal wheel, beginning at the primary angle known as the *Midheaven*, or MC. It is at this summit in the twelve-fold cycle of astrology's archetypes that the manifested creation reaches maximum structural definition. Advancing from the previous evolutionary plateau, beliefs and viewpoints explored through Sagittarius become the cement mix (prima materia) for the building of dimension through the Capricorn archetype. In Sagittarius, we conceptualize; in Capricorn, we manifest.

Completing the zodiacal triad of the element of earth, the manifestations of the Capricorn archetype correlate to the stage of ripening—in other words, to the maturation of environmental conditions and physical circumstances—and to the conclusions formed by the experienced, educated, and thereby progressively conditioned awareness.

Capricorn's chief attributes are form, substance, boundaries, borders, and limits. The Capricorn archetype also corresponds to the principle of gravity. The gravitational force behind any accumulated mass largely regulates baselines and dictates boundaries. For example, in human consciousness, once a sufficient amount of emotional energy (fear, mistrust, love, etc.) is amassed within the psyche, it will most naturally define and influence (organize, control, rule, dominate) the boundaries of perceptions.

Physically, Capricorn correlates to the skeletal structure of the human body, which represents the inner foundation or support structure, and it also correlates to the outer casing known as the body's skin, which serves to house, protect, regulate, and limit the organism as a whole. Distinct in both form and function, each is a counterbalance for the other. Together, they define and determine the body's form and its function.

Psychologically speaking, the inner core, defined by its foundation mindset and conceptual boundaries, forms the regulating body called consciousness. Capricorn correlates to both the outer manifestations of physical realities and to the inner realities that crystallize to form a consensus within consciousness of an individual and within the mass consciousness of larger wholes—from one-on-one relationships to groups, societies, nations, and to the larger collective unit. The goat with the fish tail, Capricorn is a dual archetype. It is inherently both masculine (assertive, active) and feminine (responsive, retentive). Capricorn's inner and outer constructs can be referred to as its light and shadow forms.

As an earth sign, Capricorn is the archetype that correlates to the finite realms of physical reality. As a cardinal archetype, Capricorn correlates to the creation and materialization of realities. Capricorn's shadow component correlates to the perceived realms of manifestations—in other words, our experience of reality or that which is defined by the limits of consciousness in any given moment. While they are two separate and distinct counterpoints, perceived reality and actual reality are often judged as one and the same. For the willful subjective consciousness (or ego on the run), they can be experienced as virtually inseparable.

Evaluations and expectations shaped from prior experience become the basis of rationalizations known as judgments. These preconceptions set the boundaries for our creative process and function as the initiating angle (cardinal archetype) from which the casting reel is tossed. As a cardinal archetype, Capricorn's initiatory impulse manifests from a baseline of past preconceptions and experience, but the momentum is directed to new building and new formulations. Thus is demonstrated the intrinsic conflict of cardinal activation. That which is already set in place can both support and hinder new creation. Capricorn's security conflict ignites a particularly dynamic struggle-force. Capricorn's cardinality also ignites the struggle between the inner and outer experience: the pressure to accept and conform, juxtaposed with the anxiety and fear generated by potentials— i.e., the repeat struggles of the past, the threat of the infiltration or invasion of the new and overpowering, and the fear of loss, security, and control.

The perceived consensus is the invention of the socialized and learned consciousness. Once accord centralizes around a consensus reference point, this then serves as the baseline that not only defines what is most readily accepted or adhered to, but also serves as the criteria or measuring stick by which all other information or experience is received and judged.

Over time, the progressive socialization of consciousness conditions one to act and respond in alignment with that which is already assimilated, or, in other words, pre-exists.

Once the socialized consciousness has amassed enough information to formulate a structural definition, it segregates the inner and outer references, thereby setting self separate and apart through the defining of boundaries, borders, limits, and cut-off points.

Conceptualizations energized within the conditioned mind lead to the progressive crystallization of thought forms. These thought forms are the foundations of security, limits, and limitation. Once the willful subjective consciousness forms the strength of internal accord, it will strive to preserve itself and its pre-established sense of security for as long as possible, utilizing whatever means are within reach. This safety mechanism typically results in the blocking or denying of alternate definitions of reality.

Just as this moment is but a link in a chain of moments, history precedes the consciousness of the here and now. As stated previously, it is the historical frame of reference, or, in other words, the remembrances of prior experience, that constitutes a dominant driving force for the Capricorn creative process in its search for security, control, and self-consistency (Cancer polarity). Thoughts, judgments, and behavior patterns reformulated from the memory pools of the past (Cancer polarity) progressively saturate and program the consciousness, nudging it toward a crystallization apex.

The rational (logical/left brain) perspective most commonly perceives in terms of separateness. Consciousness commonly holds to a perspective that seemingly "stands outside of its own creations." Through this kind of limited perspective, the workings of displaced emotions commonly translate into disowning our own involvement in the process of creation. In truth, outside forces reflect inner needs. As we perceive, so we create—and re-create. Link after link forges in the action/response chain.

It is a natural propensity for the subconscious to project a possible outcome and then to manifest it. Extracted from the consciousness, in other words, the understandings and experiences of one's evolutionary state, what is called into being, are a mix of memory recall and one's pre-constructed viewpoints (the response mechanism). Perpetuating creation, this subconscious projection process animates as the karmic law of cause and effect, also known as fate or destiny. Free will correlates to the internal response mechanism and choice-making present in each evolving moment.

BEHAVIORAL RESPONSES

1. Developing a relationship with externalized authority

When we resist or block seeing alternative realities beyond our own preconceptions, we often find ourselves limited by our circumstantial realities and overpowered by life's hardships. So often, we do not recognize that we have been part of our own creative process and that we have called forth the circumstances we experience.

When faced with seemingly insurmountable challenges, we can acquiesce to external pressures, authority, and the "as is" of past experiences, which can result in futility consciousness. We commonly complain that life is unfair, that we are hard done by, that opportunity is limited, and that we find ourselves on the short end of the stick. We feel dried up on the inside and our outer life seems barren, too. When futility consciousness takes the lead, the re-creation process has a propensity to extend the suffering and diminish ambition, leading to a perception of failure. One often feels crippled by circumstance, as if there is "no way out." This inner emotional compression energizes the draw of the yin magnetic pole in such a way that we can bring to ourselves situations in which we feel dominated and inferior. While feelings of disappointment, depression, anxiety, self-doubt, fear, guilt, a sense of futility, etc., seemingly appear to slow down, inhibit, or even stop the forward gait, it is this exact struggle that keeps the wheels in motion and that will eventually lead to a shift in both consciousness (inner world) and circumstance (outer world).

When the struggle occurs inwardly and is funneled or projected outwardly through the yang magnetic pole, resentment, rejection (of status quo/consensus), and blame are the breeding pool for justifications leading to a sense of righteousness and deserving. Distorted judgment reflecting the distorted conceptualization of internalized authority needs tends to be the root cause of actions taken. We find ourselves harboring a sense of injustice that is motivated by a desire for the reclamation of our "rightful" position. There grows an intensified anxiety to re-establish control, along with expectations for accountability, as if something is owed, a debt must be repaid, or more homage and recognition is deserved. Ambition to "right a wrong" can intensify to the point where unacceptable boundaries can be crossed. Rather than allow oneself to succumb to outside forces, any or all means can be undertaken in order to regain control, authority, and power. When objectives are thus driven, ambition can be formidable, ruthless, even tyrannical.

2. The development of internal authority

The psychological behavior pattern can be one of inner or outer rejection of the systems, standards, and authority of others. In this case, the stance can be one of struggle, of resistance, and of chafing against external limitations or dictates, real or projected. Resistance to the status quo creates a separation impulse that serves to advance the process of individuation.

When appropriate means and steps have been taken, Capricorn's search for inner and outer control can result in solid emotional security, self-sufficiency, self-reliance, and united fronts, leading to long-lived benefits. Conversely, when Capricorn's creative process begins construction with selective justification based on the release of previously suppressed emotions, the industriousness of distorted response mechanisms builds false walls and distorted security. Eventually, the control fortress collapses.

3. Acceptance and conformity

At this stage of ripening, an appropriate alignment with authority facilitates a more harmonious integration—internally, externally, individually, and socially. Contributions to the larger whole result in achievements that fortify the life force or structure of the whole, and in so doing, results in an enlivened momentum that expands viable opportunities (choice-in-action) rather than shrinks them.

In the broader scope, the manifestations of crystallized thoughts and behavior patterns also establish the features—platforms, policies, politics, realities, anxieties, necessities, and crowning achievements—that define the consensus formulae of mass consciousness and that also identify the feature characteristics, personality, and achievements of a collective era.

As the archetype that correlates to time (a finite measurement), it is through Capricorn that we become increasingly more aware of time spans and of the limits of our own existence—in other words, our own mortality. Through the Capricorn vehicle, we come to recognize or learn that we have a limited time in which to function, to build, and to create life. Growing recognition of our physical limitations also draws added attention to environmental or external restrictions. This in turns prompts greater internal emotional compression. The pressure generated from the perceived and/or actual experience of lack, or of time running out, results in the build-up of anxiety, a base emotional trait of the Capricorn psychology. Anxiety and its counterpart emotion, fear, most commonly fuel Capricorn's drive toward accomplishment and achievement.

The Capricorn motto may be aptly described by the axiom "control at all costs." The as-yet unknown, unformed, and undefined, the random, the out of control or seemingly beyond control can be initially viewed as counter to the pre-existing focus of security and therefore can be readily judged as threatening. Lack of security commonly builds anxiety in varying degrees of expression. Coming from this emotional reality, Capricorn typically builds (false) walls, holds guard, shuts out, closes off, staves off, blames, suppresses, or denies in varying degrees. When in anxiety or fear-based mode, self-preservation emotions are the compelling forces that come to dictate, dominate, and limit every move, and that typically build false protection that can only temporarily bolster or buttress the bastions.

Traits commonly associated with Capricorn are resistance, dread, apprehension, foreboding, skepticism, fear, paranoia, blame. When extreme, these traits can display as domineering, berating, condescending, persecutory, and tyrannical; acts of self-preservation and self-protectionism can lead into moral decay and physical corruption. Terrorism or sadistic acts are common by-products. Emotions can range from dried-up, cut off (the castration complex), or shut off to numbed, stone cold, frozen, or deadened. Emotional complexes can develop into emotional or physical paralysis, and even catatonia.

The regulating function of the Capricorn archetype, relative to the Cancer polarity in search of self-consistency, creates a repetition dynamic. Familiarity may breed familiarity, but the results of this action/response mechanism do not necessarily guarantee safety, security, or control. In fact, often the creations/manifestations generated from the perceived security needs and security measures undertaken can be antithetical to intentions, especially when insecurity is the base breeding agent. Rather than running a tighter ship, pre-existing anxieties and fears become the lead programs that drive and control.

It is in the sign of Capricorn that we learn to establish and refine a relationship with authority. Conformity to external authority is our first lesson; our first school is the parental influence and the family unit, and it extends throughout our engagement in various stages of socialization and collective experiences, where we come to learn how to navigate the rules and rankings of our economic, political, national, and religious systems. Throughout each level, we learn about support and containment, dominant forces, sacrifices, and consequences. We learn the ins and outs, the pros and cons, of our contributions in support of the system, and we find purpose and distinction through professional undertakings and social status. We learn what it means to stand embraced within the circle, or to be rejected and to stand outside of it.

As we discover the workings of what is acceptable and appropriate to external authority, we learn lessons of how we are limited and controlled by forces larger than ourselves. Our consciousness becomes conditioned, programmed, tamed, and "domesticated," both with regard to our relationship to the externalized world and also within our own being. This process leads to progressive programming and conditioning of internal judgment. Once trained and harnessed, internal judgment becomes a stringent regulating force regarding acceptable standards of conduct. Deviation from this established regulating system, called conformity, commonly results in the reactionary impulse/judgment known as internalized guilt.

Internalized guilt becomes another vehicle through which we suppress our natural tendencies and emotions, resulting in the experience of division and separateness both from our core and from externalized status quos. When we disown our own hand in the creative process, we externalize it and we meet with blame, criticism, and failure, whether sensed or actualized, or we project it onto others. When facing our true need is too painful, too frightening (fear-based), or too costly (loss of security) to view directly, we approach it indirectly (Cancer polarity); we cover up, we deny reality, and we suppress the truth. Our distorted perceptions of reality translate into displaced emotional needs. These displaced emotional needs commonly result in unconscious projection and compensatory actions. In other words, we act out.

As we grow and mature, we become more aware of the contrast of the polarizations (Libra evaluations/crisis in consciousness) of our outer and inner realities. This contrast serves to further define a sense of our separateness from the dictates of external authority. This differentiation process prompts the further examination and development of inner needs and internal authority. Whether the process involves resistance or acceptance, or a combination of both, the process serves to advance the process of individuation, which leads to the skilled usage of resources and to developing mastery over systems. The educated, experienced, and adept Capricorn has a talent for working the system to his or her advantage. When self-serving motivations prompt the use of inappropriate means to gain a dominant position, Capricorn ambition for control displays the workings of the hungry opportunist. This tendency is common to Pluto in Capricorn.

Capricorn prompts lessons in standards of conduct: the honing, managing, usage, and limitations of our own authority, regarding both the inner and outer experience. It is through the Capricorn stage that we first learn to develop a relationship with external authority, and then to internalize it. This impregnation within our own consciousness teaches lessons in self-regulation and behavior modification; we learn to qualify our socialized context and find purpose based on this internalized programming.

It is at the peak of the Capricorn stage in the twelve-fold process of evolution that the internal and external structures become fully formed, fully functional, and fully regulated. Results come under the jurisdiction of the Capricorn archetype. At this point in the wheel, we meet with the fullness of success, recognition, achievement, and rewards, or the fullness of failure, disappointment, loss, and the end of life.

As a culmination point, the Capricorn archetype brings an entire chapter of evolution to an end. As a cardinal archetype, Capricorn also represents an initiating point for a new evolutionary chapter.

There are two sides to the mountain, of course. Observation will tell us if the goat is scaling the ascent or descent part of the journey. The conditioned consciousness of the Capricorn archetype can be found to be at the stage of amassing, mobilizing, and climbing toward a ripening or maturation peak, or the conditioned consciousness may be found to be mobilized in the declining stage, when the harvest residues are in the process of withering, receding, decaying, and dying. Whether in the build-up or tear-down stage, Capricorn continues to use previous experience and previous structures as fodder; always the historical frame of reference provides the foundation for contemporary constructs and is also the place to start when attempting an assessment of any chart, be it the individual's journey or that of a larger whole or grouping.

PLUTO IN CAPRICORN

In astrological terms, Pluto represents the cyclical regenerative process, and as such correlates to the theory of reincarnation. Evolutionary astrology looks to Pluto to provide perspective on the nature of the Soul's evolving needs and desires.

Pluto's transit through a particular sign, a cycle that on average can span twelve to eighteen years (and sometimes more, as was the case of Pluto in Cancer, extending from 1912 to 1939), will progressively fashion the defining signatures for an entire generation's identity. It also describes the advancing journeys of the individualized, socialized, and collective Soul. When Pluto is activated by contact with other planetary energies, or by sign or directional changes, it quickens the evolutionary pace of the Soul's desires and needs, at individual, interpersonal, and collective levels.

Whether Pluto's transformative process is experienced as a steady and natural progression or as a cataclysmic experience will depend on the degree of resistance generated at any given point along the timeline. Resistance, caused by fear of loss associated with vulnerability and disempowerment, creates friction, which in turn increases the degree of polarization and intensifies the building momentum. Repetition, occurring through the process of an action and corresponding response mechanism, creates more links in the chain of experience. Eventually, the energy of this repeating process reaches a saturation point. It is at this crisis or turning point in the cycle that polarized resistance exhausts itself, giving way to an evolutionary leap of significance.

Pluto's entrance into the sign of Capricorn marks a culminating point of great historical significance, as yet another chapter of our collective experience winds to a close. As we witness the waning hour from this particular vantage point along the timeline, the necessities of an emerging new reality are becoming progressively more evident.

Pluto first dipped into the sign of Capricorn from January 26 to June 14, 2008, and returned to this sign on November 27, 2008, to stay through November 19, 2024. The archetype of Capricorn will remain as the predominant astrological signature for this next important stage of collective, social, and individual evolution.

Pluto in Capricorn ushers in the creations of the collective Soul and the individualized journey through a greatly intensified core reformulation. While traveling through cardinal Capricorn, Pluto swings the wrecking ball toward outmoded structures, which include not only the physical structures and institutions of everyday realities, but also the conditionings and security anchors of consensus and individualized consciousness.

Sounding the wake-up alarm on the lateness of the current hour, this planetary transit generates an intensified awareness of encroaching endpoints, while also inducing counterpoint recognition of new necessities that grow increasingly more urgent. In other words, Pluto's transit through Capricorn propels the big-picture evolutionary chapter through the advanced stages of closure and completion; simultaneously, it also begins construction on a new reality base that will eventually support and house the collective Soul's upgraded requirements.

Stifled as we now are by the heavy pressure of atmospheric ceilings (figurative and actual), the recycling experiences of a world weary of perpetual crisis, and the increasing threat of species extinction (ourselves included), Pluto in Capricorn's next task is no small feat for we who exist now. Monumental history will be written in the coming years.

Noting that Pluto in Capricorn brings an entire chapter of existence to an end, it is now plain to see that a completely altered future is just around the corner. Through 2024, we will see the paving stones of the coming Age of Aquarius set in place, as the future mandates of a new reality command (and demand) more of our urgent attention.

As we journey across this River Styx intersection timeline, humanity will peer into the deepest and darkest recesses of its shadow. Along the way, Pluto in Capricorn's stripping-away process will confront us with devastatingly stark truths. It cannot be understated, the choices we now make are of major consequence to the future survival of life on this planet.

While Pluto's demotion to a dwarf planet by the authorities of the day changes nothing of the planet's qualities, nor the astrologer's viewpoint on the potency of its powerful influence, this re-labeling can be considered reflective of the subconscious shift now growing within the collective. A patriarchal regime has evolved during the Age of Pisces. At its base, and antithetical to Christ's true message, the Garden of Eden myth has permeated the collective consciousness for the majority of Souls.

This Garden of Eden myth has promoted three key ideologies:

1. Flesh is antagonistic to spirit.

2. Woman is to blame for man's spiritual downfall.

3. God exists as an external force, outside of us. In other words, God exists above us; we are separate from God and Creation.

These ideologies have promoted hierarchal judgment as a base of understanding and relating. We think in terms of better or worse, greater or lesser, superior and inferior. This cataloguing of existence has resulted in the acceptance of dominance and submission as an accepted fact of everyday life. It is this philosophy that has comprised the base of most world religions and, for the most part, has also set the standards for sociopolitical norms and laws. Carried over from many lifetimes, indoctrination into the philosophy of dominance and submission has led to the suppression of more natural ways of manifesting our needs, our relationships, and our realities. The distorted behaviors that result from this base have been the root cause of the educated masses gone wrong, of the brutality of man against man, and of the rampant sexual violence that exists as a cultural standard in contemporary everyday reality.

The human Soul incarnates into the physical and biological atmosphere that will best support the requirements of its ongoing evolutionary journey. Sometimes we will choose to live a life in the male gender, and sometimes we will choose to live a life in the female gender. As an inherently dual archetype, Capricorn houses both the masculine and the feminine consciousness and also the conditioned gender complexes referred to by Carl Jung as *anima/animus*. No matter what physical body we have chosen to wear in the present life, Capricorn's judgments will draw readily from the subconscious memory pools (Cancer polarity), which naturally replicate the consciousness of our past-life personalities. This consciousness recall may or may not match the gender assignment of our contemporary physical form.

That which has been absorbed into the recesses of the subconscious will be not only self-referenced from our own past-life egos, but also drawn/pooled from those who have been influential in nurturing and shaping our emerging personalities. In other words, our subconscious dilemmas, including that of gender assignments, will also reflect and perpetuate the inhabitants of our subconscious, that of our family of origin and ancestral lineage (Cancer polarity). The conflict of buried and suppressed anima/animus gender complexes can be evidenced seeping into, or filtering through, our subconscious behavior responses.

Capricorn's archetype correlates to the conditioned structure of consciousness, which has been trained by the authorities of the day— be they parents, teachers, preachers, bosses, governing officials, or those others who control our heartstrings—to accept the standards of societal norms or "cultured" status quos. These norms comprise the manufactured rules and regulations that have formed the consensus of social groupings and that have also become imbedded within the individual psyche. Over time, the man-made laws and accepted living standards that have separated "man from beast" have come to dominate the structuring of our everyday common existence. This separateness standard has mushroomed into a very wide reality chasm. Progressively, our species has grown fundamentally out of alignment with nature and its natural rhythms, with Creation, and with the universal consciousness of unity and wholeness.

The subconscious personalities that exist within the retaining walls of the Capricorn/Cancer polarity will form the baseline judgments and choices of how we move ourselves forward from the present timeline. It is the animation of these subconscious inhabitants and their emotional complexities—their strengths, weaknesses, defenses, fears, and anxieties—that pull the strings as we resist and reject, or, conversely, submit to the indoctrinations of previous exposures. Relative to Capricorn's socialized judgments and the suppression of the inherent duality of the archetype as has been described, it is easy to see how the "war between the sexes" can surface as a motivating factor within the subconscious of the individualized Soul.

Judgment relative to the Capricorn archetype establishes a subconscious sense of what is appropriate behavior, what is considered right or wrong. Relative to the issue of gender assignment and sexuality, we have progressively come to accept superiority, inferiority, dominance, and submission as the socialized norm. The hierarchal distinctions of class, race, nationality, and creed are ready testament to this pervasive consciousness. In turn, such skewed psychology has hatched society's ills—i.e., slavery (in all its forms), the inequality and subjugation of women and children, the atrocities of man against man, and the brutal rape of our planet. Pluto in Capricorn now brings these key and critical issues to a head. They encompass the wrong turns that must be righted before we can successfully transition into the coming Age of Aquarius. In contrast to Capricorn's hierarchal judgments, a key concept of the Aquarius archetype correlates to the recognition of the interconnectedness of all of life (the infinite universe) and therefore the equality of all of Creation. As such, it is representational of matriarchal consciousness, which is rooted in the base principles of respectful participation, of sharing, caring, and inclusion.

While it is a dramatic statement to say that Pluto in Capricorn puts humanity to the test, the reality of the present day bears undeniable witness. Our polluting ways (social, political, economic, physical, environmental) are now so great that we face not only the toppling of our everyday institutional foundations, but also—and more critically—we face the very real threat of biological extinction. We can only hope that we do not find ourselves in a crippling paralysis that supersedes the ability for effective action taking. Timeline margins are shrinking fast.

The BP/Deepwater Horizon oil-rig disaster of April 2010 and the resulting massive oil spill in the Gulf of Mexico, which severely threatened the fishing industry, wildlife, and coastal vegetation, is a case in point. Less corporate face-saving at the time of the disaster could have minimized the destructive impact; tighter safety regulations, overlooked by the U.S. government but standardized in other countries, could have prevented the disaster altogether.

As the backed-up-against-the-wall realities of the day threaten our emotional equilibrium and physical resources, greater degrees of personal, social, and collective anxiety will naturally ignite. While consciousness scrambles to hold tight to the last vestiges of what has previously constituted security, the consequences of varying degrees of denial, resistance, fear, and foreboding can set into motion a chain reaction of provisionary or compensatory safeguards. As Al Gore began to promote his 2006 movie, *An Inconvenient Truth*, many of those with the power to implement positive change openly refuted the need for concern or action in broadcasting their denials: "There is no global warming crisis, there is no energy crisis."

There are still a number of people who will dispute humanity's hand in climate change and global warming, and who believe that the rising temperature averages and increasing frequency of weather extremes are simply a cyclical norm for Mother Nature. At the start of threshold-crossing times such as we are now experiencing, we can typically find that the doomsday naysayer is as prevalent as the doomsday prophet. By the fall of 2007, Al Gore would come to win the Nobel Peace Prize for his participation in group initiatives on climate change and global warming.

The initial markings have long been in place; the Pluto-in-Capricorn years will create wider divides between the haves and have-nots. Many families have fallen slave to the necessity for dual-income earnings, and in many cases, it is still not enough. With social assistance and pension coffers diminishing, and the daily burden of rising grocery bills and the struggle for basic survival so commonplace, it is little wonder to see the anxiety over present shortfalls and apprehension regarding the future give way to rampant depression, grief, futility consciousness, and fear mongering.

While these disconcerting states of consciousness seemingly put evolution at a standstill, they will still continue to serve as a creative tap. Capricorn's archetype employs anxiety and the workings of the resistant or fear-based consciousness as a catalyst in order to stimulate the necessary momentum and motion. While Capricorn can manifest a range of possible expressions in order to create the necessary evolutionary advances, it is the more dominant of energies that will become the fuel of choice.

More often than not, crisis is the primary catalyst for action. Struggle, guilt, sacrifice, atonement, dominance, and submission are today's most familiarized way of life, and typically they are the most generating in terms of our conditioned reflexes. Yet, how many of us would consciously choose to live with pain, punishment, and sacrifice if we truly understood how to live life differently? The key work of our contemporary collective evolutionary mandate is the destruction (Pluto) of these firmly cemented, and emotionally distorted, programmings of the past (Capricorn). Before new paradigms can become our new flagships, the unfinished business must be exposed, confronted, and finally laid to rest. Now, through 2024, Pluto in Capricorn will serve humanity's priority requirements.

The proliferative Pluto-in-Sagittarius years have delivered growth and expansion beyond that which we have previously known. While there has been much positive development, especially in the areas of travel (terrestrial and extra-terrestrial), knowledge, communications, and the mixing of race, culture, and creed, we have also seen a growing proliferation of disease, and of tragic human and environmental conditions. Building forward from these recent Pluto-in-Sagittarius years, Pluto's transit through Capricorn will enforce a time of reckoning with a past gone wild, at the personal level and beyond. Occurring only once every 248 years, Pluto in Capricorn is set to ignite the astrological flare-signal for an emerging new world order. We can already see a significant reordering/restructuring of private-life priorities, dictated by the shrinking options and increasing urgent necessities of living on an overcrowded planet.

Throughout history, Pluto in Capricorn has typically advanced the rise and fall of empires. The last cycle brought about the American War of Independence, which led to the birth of a new world superpower, the United States of America, along with the rise of democracy and the growth of capitalism. The previous two Pluto-in-Capricorn cycles saw the rise and subsequent demise of the Ottoman Empire.

It does not take much looking around to see the signposts of a shifting world order already well underway. China and India's ranking among economic superpower nations is quickly on the rise. At the same time, democracy and its now-corrupted counterpart, capitalism, rank top among our modern-day institutions now in systemic decay. The massive financial bailouts of 2009 (Wall Street, General Motors' bankruptcy filing) saw democratic nations beginning to more closely resemble socialist governments.

Work has already begun on the construction site of globalization and economic unification (NAFTA, the European Union, and so forth). While "the world as one" (peace, respect, equality, and tolerance for all) is not only the ultimate aim but also the ultimate necessity for a new social world order, we are only at the very beginning of a long learning curve and a laborious uphill battle. As the search for new and more workable solutions necessitates experimentation, Pluto in Capricorn's reign is also likely to see intensified resistance and perhaps even more desperate measures undertaken to revive control, formulas, and institutional bodies to their previous levels. Resistance, which unwittingly aims to perpetuate the flawed systems and corrupt structures, can easily breed more loss and destructiveness. Still, there comes a time when the lack of appropriateness and the lack of workability for "more of the same" policies and practices become too obvious to ignore. Building up from an already corrupt or flawed reality base, the initial safeguards, structures, and systems that are put in place during this first phase of Pluto in Capricorn's reign can prove to be a false cushion with short-lived effectiveness.

Pluto in Capricorn's transit will leave no stone unturned. Accordingly, we must brace for the potential of a confrontation with the darker forces of the manifested creation before we can climb to safer and higher ground. The powerful Pluto-in-Scorpio generation (born from 1984 until 1995) will rise to adulthood and leadership during the Pluto-in-Capricorn years. Pluto in Scorpio's primary agenda is to confront and heal the intensified traumas that reside within the individual and collective Soul structure and to transmute this experiential knowledge into a rich and generating compost for the journey forward—this in terms of individualized, socialized, and collective contexts. The particularly difficult and dark histories retained within the cellular memories of this generation are at their ready tap. Incarnated among this Pluto-in-Scorpio generation is also a percentage of Souls that are aligned with evil. Among those teetering on the dark edge, some will be seduced, and some will choose to contract themselves to become agents and recruiters of evil.

When the polarity of Capricorn and Cancer is ignited, the past holds the key to our evolutionary forward. Ever since the advances of the Industrial Revolution, which eventually led to the shaping of our world economic structure and the invention of the banking and credit-card systems as we now know them, we have come to subscribe to a belief that the well will never run dry and that we can always get more, buy more, produce more, or charge more on our accounts. Manufacturing driven by profits before all other considerations, and the spawning of voracious consumerism tied to a philosophy of discard rather than re-use, has brought us to our precarious present day, rife with its shortages and overloads.

We are beginning to recognize that we can no longer live on borrowed time or borrowed money. Pluto's travel through Capricorn will force us to acknowledge that wasteful consumerism has placed a severe burden on our planet's fecundity. We have witnessed how financial excesses, institutional overextensions, and profiteering have led to the fast collapse of worldwide money markets, which has prompted the subsequent domino demise of various industry sectors along with significant unemployment hikes. Pluto's advance into Capricorn late in 2008 cemented the cornerstone of a recessionary period that threatened to rival that of the Great Depression of the 1930s. (At the time of this writing, Greece is in severe economic crisis and the world is on watch.) Chief among Pluto in Capricorn's wrecking-ball mandate is the complete decimation of our current conceptualization of wealth and money.

Although there is now more industriousness directed to tackling the critical environmental issues, scientists continue to warn that there is no stopping what is already in rapid motion. Precious resources are dwindling at a rapidly accelerated speed. Critical time margins shrink much faster during Pluto in Capricorn's reign. We cannot ignore the most pressing challenges of the day: repair from the devastation caused by natural and man-made disasters, famine, and drought cycles; preservation of forests, agricultural lands, marine life, and freshwater reserves; waste management and disposal; growing infertility and species extinction; pollution; and, last but not least, work toward finding more encompassing solutions for Gaia's repair and healing.

Capricorn's polarity sign is Cancer, and within this sign can be found both the crises points and the resolutions for this next part of our journey. The crisis generated by the Cancer cardinal archetype takes root in insecurity that clings to the past, in the "inbreeding" of conceptual references and attachments that perpetuate distorted judgments and compensatory responses—in conflict with the birth of overpowering new life forms—and in socialized movements that threaten previously established continuity. The key to navigating successfully through these upcoming feast-or-famine years will be found in the reseeding of consciousness with an unyielding reverence for the equality of Creation and all its life forms, and in the active and attentive nurturing of both the healthy nucleus and the growing embryo. Reality "as is" must be faced and be reconciled with. Denial may prove to be a potent and perhaps lethal poison pellet.

Preservation strategies aimed at perpetuating more of the same must be completely overturned. New programs must be embraced in totality and implemented in short order. Time is of the essence, and waste—not only of resources but also of time—is a luxury that comes with too high a price tag. Pluto in Capricorn enforces the necessity to severe ties from any chokehold dependency. Corporate opportunists, government leaders, and policymakers can no longer afford to make rationalizations based on self-serving interests that sacrifice both human life and the life of our planet. Dependency on anything that diminishes or undermines self-sufficiency cannot be counted on to provide security.

Our current Pluto-in-Capricorn transit will energize an acute awareness of our shrinking planet and our shrinking choices. We will become acutely aware of have and have-not, of power and powerlessness, of the corruption of systems and the rationales that have perpetuated them. Our conscious understanding of time as we know it now will take a radical shift as we become even more aware of how the past shapes and defines the future. Our understanding of the workings of good and evil is also about to undergo a monumental transformation. Again, it is the understanding of our own hand in the creative process that will be either part of the curse or part of the cure.

Accountability is absolutely key; we cannot afford to hedge on the proper usage and honoring of all resources. With the world steeped in crisis, the next major lesson for the Pluto-in-Capricorn years will be in learning of our limitations—how absolutely connected and interdependent we are. We cannot afford to create more physical, material, social, and spiritual wastelands; we can no longer turn a blind eye to the fact that the recycling of our polluting ways is the root cause of the severely crippled body, mind, and Soul of humanity that we see is so prevalent today.

When Pluto transits Capricorn, it is also absolutely necessary to face reality for what it truly is, to turn priority attention toward the actual workability of the potentials held within the current critical time allotment, and to embrace realistic goals that will perpetuate long-lasting benefit with enduring results. Approaching deadlines cannot be ignored or put off. Today's results are the vital determinant for where we go from here. Halfway measures or halfhearted efforts will not cover enough ground in the current race against the clock. As time moves forward, we will come to realize that we have been building tomorrow's problems with today's solutions for far too long.

Pluto's travel through Capricorn ignites the cardinal-cross signs of Aries, Cancer, and Libra, and the geodetic cardinal world axis. Following is a discussion of Capricorn in reference to the cardinal signs/angles and also a brief look at the geodetic regions that will be affected by Pluto in Capricorn. These geodetic locations outline the areas of the world that are designated for key reform through the Pluto-in-Capricorn years. Of particular note are the revolutionary years when Uranus in Aries (2010 through 2018) forms dynamic (square) aspect to Pluto (March 2011 through May 2016), and the recessionary years when Saturn in Libra (October 2009 through October 2012) does the same (Saturn squares Pluto within a few degrees from late October 2009 through October 2010). Note that there will be seven exact squares of Uranus in Aries and Pluto in Capricorn: June 24, 2012; September 19, 2012; May 20, 2013; November 1, 2013; April 21, 2014; December 15, 2014; and March 17, 2015.

THE CARDINAL CROSS

The cardinal cross is formed by the four cardinal signs: Aries, Cancer, Libra, and Capricorn. Archetypically, these signs are situated on the four primary angles of the horoscope wheel. The Ascendant/Descendant axis correlates to the sign archetypes of Aries/Libra. The Midheaven/Nadir (also referred to as the MC/IC axis) correlates to the sign archetypes of Capricorn/Cancer.

Ignited through the dynamic aspects (square and opposition aspects), each angle of the cardinal cross correlates to a freshly charged and forcefully invigorated initiatory momentum. Aries propels new experiential and primal enterprise, which propels Cancer to search for greater emotional safety and self-consistency (through nesting with the familiar, or, in other words, through nurturing and preserving the past), which propels Libra to form relationships and new conceptualizations (evaluations) pertaining to socialized relativity and needs, and which propels Capricorn to self-regulate through the manufacturing of a structural housing or system in which to govern and control the functioning of the evolving form.

Capricorn/Aries Angle

Aries, positioned as the first sign of the zodiacal wheel and thus correlating to new beginnings, activates the experiential initiation process for the emerging consciousness. It is through Aries' experimentation and subsequent manifestation that the Soul will come to experience a new relationship with itself and, by extension, with all of Creation. Evolutionary astrology correlates the Aries archetype, and its ruler Mars, to the subjective will of the evolving Soul thrusting into new creative action.

The crisis of new discovery serves to unleash the Aries creative impulse, compelling an energy surge that leads to assertive action-taking. As the first sign of the zodiac, the typical Aries momentum is a coarse, raw, wild, and primal energy. In relationship to Capricorn, also a cardinal archetype, the conflicting energy momentum at this 90-degree angle brings the conditioned consciousness to a sharpened clash point between the security issues of the past and the evolving needs of the present.

It is at the Aries threshold that Capricorn's building momentum becomes sufficiently fueled for action. When linked together, Aries and Capricorn are result driven. Together they thrust desires and needs into manifestation, and in so doing they serve to accelerate the evolutionary pace.

With Capricorn as the originating point for Aries (separation) initiatives, the Aries/Capricorn creative impulse can be influenced by the distortions caused by the short-sightedness of fear-based emotions. Thus, short-lived successes, barren achievements, productions, or yields can result from the creative impulse of this limited fear-based perspective.

Conversely, when the initiating point of Aries "looks back" to Capricorn's ripened support, the Aries/Capricorn creative impulse can be reflective of "right" or appropriate timing, and of the wisdom and maturity that has been gained through experience. When the Aries/Capricorn creative impulse is built on judgment based on natural needs—not compensatory, manufactured, or artificial needs—there is an ability to move mountains, metaphorically speaking. The results then lead to the fertilization of a thriving new life force that is infused with unlimited potential.

That which has been held in check (regulated, contained, inhibited, suppressed, or resisted) through Capricorn is released with great force through Aries. When fear, anxiety, biased judgments, or distorted rationalizations are at the base of the Capricorn subconscious, unbridled Aries can cut a path of great destructiveness, setting fire to the cataclysmic experience. When this is the case, a range of emotions/behavior can be expressed: excessive paranoia leading to self-demolition, acts of aggression, anger, rage, attack, brutality, violence, sexual violation, war, and even murder. We can witness the unleashing of the critic, the rejecting skeptic, the bossy one, the bully, the user, the despot, the tyrant, the terrorist, the rapist, the criminal (the violator or guilty one). When resources become dried-up or exhausted, and defeat results, the Aries/Capricorn stance displays the veritable bone-crushing, crumbling, and immobilizing effects of failure. A sense of futility results in the loss of momentum, in pessimism, self-degradation, and self-destruction. We can witness the "walking fatality," this in reference to an emotional state or a projected circumstantial reality-in-waiting. When this self-sabotaging psychological perspective is at the base of projected creation, rising opportunity can meet with what appears as "sudden death." The quickly extinguished momentum readily perpetuates futility consciousness and circumstantial paralysis.

Coming from a secure, mature, well-built, well-fortified, and self-controlled Capricorn anchor, the Aries creative process can be one of constructive application of that which has come before. Self-rule and self-mastery (the harnessing of mind or body) becomes a channel for purpose in action, resulting in great accomplishment, often achieved in short order. The harnessing of appropriate methods and means can ignite and support an enduring creative wellspring. This lays the groundwork for successful socialization, self-determination, execution, effectiveness, command and control, recognition, acknowledgment, purpose, authority, and achievement of significance and of lasting value.

Pluto in Capricorn/Uranus in Aries
Uranus in Aries : May 27, 2010–August 13, 2010;
March 11, 2011–May 15, 2018

Pluto in Capricorn's transit will dismantle structures and systems that have outgrown their usefulness. The transit of Uranus in critical aspect to Pluto marks evolutionary peak cycles for our collective experience. This aspect delivers signature times of great revolution, devastation, upheaval, invention, and accelerated collective modernization. When Uranus is in Aries and Pluto is in Capricorn, anything that is weak, decayed, damaged, or corrupt is likely to explode or implode with intensified impact. Massive and revolutionary change occurs in a relatively shortened time frame. The defining moment may be a flash in time, but the result can deliver long-lasting consequences.

The start of Pluto in Capricorn's wrecking-ball transit delivered Wall Street's near-fatal collapse and prompted a rapid domino effect for the world's major banks. This was soon followed by the faltering of the American auto-manufacturing titan General Motors, which filed for bankruptcy on June 1, 2009. In a bailout move to circumvent even greater economic disaster, General Motors subsequently became largely owned by the U.S. government. Worldwide economic instability and uncertainty continued through 2009 and into 2010. We have

yet to witness what additional surprises, shake-ups, innovations, radical actions, or solutions will occur once Uranus advances through
Aries.

Times when Pluto tenants Capricorn see the reorganization of sociopolitical structures. Nations, governments, and leaders rise or fall
from power in a more striking way than during other times. Just as
with the more personalized transit of Pluto through the tenth house
of a natal chart, inner- and outer-world security fortresses (emotional, psychological, material, structural) are overturned as the process of a necessary reordering of existing reality begins.

Uranus will stay within a few degrees orb of a first-quarter square
(crisis in action) aspect to Pluto in Capricorn throughout most of its
tenancy in the sign of Aries. Looking back from the future, these years
are likely to be described as exceptionally revolutionary times lived on
the razor's edge.

When Uranus tenants Aries, both collective crisis and collective
evolution speed forward with much greater intensity. Lifestyles dramatically alter, especially for those living in regions under geodetic
stress where geographic fault lines and volcanoes are situated, and
where the occurrence of hurricanes and other extreme weather conditions make daily existence a perilous journey (see next section).
Natural disasters; disease; the effects of war; barren and toxic environmental conditions (Uranus in Aries); economic bankruptcy; and
obstructive, destructive, oppressive, or tyrannical politics and governments (Pluto in Capricorn) can cause many ruptured lives, and bring
about the displacement, or even death, of multitudes. At the same
time, Uranus is the planet of discovery, innovation, and of technological and scientific advance. While we can see how the rapid curve
in medicine, science, and computer technology is revolutionizing our
lives, we have yet to see the full extent of what is invented and how it
will change our everyday realities.

While Pluto in Capricorn can put our backs against the wall, Uranus in Aries serves to intensify the drive to find unique solutions to our age-old problems. Historically, the acceleration years when Uranus tenants Aries and Pluto tenants Capricorn are ones of disruptive and chaotic circumstances. At the same time that established ways of doing business and of organizing life "burn to the ground" (in some cases figuratively, in other cases literally), the prompt of Uranus in Aries sees innovation and invention rapidly replace the inferior, outworn, or defeated, and also supersedes previous benchmarks and high bars.

On the mental plane, the revolutionizing influence of Uranus liberates the crystallized consciousness (Capricorn) and the structural realities that underlie modern societies and modern life. The coming years of Pluto in Capricorn and Uranus in Aries are sure to bring rapid, dramatic, and extreme change to our social, political, and economic status quo. The last time Uranus tenanted Aries and Pluto tenanted Cancer, the stock market crashed, the atom was split, and Hitler was on a rapid rise to power.

The combination of Uranus and Pluto serve to advance major social, cultural, political, scientific, and technological breakthroughs. When these planets are in aspect, everyday lifestyles are rapidly and radically transformed. For example, note that the conjunction of Uranus and Pluto in the 1990s brought the personal computer into our homes and forever revolutionized our lives.

Prompted by the formidable ultimatum delivered by Mother Nature's hand, the most revolutionizing mark left by the pivotal Uranus in Aries, the Pluto-in-Capricorn years are sure to be seen through the inventions and advances made to combat global warming, the energy crisis, and the destruction caused by wasteful consumerism and environmental pollution. While unemployment is a key propeller of economic crisis, increased employment is a key factor that stimulates economic recovery. Uranus in Aries, a revolutionizing planetary signature that enlivens new energy initiatives, is set to spawn plenty of new industry that will surely liberate us from our present economic parameters. The math is simple. New energy initiatives, sustainability solutions, and quality-of-life upgrades will spawn new industries and new jobs that can create not only a rapid economic correction, but can also create critical healing for our planet's biosphere.

Libra/Capricorn

The orientation of 90-degree square aspect between the air sign of Libra (mental planes) and earth sign of Capricorn (manifest planes) is one of crisis in consciousness (internalized, philosophical, moral energy) rather than crisis in action (externalized, projected, manifested energy). At this intensification threshold, the momentum builds toward cohesion, united fronts, integration, regulation, and containment, rather than separateness, independence, and individuation.

The sign of the balancing scales, it is through the Libra archetype that we seek to reconcile with our observation of self in an externalized or projected context, and, by extension, that we begin to form a sense of worth, value, and meaning. The contrast supplied by our outer (Libra) experiential (Aries) realties (Capricorn), prompts the forging of relationships, relatedness, and relativity. Our external circumstances and environments become the breeding ground for the next stage of evolution. As we respond to external stimuli, we begin to formulate a sense of context based on our evaluations of experience. This consciousness-raising ignites the Capricorn angle.

Libra's initiating impulse or drive is compelled to seek unity rather than singularity and individuality, and to combine or join together rather than to create separateness. To some extent, Capricorn's drive to establish consensus and to regulate the workings of the whole is in harmony with Libra's basic drives, and it is for this reason that Saturn in Libra is considered exalted. Still, it is the intentions and goals behind the momentum that are critically defining at this 90-degree crisis angle. Socialized values and evaluations are the key segregating factors that challenge more cohesive or encompassing integration.

Libra's evaluations lead to the formation of judgments (Capricorn) that will dictate how we moderate and regulate when we interface with larger wholes—in other words, that which is outside of self. In contrast to the coarseness of the Aries pioneering initiative, Libra's initiative is directed to a refining of needs and desires.

The angle of Libra in square to Capricorn's zenith point correlates to the progressive socialization of consciousness seeking to correct imbalance or extremity and to (re-)establish a new level of equilibrium and conformity. The objectives defined at this 90-degree crisis angle will shape what comes next. The Libra archetype combined with the Capricorn archetype brings consciousness to the stage of evolution where it begins to formulate a law of averages. This system of measurement is then used to find and establish middle (Libra) ground (Capricorn).

The Libra/Capricorn intensification threshold is one that energizes and accelerates the drive toward the achievement of a bettered equilibrium. Prompted by clashing contrasts and polarizations now reaching maximums, the Libra/Capricorn square seeks to reconcile, streamline, and corral the diverse and multifaceted expressions into an organized whole, and to bring extremes to a better balance point. Industry will be directed to the regulating of standards and status quos, which will lead to the progressive shaping of consensus-based opinions (Libra/Capricorn). These consensus-based opinions are the security linchpins from which all other judgment tracks will be laid. At this cardinal apex point, society's evaluations (Libra) will begin (cardinal) to form the standards of the judicial systems (Capricorn) of contemporary civil and social laws. That which becomes labeled as necessary will form the boundaries, dividing lines, and base shape of what is built next.

In its positive application, Libra regulated through Capricorn results in the construction of a supportive equilibrium. Balanced judgment leads to governing within appropriate boundaries and secure structures/frames of reference (psychological, emotional, material, and conceptual) that take into consideration the diverse needs of the one as a reflection of the many. When harnessed in its purest, most natural expression, we see the results of mature and wise judgment, self-regulation, self-consistency, genuine authority, and disciplined achievements.

When filtered through the emotions of fear and anxiety, the building momentum reflects the imbalances of judgment that naturally translate into a battle for control that sees forceful, restrictive, or constrictive means employed in order to achieve objectives. Justifications and rationalizations based in a singular rather than plural or cooperative orientation result in hierarchal evaluations and relationships shaped by dominance, submission, withholding, entrapment, and enslavement. The sociopolitical system is then used to serve the one or the few, rather than the many. Rather than achieving integration, we see further segregation and abuse of the system. At this distorted level, uniformity translates into forced conformity, and conformity is forced to bent knees by restrictive regimentation, laws, and regulations. Authority then uses the system and its rules to its convenience; fair play turns foul with opportunistic self-serving; social inequality, racism, and bigotry become the norm; and social injustice is sanctioned through political policy and government enforcement.

Saturn combined with Libra can be restrictive, inflexible, and intolerant of any idea or person that does not align with its specific rules and guidelines. In this state of imbalance are born the social climbers who use their position and the system; the government rules over the people rather than with or for the people. Libra square Capricorn can see the devaluing, diminishment, and disposability of the individual and his or her social rights; the needs of the one can be sacrificed for the rationalization of a private, political, or social goal—"the cause is more important than the foot soldier." When this is the case, Libra square Capricorn can set in play sociopolitical "means justify the end" strategies that turn subjects into objects, that marginalize social groups, that reduce individuals into faceless names and numbers, and that create rationalizations and justifications that allow for the crossing of inappropriate boundaries. This includes infiltrations into private systems and personal lives (invasive tracking and surveillance). When Capricorn dominates Libra, conformity leading to regimentation and social convention, rather than uniqueness or individuality, is both lauded and enforced. Individualized rights, free enterprise, and true capitalism lose their previous ground.

Social, political, and ideological inequalities can stew along with racial and national tensions, while that which is suppressed can be unleashed with great destructive force. Taken to extreme, Libra square Capricorn ignites the conflict between fair play and authority's dictates, and prompts increasingly forceful means in order to establish the desired necessary control. In other words, we experience war rather than peace.

Adding the Cancer angle to create the T-square configuration, fears concerning lack of security and mistrust tend to be found at the base of such safeguards as government surveillance, which is likely to prove to be a more widely used tracking system than the average person may suspect. Monitoring has come to such extremes that some now advocate the implanting of computerized chips into the human body as a medical and safety precaution. Whether or not it is simply the paranoia of conspiracy theorists, there has been speculation that these controversial chip implants may have useful tracking applications for other than medical reasons. Perhaps the merging of man and machine is not as far-fetched or as far off as most of us would think.

Saturn in Libra (Sign of Exaltation)

Saturn tenants Libra from October 29, 2009, through October 5, 2012. (Note: Saturn dips back into Virgo from April 7, 2010, through July 21, 2010.) Saturn in Libra draws attention toward the normalizing and legitimizing of a conceptual frame of reference. Saturn's transit through Libra prompts a refinement process that will qualify who and what is acceptable, and that defines rules or regulations in regard to what methods or what means need be employed in order to enforce an "upgraded" equilibrium and to gain better control.

Will the results deliver greater tolerance, or more judgment, hypocrisy, and double standards? The scales can tip to either side, and they can swing to the extreme, too. Attitudes toward social issues such as gay marriage, sexual abstinence, and abortion can become more contentious, especially in areas in which the fundamentalist-religion faction and repressive sexual morality grows. As a tightening influence, taxing Saturn in Libra can set in place more stringent legislation that eliminates many previously taken-for-granted privileges. The restraints of the Saturn-in-Libra years may also bring a greater slide to the side of anti-choice regarding a woman's legal rights to her own reproductive system. At the very least, wider social intolerance, dissension, and division over social morality can become more evident.

As Pluto transits Capricorn and Saturn transits Libra, the demands of overpopulation will prove to add an increasing burden to our already limited natural resources. The harvesting and decimation of our forests, along with the endangerment and extinction of species, have long been recognized as a threat to the delicate balance of our ecosphere. At the same time, the increasing infertility of our own species is sure to grow more concerning, proving, as we have suspected for some time, that we are sabotaging ourselves—that food and water contaminants, vaccinations, chemicals in everyday usage (cleaning, hygiene supplies), and such are root causes of human infertility (the Cancer angle).

While more rigid sexual morality and practice can attract a larger following, on the flip side of the scales we can see surrogate parenting and in vitro genetic manipulation become standards, too. As populations diversify and increase, hopefully our humanity will not only keep pace but exceed it, too. We can already see more commonplace acceptance for those who have been previously marginalized through such issues as sexual orientation and couplings, skin color, and physical deformity or debility. When push comes to shove, as we have seen demonstrated through 2009's threatening worldwide economic crisis, and 2010's Haiti earthquake disaster response, the world is forced to tackle more cooperative global initiatives. Ultimately, the crisis produced by these (potentially desperate) transit years can serve to narrow the social or political divides.

Saturn in Libra relative to Pluto in Capricorn may also see less distinction between the implementation of democratic and socialist policies. Positively, this could translate into proactive government reform and funding for such essentials as health care (Cancer polarity), recycling and waste management (Pluto in Capricorn), education, air-pollution control (Libra angle), humanitarian aid, and other such essentials, which will serve to improve the quality of life for all. Case in point: in the year 2009, the bankruptcy crisis of auto giant General Motors saw the U.S. government become a 60 percent owner and the Canadian government own 12 percent of the company. In a positive move, the U.S. government placed stringent requirements on General Motors to undertake green restructuring in a greatly shortened time frame. The shaping years of Saturn in Libra relative to Pluto in Capricorn can see the rise of leaders with noble ambitions, and cooperative alliances formed. Conversely, this transit can mark the rise of despots on a power grab, and see the few controlling the many.

The transits of midsummer through fall of 2010 are of particular note. Saturn formed a close opposition aspect with Uranus (mid-July through mid-August 2010), to mark the final of five opposition contacts over two years. This last opposition aspect (perfected July 26, 2010) departed from the previous four oppositions across the mutable sign axis of Virgo/Pisces, to oppose in the cardinal signs of Libra/ Aries. Pluto and the transiting North Node in Capricorn were found positioned at the T-square apex angle (square aspect position).

Jupiter, intensified by retrograde, is in the sign of Aries and conjunct Uranus. The transit trigger of Mars, in the sign of its detriment Libra, is an influence of shorter duration but of potent significance nonetheless. These retrograde transits, a giving-way (externally dismantling) and heating-up (internally energizing) influence, provide the incentive for David-faces-Goliath action taking. The summer and early autumn of 2010 may come to be viewed as a historical boiling point or trigger time, quickening a wider divide between the fast-receding past and the increasingly urgent dictates of the rapidly overtaking new reality. These transits typically ignite intensification of political conflict, civil unrest and social uprisings, economic strife, and weather extremes (drought, wildfires, poor crop yields, etc.). They also prompt a rapid call to action and the implementation of stringent, perhaps even desperate, correction remedies. (Archetypically, the T-square formation is a pressurized one that serves as a catalyst to prompt creativity in action.)

Capricorn/Cancer

The momentum of the 180-degree aspect known as the opposition can be energized in two distinct manners: as polarized and competing, or as complementary and reconciling. Evolutionary astrology looks to the integration point 180 degrees away from Pluto, the Soul's significator, in order to discover the Soul's intended forward destination. Before this evolutionary synthesis can be achieved, polarizations and divides must be revisited and resolved. The nodes of the Moon and their rulers provide key information and shaping tools.

In the case of the Capricorn/Cancer polarity, both archetypes seek security, control, and continuity. Capricorn's security needs focus primarily on external manifestations (physical/material, external relationships/relatedness/authority), while Cancer's security needs focus primarily on internal manifestations (emotional/psychological, inner/personal relationships, internal relatedness). Both archetypes are motivated by insecurities that lie within consciousness; both seek to achieve self-consistency, and both archetypes seek to gain protection and to safeguard from vulnerability. Capricorn builds walls to shut in what is on the inside; Cancer builds walls to shut out what is on the outside.

Both Cancer (personalized) and Capricorn (socialized) are initiating points for new cycles of evolution. Both bring the past to culmination. Building from the support foundation of the past, Cancer's main industry is focused on the creating of a new and separate life force that will eventually advance to independent functioning. In contrast, Capricorn's main industry is to work toward the completion and culmination of the previously established agendas and goals, and while setting about this task, a new life or a new form will emerge to eventually overtake the functioning of the system.

Cancer's primary lesson is to learn how to create independence from the matrix (symbolized by the Capricorn structure), to minimize external dependencies and needs, and to develop self-consistency and emotional reliance from within. Through the Capricorn archetype, the primary lesson for the individual or socialized unit is to learn to become a purposeful contributor to the socialized whole, to maximize externalized self-effort, to develop self-sufficiency and intactness, and to become self-reliant and self-regulating as well as accountable and responsible. Through the Capricorn archetype, the individual or socialized unit will be prompted to learn to maximize externalized self-effort and to develop accountability, responsibility, self-regulation, intactness, control, and appropriate boundaries that will allow the forging of a productive relationship with both personal and externalized authority. The lesson in so doing is for the individual or socialized unit to learn to become a purposeful contributor to the socialized whole.

Inner projection/Outer projection

When Capricorn's reasoning regarding appropriate standards of conduct is projected through Cancer, it translates into emotional expectations. When one does not meet one's own emotional expectations, a range of castrating, self-debasing, and self-punishing emotions are ignited: guilt, grief, disappointment, sense of failure, sense of loss, resignation, futility consciousness, inner criticism, depression. We can find ourselves immobilized, crushed, or crippled by any of these psychological/emotional states.

When others do not meet our expectations, we ferret out blame, resentment, judgment, and various punishments, which range from the withholding of emotions to various levels of rejection: coldness, distancing, dry or wry response, disdain, stand-offs, or unresponsiveness. We can take to inflicting our "law" or disciplinary measures on others; the analogy of wringing a towel out to dry is a befitting description here. We can feel stifled; we can become stuck in a sense of underachievement or lack of deserving. We can feel dominated by those who judge us, and find ourselves forced to submit to the dictates of an authority that we do not agree with, that we are diametrically opposed to. A high-priced and punishing struggle can ensue.

When the polarity of Capricorn is well blended with its polarity sign, Cancer, a state of emotional and social maturation results. The realities built from such foundations pave the way for future growth of fecund longevity.

THE MOON'S NODES

Evolutionary astrology considers the Moon's nodal axis to be of key importance. The Moon correlates to the evolving ego and self-image, and to emotional-memory imprints retained by the personality of the subconscious ego. The Moon's nodes in an individual chart will correlate to that of personal imprinting; the primary shaping factor is seen in the previous direct exposure, experience, and conceptualization of parental influences. Beyond the self-referencing/influence of the parental experience, the Moon's nodes will also describe the origin imprints of past public exposure or, in other words, the environmental conditions that lead to social and collective grooming. (The Moon in astrology also signifies the public.) In tandem, the North and South Nodes reference the blended resources of past experiences and future potentials, and are considered as key integration and synthesis points regarding the Soul's contemporary (present) and evolving journey.

Transiting Nodes in Cancer/Capricorn
North Node in Capricorn, South Node in Cancer:
August 21, 2009–March 3, 2011

When the nodes are found in the cardinal signs of Cancer/Capricorn, significant evolutionary chapters close and others begin; the past and future are intertwined. When this nodal transit occurs for the individual, added attention becomes focused on personal issues of self-consistency, personal safety and security, and the polarizations of (internalized, externalized) gender assignments. In reference to the socialized or collective unit, the transit of the nodes in this sign polarity will ignite a cycle when physical, material, and emotional/moral security needs intensify, which also encompasses the conflict of interrelatedness and gender assignment in the socialized, or outer world, context.

The transiting nodes spend approximately eighteen months traveling through a sign axis. In doing so, they highlight the featured evolutionary programs and work that will consume priority attention over the transit's time interval. When the transiting nodes travel through a cardinal axis, they serve to energize and prompt the necessary momentum for decisive, and often critical, action taking. As the transiting nodes began their travel through the sign polarity of Capricorn/Cancer in August of 2009, Pluto was found at the start of its transit through cardinal Capricorn. Saturn (ruler of the transiting North Node in Capricorn) advanced into cardinal Libra (October 2009), and

Uranus continued to advance through the late degrees of mutable Pisces. The T-square configuration continues to hold court as Uranus began its first foray into the cardinal sign of Aries in the summer of 2010. Once the transiting nodes fill in the grand-cross angle in cardinal signs, a compelling intensification dynamic is set to task on the core restructuring of both external and internal programming. A grand-cross configuration keeps the pressure alive from all sides. A critical transit such as this is sure to create a testing time of mounting challenges, greater insecurity and inconsistency, and a more rapid demise of that which is already crumbling or in a state of decay.

THE CARDINAL CROSS AND THE WORLD AXIS

When Pluto tenants Capricorn, the cardinal signs of Aries, Cancer, and Libra are also activated. Correlating to both the ending and beginning of a key chapter regarding the evolution of the collective Soul, Pluto's tenancy of Capricorn in reference to the geodetic cardinal world axis is of particular note, as it designates the regions of the world that are most strongly earmarked for radical restructuring. The contemporary added influences of Uranus in Aries, and for a shorter time, Saturn in Libra, greatly intensify this particular history-making chapter.

Simply described, the 360-degree wheel of the zodiac is overlaid on the world's geography—starting at the 0 degrees Prime Meridian, located in Greenwich, England. These astrological geodetic equivalents form the base of mundane, or world, astrology (the study of nations and of geological phenomena) and locational astrology (commonly used for personal and relocation charting). The name *astrocartography* was popularized by astrologer Jim Lewis.

Natal-chart signatures will resonate with corresponding geodetic locations. A heightened emotional response or pull to a particular location or culture can also be suggestive of past-life connections. Please note that the theory of correlating past-lives to geodetic locations is an

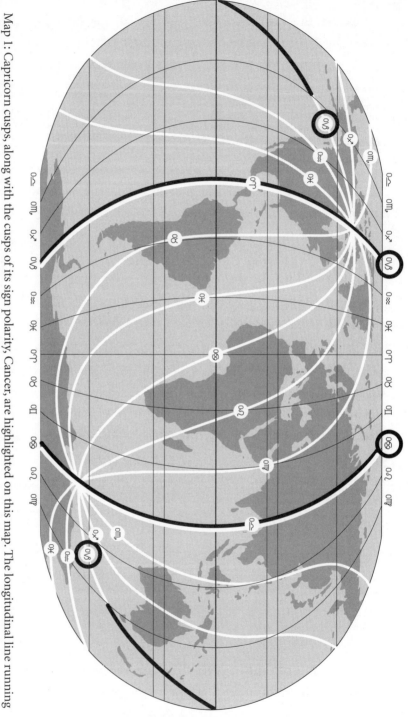

Map 1: Capricorn cusps, along with the cusps of its sign polarity, Cancer, are highlighted on this map. The longitudinal line running through North America, Central America, and the southern Pacific Ocean correlates to the 0 degree of Capricorn for this geodetic region. The longitudinal line correlating to the 0 degree of the polarity sign of Cancer on the Midheaven is also highlighted on this map. Note: the light-colored curved lines correspond to the Ascendant angles.

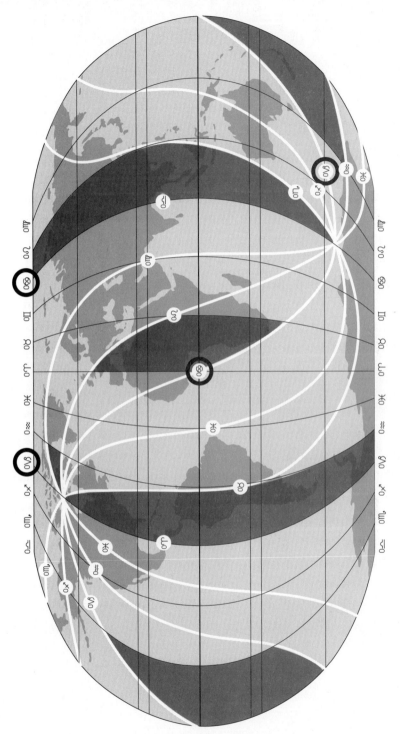

Map 2: As is discussed in this chapter, the map's shaded areas correspond to the cardinal world axis—in other words, the regions that have the cardinal signs (Aries, Cancer, Libra, Capricorn) situated on the angles (Midheaven, Ascendant, Nadir, Descendant). When one angle of the cardinal cross is ignited by transit stimulation, all the angles become stimulated. The dynamic transit alignments of Pluto in Capricorn, Uranus in Aries, and Saturn in Capricorn—enhanced by the shorter intervals of Jupiter, Mars, and the moon's nodes forming aspects in cardinal signs—will greatly activate the corresponding geodetic regions.

extremely complex and controversial topic. Readers are invited to do their own research and form their own opinions.

MAPS

The twelve signs of the zodiac overlaid on the world's longitude lines correlate to the angle of the Midheaven. These sign correlations are fixed—that is to say that the 0 degree of Aries will always be found at the 0 degree Prime Meridian longitude (which separates the Eastern and Western hemispheres). Ascendant lines are indicated by the white curved lines.

Areas that feature Capricorn are listed on the maps supplied. Note that Capricorn can be found at all four angles—the Midheaven, the Ascendant, the IC, and the Descendant. Note also that the Midheaven longitude lines are intersected by curved Ascendant lines. While Capricorn/Cancer may appear across the Ascendant/Descendent or MC/IC axis, the latitude of a location will determine the other corresponding chart angle; it is not always found in the cardinal signs. Note that when ignited by transits, the 0 degrees of the cardinal signs can be particularly dynamic. As they move into position to ignite the cardinal world axis, the ingresses of Pluto into Capricorn, Uranus into Aries, Jupiter into Aries, and Saturn into Libra are likely to energize with forceful and catalytic intensity, the results of which are likely to produce significant physical, political, and socioeconomic restructuring perhaps prompted by a crisis of significance. For more instruction on geodetic astrology, please see the work of Jim Lewis, Chris McRae, and other experts.

Following is a brief look at the geodetic regions that will be most affected by Pluto's transit through Capricorn.

1. Capricorn Midheaven, Aries Ascendant, Cancer IC, Libra Descendant

This geodetic region covers the following areas: the eastern half of the Gulf of Mexico; Cuba; the eastern portion of the United States, including New Orleans, the Great Lakes region, Florida, Washington DC, and New York City, the home of Wall Street; the Canadian province of Ontario, including the country's capital, Ottawa; a western portion of Quebec; the Caribbean Sea and its islands: Barbados, Jamaica, Haiti and the Dominican Republic, and Puerto Rico; Mexico's Yucatan; Central America's Honduras, El Salvador, Costa Rica, and the Panama Canal; and the western half of South America, including Argentina, western Brazil, Bolivia, Peru, Chile, Columbia, and the western half of Venezuela. (See the appropriate shaded section on map 2.)

The years when Pluto tenants Capricorn will see the geographic region with Capricorn on the Midheaven in an active social, political, national, economic, and physical teardown-and-rebuild cycle, as a historic evolutionary chapter concludes and a new one begins. That which was previously considered as rock solid can topple, perhaps like a deck of cards. The laborious, all-consuming industry of the day is likely to become more sharply focused on surviving through the decay, decadence, and destruction (of systems, safeguards, and security) caused by corporate and government mismanagement, political oppression or tyranny (loss of freedoms and human rights), social pollution and disease, and other natural causes. Geographic regions and borders can be redefined, through hostile takeover (war, invasion), political vote, or Mother Nature's harsh hand. Altered landscapes caused by climate change, atmospheric extremes, and natural disaster are a likely signature of the acceleration years when Uranus in Aries squares Pluto in Capricorn. The increasing volumes of human and chemical waste (industrial fertilizers, pesticides, etc.) dumped into our precious waters are destroying vast quantities of marine life. Note also that this is the geodetic region compromised by the catastrophic BP oil-rig spill of 2010. Mother Nature's wrath has already proved painfully evident through the Gulf of Mexico, Haiti, Chile, and the Caribbean. We can expect to see more turbulence ahead.

On a positive note, the groundbreaking transits of Uranus in Aries square Pluto in Capricorn can see rapid social and political reforms and outstanding initiatives taken by the many or by the one. Scientific advances aimed to stimulate economic growth and improve quality of life can create new industry, productivity, and uses for the lands in the area (for example, refertilization of the land through irrigation systems and such, active reforestation, etc.). Uranus in Aries adds speed to scientific advances and new energy initiatives, signaling the potential for a fast turnaround and rebuilding period. (Sustainability is a Capricorn archetype.)

Resource-rich Canada's economic and political future is intertwined with that of its southern neighbor, the United States, and so it is not surprising to see this geodetic zone house the political and economic hub for both countries. (Canada's capital is Ottawa; its manufacturing and economic center is the province of Ontario.) The political decisions and advances made through the Pluto-in-Capricorn years are crucial not only to both countries' individual futures, but they will also hold significant sway on the global future.

Note also that a great deal of South America is under the same geodetic influence. The politics of this resource-rich (oil, mining) and largely underdeveloped region is rife with socialist extremes, political tyranny, regime takeovers, covetous ambitions toward economic imperialism, and nationalism with strong anti-American sentiments. Natural disasters are also likely to threaten civilization. At the same time, as we have seen with Brazil's economic rise, this geodetic area holds great potential for growth.

Of added note, the ancient Mayan civilization thrived in parts of this geodetic region (Central America). We have yet to witness what coincidence or impact, if any, December 21, 2012 (or June 6, 2012, when Venus retrograde conjoins with the Sun), will have on our collective history. This key date is known as the end of the Mayan calendar, an ancient timekeeping (Capricorn) measurement. In contrast to the turning of a new millennium (Y2K) which sparked anticipation of destructive global fallout as computer clocks struck 2000, the symbolism of the Mayan calendar's end has sparked a romantic view of a new dawn of enlightenment and of humanity coming together as one. While it is true that the Mayan calendar is based on celestial movement, it is simply a man-made timekeeping device. Should there be a notable and rapid reshaping of collective consciousness, it is more likely to be prompted by our back-against-the-wall realities—in other words, as crises dictate a more urgent need to embrace more encompassing change.

2. Capricorn IC, Cancer Midheaven, Libra Ascendant, Aries Descendant

The geodetic region that houses Capricorn on the IC (security, preservation, rule over homelands, nationalism, traditional culture, domestic and agricultural production, hardships associated with daily existence, population isolation, geographic remoteness or desolation, political oppression, economic strife) and Libra Ascendant (social and cultural identity) covers much of Siberia, most of China, as well as Thailand, Malaysia, and part of Indonesia. (See the appropriate shaded section on map 2.)

When the transit of Pluto in Capricorn crosses the geodetic nadir or IC, and moves into the fourth house of the vicinity in question, the Cancer Midheaven polarity is also ignited. Local resources can become scarce, dry up, or be lost altogether. Domestic systems, norms, and traditions of the past can be destroyed or forever altered. When Pluto transits Capricorn, the old ways and means are swept away to make room for a new reality base.

Pluto in Capricorn's transit through this geodetic region can rock not only security, but even the physical land and life itself. When the gestational hatches, the latent unleashes, or the suppressed erupts, it can do so with relentless, crippling, or rampant force. That which was previously considered as secure can become increasingly vulnerable, even targeted.

Cataclysm caused by natural disaster or oppressive or tyrannical government regimes can turn daily life into a daily struggle, which in turns sees impoverished people grow more needy and desperate. Destroyed lands and decimated lives can become the defining catalysts that finally elicit long overdue and lasting progress. When such critical times drive evolution, previous safeguard measures can hold little relevancy or feasibility to the tasks of the present. Industry is focused on rebuilding, refortifying, and re-securing through any and all means. Sometimes this may occur through martial law, exploitation of the people, and the diminishing or denying of personal rights. Rising from the ashes of brutally ravaged homelands, domestic recovery and rebuilding is a long, slow, and laborious project (reflecting the length and effect of the transit itself). As we have seen in the wake of the Indian Ocean tsunami disaster, basic needs such as shelter, food, clean water, waste management, safety, medical attention, and the rebuilding of morality become the all-consuming work of the day.

Stimulated by Pluto's transit mentioned above, the region with Cancer on the geodetic MC is likely to experience an unstable economic cycle. Government, political systems, banks, and corporate leadership can prove to be weak or vulnerable. At the same time, the transits prompt the necessary interior refortifying and rebuilding that will eventually lead to greater self-consistency. The transit stimulation concentrates significant attention on the safeguarding of territorial homelands and on domestic concerns and challenges, such as agriculture and food sources, depletion or lack of commodities and resources, domestic industries, population matters (densities or diminishing numbers), medical services, water safety, and pollution issues. Challenges also mount regarding self-rule, social reform, reliance or dependency on political or economic alliances, and territorial jurisdiction/rights.

The transit stimulation igniting Libra on the geodetic Ascendant region also births a new blend of social and cultural identity. Capricorn on the geodetic IC describes the harshness of extreme climates, locality, and agricultural limitations or barrenness that is factored into everyday existence. Pluto's transit influence on the geodetic IC region can transform that which has been taken for granted. In the wake of erosion, that which has been previously buried, untapped, or hidden from view can become the new "feeding ground" or resource from which to create new life. Some of these extreme areas will prove to yield lucrative new resources for mining and drilling operations, resulting in a significant lifestyle change for people living in the region. So, too, climate changes may prompt a radically altered lifestyle. For example, note that rising temperatures caused by an intensifying hothouse climate are causing rapid melting of the permafrost in the extreme northern regions, such as Siberia. This climate advance gives way to a longer agricultural growing season and facilitates greater potentials for drilling and mining operations.

There is no doubt that Thailand, Malaysia, and Indonesia will spend many years in recovery from the devastation of the 2004 tsunami. Typhoons have continued to pound the area. As of the time of this writing, China's waters are dangerously polluted and people are being slowly poisoned by the toxic substances that are commonly used in manufacturing and food production. Overcrowding continues to be of critical concern. An oppressive political government continues to keep a stranglehold on the people. At the same time, China has continued to grow more powerful as an economic investor and trader (holding a majority of the U.S. debt), manufacturing supplier, and technological leader in the world.

3. Capricorn Ascendant, Cancer Descendant, Libra Midheaven, Aries on the IC

The region that has Capricorn on the Ascendant, Aries on the IC, and Libra on the MC is found in the Pacific Ocean, and includes part of Hawaii and Samoa. The Capricorn Ascendant also covers New Zealand to the south (with a Virgo MC) and the Pacific Northwest (with a Scorpio MC). See the appropriate shaded section of map 2.

When Pluto transits the geodetic region where Capricorn is on the Ascendant, a new national identity is formed, a new way of governing comes into being, and new priorities see a fundamental reshaping of existence and everyday life. Territorial rights can become a contentious battleground. Note this geodetic area is primarily an island and aquatic region, and as such, existence and self-sustainment can be inhibited by distance or isolation. Threatening extinction has already been noted in pockets of the ocean. The dying-off of the coral-reef ecosystems is particularly alarming to scientists.

As this geodetic region falls under the stress of the ignited cardinal-cross alignments (especially so under the dynamic influence of Uranus's transit through Aries), the land—both the floor beneath the ocean and the islands above—can fall vulnerable to a significant increase in seismic and volcanic activity. Aries correlates to the IC (or terra firma) for this geographical region, and noting that Uranus in Aries greatly increases the potential for earthquakes, volcanic eruptions, and atmospheric extremes, landmasses could physically alter—perhaps some will go underwater.

Tidal waves, shock waves, aftershocks, and such could cause major destruction; inhabited areas could become more difficult to reach. We have yet to measure the true effects of nuclear testing from previous years, but note that Uranus in Aries, correlating to radiation, dehydration, and sterility, is likely to expose the radical damage done to the ocean's eco-structure. Vast areas of dead ocean have already been discovered. On the other hand, perhaps new discoveries will lead to cultivating the oceans in this region in some new way. Noting Cancer on the Descendant, the region could become coveted for its resources or strategic location. (The islands of Hawaii and Samoa have long been popular tourist destinations.) The geodetic region could also fall prey to economic over-harvesting, political or territorial wrangling, or takeover bids.

As an aside, Capricorn is on the Ascendant with Pluto-ruled Scorpio on the Midheaven for the Pacific Northwest region, which includes Seattle and the rest of Washington State, as well as Vancouver Island and the Canadian province of British Columbia through the Queen Charlotte Islands, the Yukon Territory, and a very small tip of southernmost Alaska. Considering these regions are adjacent to the Pacific region discussed above, there could be some vulnerability or fallout effects from weather extremes, particularly those created by earthquakes, tsunami aftershocks, or ice-cap melting—especially along the coastline, where a change in topography could have significant repercussions for inhabitants. Noting Scorpio on the Midheaven, there can be undermining through excessive consumerism or power plays made by those in possession or in authority. The coveted yields from this resource-rich region (mining, drilling, logging, fishing, water-resourcing) are likely to become more in demand and therefore more exploited.

The selling off and privatization of rivers in British Columbia has been of great political concern to Canadians, especially those living in the province. First Nations (indigenous) peoples are still fighting for their territorial rights. Massive forest areas have fallen prey to wildfires, while extreme weather has created havoc for growing seasons.

4. Capricorn Descendant, Cancer Ascendant, Aries Midheaven, Libra IC

The geodetic region with this profile covers the main portion of Europe, including England, the Netherlands, France, Switzerland, Monaco, the eastern coast of Spain, most of the Mediterranean area, the western coast of Italy, Vatican City, and a large portion of Africa (See the appropriate shaded section of map 2.)

When Capricorn is on the Descendant, nationalist needs rather than alliance needs, world status, respect, leadership, and political positioning take center stage. Dependencies on the resources of other countries can bring liabilities, indebtedness, and obligation. Aid committed to other countries, war, and peacekeeping initiatives become weighty or even crushing burdens. Socioeconomic standards undergo a significant metamorphosis, too. Moral and social corruption and decay, along with the aftermath of destruction, can lead to a mass consciousness of anxiety, despair, or apathy. Social inequality, social unrest, inhibited freedoms or mobility, caste systems, racism, martial law, and threats of terrorism can be commonplace. The needs of the many can be controlled by the few or the one.

With Aries on the Midheaven and Capricorn on the Descendant, despots and tyrants can be on an intensified power grab, but their rule, along with the life spans of elected political parties, can be short lived. Replacement regimes or governments may occur in higher frequency. In less developed areas (such as much of Africa), brutality, tyranny, hostile takeovers, and extreme subjugation can continue to be inflicted on the masses. Political strife igniting riots or coups can also occur more commonly while the transiting Pluto tenants Capricorn (the geodetic seventh house of the region), Uranus tenants Aries (tenth house), and Saturn tenants Libra (IC). So, too, this region can be a target of attacks or terrorist activity. European countries are an easier geographic target than the United States for al-Qaida and other such groups.

More positively, the region can be home to increased social responsibility and self-autonomy. Small grassroots groups can grow into major movements. Core values, lifestyles, social welfare programs, and monetary systems can also undergo significant metamorphosis.

As the Aries Midheaven, Libra IC, and Capricorn Descendant were ignited by the transits of Uranus in Aries, Saturn in Libra, and Pluto in

Capricorn, we have witnessed the beginning of a new coalition form in Europe. Examples of pooling the many into the one can be seen in the movement toward centralizing the economy with the introduction of the euro and the economic unification of Europe through the European Union (EU). The EU was a quick responder as the financial crisis of 2008–09 began, and was called upon again in the spring of 2010 to help bail member state Greece out of economic collapse.

The Vatican is also found within this geographic region, so we can expect that there will be more corruption, turmoil, and controversy from within the ranks of this institution, along with a religious revival and the (attempted or actual) wielding of more influence on its followers. Pluto in Capricorn suggests a resurrection of more conservative or traditional viewpoints and religious ideologies. Indoctrination into guilt (Capricorn) has been a most effective weapon for religious discipline and the controlling of the masses during this Age of Pisces. The unleashing of Capricorn suppressions are a root cause of today's rampant criminal activity and sexual violence. Pluto in Capricorn serves to purge this philosophy of dark Eros, of sin and repentance, from our collective consciousness, but first it must be exposed. On another note, predictions have purported that the present pope may be the last. Will the Catholic Church as we now know it come to an end, or is it slated for a significant overhaul or resurrection? Time will tell.

The Sudan and Darfur, historic regions of mass genocide, exist in this geodetic region. Let us hope that the horrendous strife so long experienced in so much of the African continent will one day not only be countered by the world's humanitarian support, but also ended once and for all.

In addition to noting the important transit stimulation in the regions of the geodetic cardinal world axis, the charts of nations outside of these regions, just like individual charts, will be ignited by the major transits contacts. For example, the Islamic Republic of Iran exists outside of the geodetic zones discussed above, but, noting that its birth chart displays the Sun in Aries opposed by Pluto in Libra, the country, currently ruled by a defiant ruler in a polarized relationship to Western countries, is sure to be radically affected by the transits of Pluto in Capricorn and Uranus in Aries. (Many consider President Mahmoud Ahmadinejad to be a dangerous loose cannon capable of much tyranny. At the time of this writing, the United States is advocating tougher sanctions to deter Iran's rebellious nuclear production, which Ahmadinejad insists is for civilian, not weapons, use.)

Forming a close tie not only geographically, but also astrologically, note that the USA's Sun is located at 12 Cancer, while Canada's Sun is found at 9 degrees of Cancer. Within a close time frame, the transits of Pluto in Capricorn (opposition) and Uranus in Aries (square) will aspect the natal Sun of both countries, marking a critically transforming economic, social, and political history-making chapter for both of these world powers. Signaling the end of an era for a modern empire, both Uranus in Aries (in square, 2016–19) and Pluto in Capricorn (by conjunction, 2019–24) will form dynamic aspects to the USA's natal Pluto before advancing into new signs.

In summary, Pluto's momentous transit through Capricorn demarcates a crucial reformatting cycle, for both the individual and the collective Soul. Everyday realities are likely to be forever altered beyond what we can fathom now. These confronting and critical years are sure to seem long and hard, but when they're measured against the bigger-picture backdrop, we will come to see that significant collective evolution was accomplished over a relatively short span of time. Emerging from these years, we will find ourselves poised on the threshold of our completely reshaped future. The ending of an Age is at hand and the beginning of a new one approaches. Astrologers will watch these important transits with great interest.

Country birth time data:

Canada: July 1, 1867, 12:05 p.m. EST, Ottawa, Ontario.

Islamic Republic of Iran: April 1, 1979, 3 p.m. IT, Tehran.

United States of America: July 4, 1776, 2:13 a.m. EST, Philadelphia, Pennsylvania. (The Sibley birth chart lists the USA's birth time as 5:10 p.m.)

The times listed above are the widely used standards.

MORE ABOUT ROSE MARCUS

For information on Rose's astrology career, please see her biography at the front of this book, and visit her website at www.rosemarcus.com.

Prior to Rose's full-time career in astrology, she built a successful art career (with her then-husband and business partner), gaining international acclaim for one-of-a-kind wearable art jewelry and mosaic sculptures made from unique materials, such as prehistoric mastodon ivory, exotic hardwoods, and semi-precious stone inlays. Some of these sculptures are housed in two public museums and a royal collection. Rose is also an honors graduate (with a speciality in fine arts photography) of the esteemed Vancouver School of Art, today known as the Emily Carr University of Art and Design.

Bibliography

Allen, James. *As a Man Thinketh*. Marina del Rey, CA: DeVorss & Company, 1983. (First published in 1902.)

Baigent, Michael, Nicholas Campion, and Charles Harvey. *Mundane Astrology*. Wellingborough, UK: The Aquarian Press, 1984.

Campion, Nicholas. *Book of World Horoscopes*. Bournemouth, UK: The Wessex Astrologer, 2004.

Carter, Charles E. O. *An Introduction to Political Astrology*. London: L. N. Fowler, 1951.

Eisler, Riane. *The Chalice and the Blade: Our History, Our Future*. San Francisco: HarperCollins, 1997.

———. *Sacred Pleasure: Sex, Myth, and the Politics of the Body—New Paths to Power and Love*. San Francisco: HarperOne, 1996.

Eliot. T. S. *Four Quartets*. London: Faber and Faber, 2001.

Evans-Wentz, W. Y. *The Tibetan Book of the Dead*. Oxford: Oxford University Press, 1960.

Fernandez Maurice. *Astrology and the Evolution of Consciousness, Volume One*. Lutz, FL: self-published, 2009.

———. *Neptune, the 12th House and Pisces*. Victoria, BC: Trafford, 2004.

Forrest, Steven, and Jeffrey Wolf Green. *Measuring the Night, Volumes One & Two*. Boulder, CO: Seven Paws Press, 2001.

Green, Jeffrey Wolf. *Pluto, Volume I: The Evolutionary Journey of the Soul*. St. Paul, MN: Llewellyn, 1985.

———. *Pluto, Volume II: The Soul's Evolution Through Relationships*, 2nd edition. St. Paul, MN: Llewellyn, 2000.

Herman, Judith Lewis. *Trauma and Recovery*. New York: Basic Books, 1992.

Jacobs, Donald. *Astrology's Pew in the Church*. San Francisco: Joshua Foundation, 1982.

Johndro, L. Edward. *The Earth in the Heavens*. New York: Samuel Weiser, 1970. (First published in 1929.)

Landscheidt, Theodor. *Sun, Earth, Man: A Mesh of Cosmic Oscillations, How Planets Regulate Solar Emissions, Geomagnetic Storms, Conditions of Life and Economic Cycles*. London: Urania Trust, 1989.

Levine, Peter. *Waking the Tiger: Healing Trauma*. Berkeley, CA: North Atlantic Books, 1997.

Lewis, Jim, with Ken Irving. *Psychology of Astro*Carto*Graphy*. London: Arkana Penguin, 1997.

McRae, Chris. *The Geodetic World Map*. Tempe, AZ: AFA, 1988.

Novak, Peter. *The Division of Consciousness: The Secret Afterlife of the Human Psyche*. Charlottesville, VA: Hampton Roads, 1997.

Sepharial. *Geodetical Equivalents*. London: W. Foulsham, Inc., 1925.

Tarnas, Richard. *Cosmos & Psyche*. New York: Viking, 2006.

———. *The Passion of the Western Mind*. New York: Ballantine, 1991.

Walsh, Patricia L. *Understanding Karmic Complexes: Evolutionary Astrology and Regression Therapy*. Bournemouth, UK: The Wessex Astrologer, 2009.

Walters, J. Donald (Swami Kriyananda). *The Path: One Man's Quest on the Only Path There Is*. Nevada City, CA: Crystal Clarity Publishers, 2003.

Wilber, Ken. *No Boundary: Eastern and Western Approaches to Personal Growth*. Boston: Shambhala, 1981.

Woolger, Roger. *Other Lives, Other Selves*. New York: Bantam, 1988.

Yogananda, Paramahansa. *Autobiography of a Yogi*. New York: The Philosophical Library, 1946.

TO WRITE TO THE AUTHORS

If you wish to contact any of the authors of this book, please write to them in care of Llewellyn Worldwide, and we will forward your request. Both the authors and publisher appreciate hearing from you and learning of your enjoyment of this book and how it has helped you. Llewellyn Worldwide cannot guarantee that every letter can be answered, but all will be forwarded. Please write to:

Rose Marcus
℅ Llewellyn Worldwide
2143 Wooddale Drive
Woodbury, MN 55125-2989
Please enclose a self-addressed stamped envelope for reply,
or $1.00 to cover costs. If outside the USA, enclose
an international postal reply coupon.

Many of Llewellyn's authors have websites with additional information and resources. For more information, please visit our website, at
http://www.llewellyn.com